JOHN DAVID BORTHWICK

University of Utah
PUBLICATIONS IN THE AMERICAN WEST

VOLUME 1 *The Montana Gold Rush Diary of Kate Dunlap,* S. Lyman Tyler, ed., 1969 (Out of Print)

VOLUME 2 *Attitudes of Colonial Powers toward the American Indian,* Howard Peckham and Charles Gibson, eds., 1969

VOLUME 3 *Early Utah Sketches: Historic Buildings and Scenes in Mormon Country,* A. Russell Mortensen, 1969 (Out of Print)

VOLUME 4 *The Reminiscences and Civil War Letters of Levi Lamoni Wight: Life in a Mormon Splinter Colony on the Texas Frontier,* Davis Bitton, ed., 1970 (Out of Print)

VOLUME 5 *Erastus Snow: The Life of a Missionary and Pioneer for the Early Mormon Church,* Andrew Karl Larson, 1971 (Out of Print)

VOLUME 6 *William Spry: Man of Firmness, Governor of Utah,* William L. Roper and Leonard J. Arrington, 1971 (Out of Print)

VOLUME 7 *A Guide for Collectors of Folklore in Utah,* Jan Harold Brunvand, 1971 (Out of Print)

VOLUME 8 *The Nicaragua Route,* David I. Folkman, Jr., 1972 (Out of Print)

VOLUME 9 *"Photographed All the Best Scenery": Jack Hillers's Diary of the Powell Expeditions, 1871-1875,* Don D. Fowler, ed., 1972 (Out of Print)

VOLUME 10 *The Golden Spike,* David E. Miller, ed., 1973 (Out of Print)

VOLUME 11 *To Utah with the Dragoons and Glimpses of Life in Arizona and California, 1858-1859,* Harold D. Langley, ed., 1974 (Out of Print)

VOLUME 12 *Tending the Talking Wire: A Buck Soldier's View of Indian Country 1863-1866,* William E. Unrau, ed., 1979

VOLUME 13 *North to Montana! Jehus, Bullwhackers, and Mule Skinners on the Montana Trail,* Betty M. Madsen and Brigham D. Madsen, 1980

VOLUME 14 *Buried Unsung: Louis Tikas and the Ludlow Massacre,* Zeese Papanikolas, 1982 (Out of Print)

VOLUME 15 *Orrin Porter Rockwell: Man of God, Son of Thunder,* rev. 2d ed., Harold Schindler, 1983

VOLUME 16 *Mormon Graphic Image, 1834-1914: Cartoons, Caricatures, and Illustrations,* Gary L. Bunker and Davis Bitton, 1983

VOLUME 17 *Saints on the Seas: A Maritime History of Mormon Migration, 1830-1890,* Conway B. Sonne, 1983 (Out of Print)

VOLUME 18 *Gold Rush Sojourners in Great Salt Lake City, 1849 and 1850,* Brigham D. Madsen, 1983

VOLUME 19 *Search for Sanctuary: Brigham Young and the White Mountain Expedition,* Clifford L. Stott, 1984

VOLUME 20 *Homesteading the High Desert,* Barbara Allen, 1987

VOLUME 21 *Hanging the Sheriff: A Biography of Henry Plummer,* R. E. Mather and F. E. Boswell

VOLUME 22 *Exploring the Great Salt Lake: The Stansbury Expedition of 1849-50,* Brigham D. Madsen, ed., 1989

VOLUME 23 *John David Borthwick: Artist of the Gold Rush,* R. E. Mather and F. E. Boswell, 1989

ARTIST OF THE GOLDRUSH

John David Borthwick

R. E. Mather
and
F. E. Boswell

University of Utah Press
Salt Lake City
1989

Volume 23 of the University of Utah Publications
in the American West

Library of Congress Cataloging-in-Publication Data

Mather, R. E. (Ruth E.), 1934-
John David Borthwick : artist of the Gold Rush / by R.E. Mather and F.E. Boswell.
p. cm. — (University of Utah publications in the American West ; v. 23)
Bibliography: p.
Includes index.
ISBN 0-87480-307-1
1. Borthwick, John David. 2. Artists—Scotland—Biography.
3. California—Gold discoveries. I. Boswell, F. E., 1941-
II. Title. III. Series.
N6797.B655M3 1988
759.2'911—dc19
[B]
88-20671
CIP

To Micki Dakis
for her invaluable assistance
with the genealogical research of the Borthwick family,
and to Marty Dakis
for his special help with the entire project.

CONTENTS

ILLUSTRATIONS

MAPS

ACKNOWLEDGMENTS

We are indebted to the following historical societies and libraries for their assistance in our research:

California State Library
Stanford University Libraries
Bancroft Library, Berkeley
The Church of Jesus Christ of Latter-day Saints
  Genealogical Library, Salt Lake City
Santa Clara Branch Genealogical Library
California Historical Society
San Jose State University Libraries
University of California at Davis
Society of California Pioneers
Clan Borthwick Association

INTRODUCTION

As a young man, artist-correspondent John David Borthwick left his native Scotland to see first hand the New World, about which he had heard and read so much. During his travels in the 1850s, he witnessed three momentous historical events: first, the California Gold Rush, that feverish stampede from all corners of the earth in pursuit of the ultimate dream of self-reliance; second, the rush to Australia, where a ragtag band of gold miners from all nations rose in arms against a superior British military presence to demand democratic reforms at the mines; and at last, a Nicaraguan revolution, in which an American adventurer attempted to turn internal strife to his own advantage by taking control of the country.

Borthwick viewed the entire panorama of the New World through the eyes of an artist, recording for posterity what he called "a picture of universal human nature boiling over."[1] His drawings, whether of raucous celebrations in pleasure halls or of mining ventures in which men joined forces to divert an entire river so they could gather the precious flecks buried in the exposed bed, capture the ebullient mood of the times. His articles and book display a delightful sense of humor, a flair for direct, compelling narrative, and the same eye for color and detail found in his art. In fact some California historians consider Borthwick's *Three Years in California,* with its eight drawings, superior in both style and fidelity to all other accounts of the Gold Rush. Professor Erwin Gudde described it as "one of the best, if not the best book of the period."[2] Certainly the book is unsurpassed in its ability to stimulate the reader to visualize scenes of Gold Rush days.

But the young artist's contribution to the history of the American West rests on more than having written a captivating story and illustrated it well. As Borthwick observed the tumultous events going on about him, his mind was constantly at work—interpreting, analyzing, and pondering the influence of these events on the progress of humanity. He consistently took an overview and sought patterns of behavior that revealed the character of each culture represented in the great movement toward democratization. He was fascinated by the developing American character and probed it in depth, reaching conclusions later echoed by Frederick Jackson Turner in his well-known address delivered before the American Historical Association in 1893 that stressed the significance of the frontier in America's history. Nor is it uncommon while reading Borthwick's *Three Years in California,* to come across ideas other historians have presented in response to Turner's theory. Also, Borthwick's illustrations and reports have special value in documenting a transition in mineral development. Earlier gold and silver mining operations, such as those resulting from the series of spectacular rushes to Brazil, utilized forced or slave labor. However, in both California and Australia, metal production relied upon free labor, with claim owners working their own placers or hiring others to help. The democracy prevalent on the mining frontier, representing a new era in the history of gold and silver mining, is a recurring theme in Borthwick's writings and art.

Though his works reflect romantic notions that evolved from his education and upbringing—such as a belief in the nobility of the common working man or the inspiration to be found in contemplating Nature—they are basically realistic and faithfully depict less attractive sides of frontier life such as crudity, greed, chauvinism, prejudice, and oppression. He praised the American traits of self-reliance, ingenuity, and adaptability, but being more objective than American writers, he also acknowledged the great contribution Old-World cultures made to progress in the New World, pointing out that America had the best of worlds to draw on during its development.

Aware of the sweep of the large movement, Borthwick never allowed his writing to sink to the level of mere personal narrative, as most Gold Rush accounts do. Always, he remained the professional journalist. As a result he revealed almost nothing about his personal life, and early attempts to research his lineage yielded only sketchy details. Though he was recognized as a talented artist of the West, what was known about him could be expressed in a few brief paragraphs crediting him as one of the first artist-correspondents to cover America for a British newspaper and the author of a fine illustrated book about early California. His other works of art, though of the same high quality as the drawings in his book, were rarely mentioned, and few today have seen them. Also few are aware he published articles and drawings in leading periodicals of his day: *Harper's, Illustrated London News, Blackwood's Magazine,* and *Hutching's California Magazine.* Prior to research conducted for this biography, events of Borthwick's life before and after California were hazy, and no attempt had been made to probe the source of the special sensitivity he brought to his task. Borthwick's writings, quoted extensively in our study, take on added meaning when interpreted in light of his personal life. The present volume, in addition to presenting fresh biographical material, also represents the first attempt to collect Borthwick's drawings of the American West. This collection also includes one of the missing miner portraits formerly considered forever lost.

John David Borthwick's journey to America can be viewed as the young artist's quest to understand himself in terms of the world about him. His story parallels that of young America grappling for a national value system as it debated how much of the world to add to its growing domain. As Borthwick came to realize, the emerging American character would play a lively role in determining future rights of citizens of the rest of the world. Such insight into the flow of historical events, combined with a rare sense of wonder and delight at the epic events of the 1850s, set this artist apart from the restless adventurers he so meticulously described, yet he had much in common with them. The very traits he recognized as representative of that amazing period Borthwick also possessed. Like his fellow gold seekers, he was driven from continent to continent by an impelling curiosity to see the world and a love for adventure, and with them he courageously endured dangers and hardships of the frontier. And, in the end, much like many a heartsick miner who made the long trip home in poorer health and with less wealth than he had at the outset, the young Scottish artist returned to his native land only to experience disappointment in the fulfillment of his most cherished dream.

JOHN DAVID BORTHWICK

PART I

Boyhood and Youth in Scotland

EDINBURGH

On his visit to America, John David Borthwick was deeply impressed with the young nation's blossoming democratic tradition, even though his own roots were deeply implanted in the soil of feudalistic Scotland. On both his father's and mother's sides he was descended from ancient noble families. Only a few miles from Edinburgh, where he was born and reared, rose the ruins of magnificent Borthwick Castle, home to the Lords of Borthwick for over two hundred years before falling into disuse. Sir Walter Scott had admired the massive square-towered edifice and written about it, explaining that it soared to such heights, nearly one hundred feet, so its owners could send distress signals to a neighboring fortress when under seige.[1] Within the castle's fourteen-foot-thick, hewn-stone walls, the fifth Lord Borthwick had in 1567 provided sanctuary for the beleaguered defender of Catholicism, Mary, Queen of Scots, and her husband, the Earl of Bothwell. Four days after the queen's arrival, the confederated lords surrounded the walls with more than a thousand troops, and she was forced to make her escape disguised as a page. In a second instance Lord Borthwick came to Queen Mary's assistance, riding to her support with a band of armed men only to discover he had arrived too late. The queen was being rowed across the lake, bound for eventual imprisonment and execution.[2]

In 1573 David Borthwick was appointed the first lord advocate and served as judge-counsel in the suit brought against the Earl of Bothwell for "outrage on the Queen's person."[3] The history of the Borthwicks reveals a long tradition of similar services. Back in the fourteenth century, a young Knight Borthwick had set the example of dedication to God and King. While keeping vigil at the bedside of the dying ruler, Robert Bruce, the knight promised that on His Majesty's passing, His heart would be carried to a final resting place in the Holy Land. During the ensuing pilgrimage, the party, bearing King Robert Bruce's heart in a small silver casket, was asked by an army of Spaniards to assist them in attempting to force the invading Moors back across the Straits of Gibraltar. Driving the Moors before them, the fierce, fervently Christian Scots led the attack, but were soon deserted by the Spaniards, who dismounted to gather plunder from fallen victims. Knight Borthwick, seeing his countrymen abandoned, quickly attacked and killed the chief of the Moors. Raising the severed head of the chief on his pike, he rallied the other Scots beneath the Borthwick standard and proceeded to rout the enemy. The crest of the Borthwick coat of arms, a Moor's head, as well as the motto "He who leads," are memorials to that battle in which the young knight distinguished himself as one of the bravest warriors on the field.[4] This same coat of arms—two golden-winged angels supporting a silver shield—was once found upon a tomb in a timeworn cemetery, and beneath the Borthwick coat of arms was the following epitaph:

> Here Lyes interr'd within this pile of Ston,
>   A Borthwick bold
> Scarce left he such a one
> Treu to his God and loyal to his King
> Ane galand man and just in everything.[5]

Over the years the tombstone crumbled, but its message endured in the minds of modern Borthwicks, a reminder of their noble heritage and an inspiration for their daily conduct.

John David's mother was of equally distinguished lineage. The Kinnear family had, for their bravery in military feats and their fidelity to the crown, received in the year 1165 a large land grant from King William. Four centuries later, the inheritor of this estate was elected to Parliament. The Kinnear coat of arms, reflecting the Scottish seafaring tradition, consisted of two seagulls, each raising a foot to support a shield emblazoned with an anchor and the motto "I live in hope."[6] Two modern Kinnears held the prestigious positions of Writers to the Signet.[7]

The marriage of John David's parents thus united two illustrious families. Dr. George Augustus Borthwick and Janet Kinnear were married in Edinburgh on March 19, 1821; the groom was thirty and the bride twenty-three. Since both families possessed considerable wealth, a marriage contract had been settled on before the wedding granting Janet possession of her husband's resources in the event of his death. On February 26, 1822, the couple had their first child, a son. The proud parents named him George, after his father and after Janet's father, George Kinnear, an Edinburgh banker. The child was cherished as a most promising heir, receiving George and Janet's undivided attention. It was only natural that in 1824 the birth of a second son failed to generate the same excitement and intense pride as the firstborn's had. Still the infant was warmly welcomed. Like his older brother, he was named for relatives—Janet's brothers, John and David Kinnear, and George's cousin, John Borthwick. Young George's distress at being replaced as the center of the household created a few minor problems, but the newest addition to the family held the spotlight for only a brief period. He was soon followed by three sisters: Fearne, Catherine, and, lastly, baby Janet, named for her mother. With parental attention focused on the three younger children, the two brothers were forced to turn to each other for company. Gradually they formed a close bond, John David unbegrudgingly accepting his older brother's dominance.[8]

The family's first residence was located at 5 Forres Street, but shortly after the birth of baby Janet, they moved to a new home at nearby 10 Darnaway Street.[9] Both the Forres and

Darnaway homes were part of a housing development on thirteen acres of land belonging to the Earl of Moray, also the proprietor of Darnaway Castle. The construction of these "fashionable" homes had been governed by a master plan that guaranteed they would be "convenient for the Inhabitants" and "ornamental to the City."[10] The sloping terrain, reinforced by several retaining walls, provided a view of one bank of the Waters of Leith, whose wild beauty the earl had preserved. Also, the multistoried homes, built of "neat, hammer-dressed" gray stone and ornamented with graceful iron railings, adjoined the earl's "pleasure ground," a vast natural park of hills and vales, overgrown with trees, shrubbery, and vines and laced with a wandering stream and a stone-paved path.[11]

Darnaway Street was in St. Stephen's Parish, which boasted a new church designed to accommodate sixteen hundred worshipers. A delicate tower soaring skyward over one hundred sixty feet capped the elegant structure. Not far from the church stood Edinburgh Academy, founded the same year John David had been born. The Academy—an impressive edifice with Greek doric portico and an elaborately decorated, oval-shaped assembly hall—was dedicated to providing quality education for those students who could afford to pay the two-guinea entrance fee.[12]

When their first son was eight, George and Janet Borthwick enrolled him in the Academy. For the first time in his life, little John David was deprived of his brother's presence, and his loneliness was intense. Though his older brother returned home each afternoon, there was a marked change in their relationship. George was now a "scholar." In waiting out the two-year period before he would be old enough to attend school, John David recognized the pattern his life would take. George would set the example and he would follow. As a member of the class of 1830, young George would remain throughout the entire seven-year course under the tutelage of a Mr. Mitchell. As his parents had fully expected, George proved to be an excellent student, showing special aptitude for mathematics. The 1830 enrollment statistics of Edinburgh University reveal the careers for which the Academy was preparing its students—medicine, 896; literature, 716; divinity, 297; and law, 277.[13]

Four momentous events marked the years immediately following George's enrollment. In 1830 Charles X, the abdicated king of France, brought his family to take up residence in Holyrood Palace, thus providing Edinburgh with an aura of royalty known in former times. Then on September 31, 1832, beloved poet and novelist Sir Walter Scott died. That same year an outbreak of Asiatic cholera ravaged the city leaving thousands dead in its wake. Fortunately all members of Dr. Borthwick's family were spared. A fourth occurrence shows the temper of the times: reformers succeeded in passing a bill that greatly increased the number of citizens given the voting privilege. In celebration, a grand procession of fifteen thousand tradesmen marched through the streets. The agitation for higher pay and better conditions for the lower classes continued, however. These events were typical of the juxtaposition that was always present in John David's environment—the privilege of aristocracy versus reform to bring equality and the glory of an idealized past versus the reality of suffering and death in the present.

Even within the boy's family there existed a strange blend of the old and the new. Dr. George belonged to the gentry, yet he worked for a living and espoused liberal ideas regarding social equality. Though the doctor and his friends boasted that the Scottish education system served all social classes equally, they also spoke of the need for opening a "ragged school" for the benefit of poor children in a section of the city where families were crowded into small apartments in seven-story tenements with no running water and no sewer.[14]

Like the poor children, John David also had relatives (Borthwick, Kinnear, and Nicholson aunts, uncles, and cousins) living close at hand, but they lived in elegant homes like his own that were worth more than three thousand pounds. His Uncle Alexander Kinnear, for example, lived on prestigious Heriot Row, later to be the home street of author Robert Louis Stevenson. Yet despite the family station and affluence, Dr. George taught his children that all men were brothers, united by the Fatherhood of God. The doctor, so respected by his peers that they elected him an officer of the Royal College of Physicians, was a God-fearing man who shunned the veneer of respectability and stressed the importance of depth of character. He was a family man whose love for his wife was matched only by his love for their children. Janet Borthwick, from a background fully as aristocratic as her husband's, and known for her intelligence and cultivation, shared her husband's concern for providing a genteel home. Yet her natural piety also prompted her to instill in her five small children a love for God and their fellow beings. The spacious, grandly furnished home at 10 Darnaway enclosed a tightly knit family unit and provided a warmth and security not found in the outside world, as little John David was soon to learn.

When the Borthwick's second son turned eight, he joined his brother at the Academy and was assigned to Dr. Cummings's class. John David was a serious, thoughtful child, who possessed many of the traits commonly associated with a middle son, such as being unassuming, sweet natured, and somewhat withdrawn. Though he greatly admired his older brother and attempted to follow in his footsteps, it soon became apparent he was not going to match George's scholastic performance. The Scottish school system unfortunately was not well suited to a child of his particular temperament. True, the country had since early times shown a dedication to education by the close of the seventeenth century requiring that each parish provide a school. The accepted method of instruction, however, relied on rote memorization, and schoolmasters tended to adhere to the Calvinistic doctrine that art was an immoral pursuit. Thus any student who had a passion for drawing pictures, like little John David, was apt to be disciplined for indolence. But the enlightened attitude of his parents softened the negative effect this educational experience must have had. Dr. George held a more worldly view regarding the arts than did school officials, and several men dedicated to the arts lived in the Moray housing development. Both a sculptor and a writer resided on Darnaway, and the Borthwicks' next door neighbor, Mr. D. F. Surenne, conducted a drawing academy for girls in his home. In fact there had been an artist in the doctor's own family, David Borthwick, a young painter, who had died of "decline" only four years before John David's birth.[15] Thus the doctor encouraged the artistic interests of his second son by arranging for Mr. Surenne to instruct the boy privately in drawing and painting.

Despite the shortcomings of the Scottish schools, their curriculum did produce students with a broad background in science, mathematics, literature, politics, and history. Of course growing up in Edinburgh, the country's capital since the 1400s, was in itself a lesson in history. In the city, whose old and new towns were separated by only a narrow valley, the merging of past and present could be seen and heard each day. Dull, repetitive blaring of foghorns from the modern port was momentarily interrupted each afternoon at one o'clock by the cannon's boom from the castle on the hill. The stone-walled passages of this brooding fortress that towered in the clouds had for centuries echoed the footsteps of kings, queens, royal children, and their attendants; and in the morning mists hovering over Old Edinburgh's semimedieval streets loomed seventeenth-century pepperbox turrets, rubbing shoulders with a labyrinth of closely set houses piled on top of each other until they had earned the reputation of forming the "tallest town in Europe."[16] The delicate, shining spires and orderly neoclassic elegance of spacious New Edinburgh stood in contrast to the antique. And though no parliament had convened in the Grand Hall since the 1707 union with England, the august structure remained, a melancholy reminder of lost independence. The stony grayness of Edinburgh, relieved only by an occasional red-tulip parterre or a blossoming plum tree, has been described by one writer as exuding a sense of time "as evocative as a perfume," misting all centuries into one.[17]

The construction of new Edinburgh on the site of the drained "loch" had been but one achievement of the previous century. The industrial revolution was the result of scientific inventions that were matched by an intellectual flowering that had made Scotland's capital a cultural center akin to Paris or

Vienna. Among the country's contributions to civilization were James Watt's steam engine, Meikle's threshing machine, John Hunter's surgical techniques, David Hume's philosophical essays, and economist Adam Smith's *Wealth of Nations*. By the early 1800s, this spirit of genius seemed to be dwindling and nobles were abandoning their estates and forsaking their nationality for the more lively society of London, though concurrently memories of the country's glorious past were being rekindled through a literary movement. Poet James Macpherson had set things off by reviving interest in ancient gaelic myths, and other writers had taken up the banner. Robert Burns composed a wealth of poems in the Lowlands dialect, and Walter Scott compiled a collection of native ballads, as well as composing his own narrative poems and popularizing the historical novel. The patriotism generated by such works as *Poems, Chiefly in the Scottish Dialect, Lady of the Lake, Ivanhoe,* and *Kenilworth* was reinforced by performances of folk dances —participants flashing the bright tartan of an ancient clan to the accompaniment of the distinctively haunting tones of the bagpipe. This boisterous patriotism was somewhat tempered by the Puritanism of the Kirk, resulting in a heritage of grave gentility characteristic of the city John David Borthwick knew throughout his boyhood and youth.

This historic city, where learning and arts had flourished, provided a nourishing background for the receptive John David, yet his influences were not confined to Edinburgh alone. Both the Borthwick and Kinnear families had at times lived in Ireland, and Dr. George had been born in that country.[18] Thus the families' allegiance to Scotland was balanced by a familiarity with another land. Still, John Borthwick, the wealthy cousin of Crookston for whom John David had been named, was inspired by the surge of nationalism to purchase their ancestor's castle. Though its basic structure was strong, it lay in a state of ruin—inhabited by small white owls and black daws, some floors collapsed, and the eastern parapet gaping from the gash cut by Oliver Cromwell's cannon. A row of huge lime trees still marked the borders of an overgrown garden sloping down a bank behind the castle. The basement of the long-abandoned structure was found to contain a dungeon, two wells, and a corkscrew stairway leading to the stateroom on the main floor. The Grand Hall, described as "imposing even in decay," was fifty by twenty-five feet, and a barrel-vaulted ceiling rose a full thirty feet above the floor. Traces of an ancient painting, quite similar to the old illuminations, revealed the towers of a castle and an inscription in Gothic characters reading "The Temple of Honor." The hall was lighted by a long window providing a view of the courtyard and was warmed by a nine-foot-by-three-foot-deep fireplace, covered by an ornately engraved stone canopy with flowered cornice. Near the hearth was the master's seat of honor, also hooded and bearing the family arms.[19]

This deserted hall had witnessed the sumptuous feast of welcome spread on the arrival of Queen Mary and had rung with peals of raucous laughter at the sacrilegious revelry conducted by the Abbot of Unreason. Then one cold, foggy day in November 1650, it had fallen into stony silence as the defeated John, the ninth Baron Borthwick, somberly handed over his ring of keys to the triumphant Cromwell, who accorded the lord, his wife, and child but fifteen days to pack their belongings and vacate the premises.

Above the Grand Hall was a music gallery where minstrels had performed, and in a nearby passageway stood a vaulted and embellished washbasin that was equipped with an outside drain. The kitchen, located in a wing, had a stone sink with drain and a huge fireplace for roasting meat. Guest bedrooms in the opposite wing bore markings where massive tapestries had hung. The second floor housed a chapel and drawing room, and the third provided sleeping quarters for the lord's garrison and the principal bedrooms. From the fourth floor rose parapets and vaulted rampart walks that attained the same level as the stone-flagged roofs of the main building and wings.[20]

John Borthwick's restoration project, carried out over a period of several decades, cost $20,000, but left the castle as sturdy as it had been in 1430. Cousin John even obtained some of the original furniture—a high-backed oak chair with arms and headrest richly carved in coronets, a lamp, and a curiously designed clock. In addition, he located and purchased Cromwell's original letter demanding surrender of the fortress in November 1650.[21]

It was not the restored castle alone that preserved the family name; there were also Borthwick Close, Borthwick Hall, Borthwick Park, Borthwick Valley, and Borthwick Parish. And the grounds of the Church of Borthwick contained the ruins of an earlier church, like the castle dating to the 1400s, and a burial plot of an early Lord and Lady Borthwick. Two handsome effigies gracefully reclined atop the tombs—the lord wore full armor and had a "sagacious and manly" countenance, and the lady, whose "beautiful female figure" was swathed in a "full robe," had a "gentle and handsome cast of features." At one time the Lord and Lady Borthwick had been surrounded by statues of their children who had died in infancy, but the lost babes had crumbled to dust.[22]

Despite a reverence for this illustrious past, Dr. George Borthwick did not hold that wealth and position were the indisputable birthrights of any member of the modern generation. His belief, passed on to his children, was that each individual must rise to success solely by his own efforts. As example of the entrenched opposition to such a liberal idea, the postal directory for 1830 classified residents as either "nobility, gentry, merchants," or "others."[23] Thus the existing establishment presented a persistent challenge to their father's philosophy, but young George and John David silently resolved to some day pick up the gauntlet, each in his own way. All about them were the effects of progress—macadamized roads, the new silk mill, canals cruised by steamboats, and railroads humming with carriages drawn by puffing locomotives—yet the influences of antiquity were pervasive, pomp and trappings from the past carried into the present. Children of Edinburgh stood wide-eyed beside their parents watching the street procession that marked the opening session of the city council. An official bearing a mace and sword marched before the city officers, some dressed in red velvet gowns and others in black silk robes, and all carrying spears. Those of special distinction wore double golden chains about their necks, and their robes and caps were trimmed in white ermine.[24] If at such a young age George and John David detected the incongruity inherent in their lives—their father's rejection of, yet admiration for, the old order—they were able to muster a childish reconciliation.

George continued to be the achiever his father had hoped for, remaining at the head of his class in mathematics. Then when he was in his sixth year and John David in his fourth, a great sorrow fell upon the family. In June their father was stricken with a mysterious illness that cost him the sight of his left eye. Dr. George serenely referred to his blinding affliction as a "visitation from God." By September, his general health had improved somewhat and, being an optimistic man, he wrote, "Relying on the mercies of God, . . . I pray that I may be fully restored to all my healthy functions." Yet his professional opinion was more realistic: "I . . . feel it a duty to be prepared for the uncertainties of this life." Deeply grieved at the thought of his family being left without their main source of support and guidance, he sat down and composed his last will and testament. Still, his stubborn hopefulness would not allow him to register it.[25]

In 1837 young George graduated from the Academy, delighting his parents by being awarded a medal for outstanding achievement in mathematics.[26] In the year of George's graduation, Victoria I was proclaimed ruler of the land. Her coronation, however, did not take place until the following year. The monarch was known for her dedication to Puritan sobriety and hard work, and since she had expressed a devotion for Scotland, the residents of Edinburgh celebrated her special day with great enthusiasm. Doors of city parks and gardens ordinarily closed to the general public were thrown open to all, and in the evening an elaborate fireworks display was presented.[27]

Young George's future was not as certain as the young queen's. Despite his dedicated preparation for the future, he now found himself in an awkward predicament. Scotland was better at producing scholars than providing them with opportunity, and therefore the unknown grass growing somewhere beyond the Firth of Forth seemed much greener than the home turf. Initially George's loyalty to family and country proved stronger than his desire for adventure, but the pull of the ocean continued to grow. His feelings were well expressed by another young Scot who was to sail to the distant bright shores of California and become a pioneer miner and founder of Downieville: "When I saw the waves rolling in through the North Channel," William Downie wrote, "I knew from my school books that they came from the great Atlantic and I longed to be on them and sail away to different parts of the world."[28]

Scots were impressed by countryman Alexander Mackenzie, who had sailed to America, crossed the Rocky Mountains, and reached the Pacific coast, thus earning fame as the first European to perform that feat. During his explorations of Canada, Mackenzie had followed a river, later to be named for him, all the way to the Arctic Ocean. Now the door had been thrown open to Scots wishing to emigrate to Canada, and members of another branch of the Borthwick family had already taken advantage of the opportunity. George, now on the brink of manhood, spent three years wrestling with the conflict between love of home and the attractions beyond. The Kinnear passion for the sea eventually held sway, and at age eighteen he took passage for the undeveloped lands of French Canada.[29] At his brother's departure, John David found himself in a dilemma. He was not only disappointed at being left behind to finish school, but also, for the first time in his young life, completely free of his older brother's domination. The freedom was as strange to him as the new role he must play as man of the house, due to his father's lingering illness. Each letter from his brother, describing his exciting experiences in the wilderness, increased his restlessness to finish school and once more follow in George's footsteps.

In 1839 he graduated from the Academy. Though he had been an avid reader, he received no medals. The Census of 1841 found the six remaining members of the Dr. George Borthwick family spending their final months together in their comfortable home on Darnaway: the doctor fifty years old, his wife Janet forty-three, John David sixteen, and Fearne,

Catherine, and little Janet, fourteen, twelve, and ten respectively. This census also reveals the conditions motivating the less fortunate to better themselves by emigration. One million Scots, that is one-third of the total families, lived in one-room homes. Eight thousand of these residences did not contain a single window.[30]

The following year Dr. George's condition became increasingly serious. His prayer to spend additional time with his family had been granted—six precious years of life, valued the more for the awareness of approaching death. Realizing his time was at hand, he summoned young George home from Canada, and then, to ease the burden soon to be placed upon his wife, set up a trust fund. Because of his strong constitution and deep desire to remain with his family, Dr. George survived yet another year, dying on November 16, 1843.[31]

His will reveals the great suffering he had endured during his final years, not for himself, but for those he must leave behind:

> I wish my beloved and most excellent wife to be my sole executrix. I well know the justice, the piety, and the excellence of her mind and disposition, and I commit the inheritance of our children to her care. But I wish it understood that she is to rely on the advice and assistance of the following persons to whose friendship I thus appeal, namely to her brothers John, David, Alexander and James, whom I hope will never desert her and her fatherless children. George Kinnear is far away, but I have no reason to doubt that he will assist her and them. To our dear sister Anne Nicholson, to dear Rachel Arthur, and Mary Heriot Kinnear I have a request that they will comfort and assist and befriend their dear sister Janet and her children in any possible way.
>
> I especially wish that my dear friend Major Maxwell, Jr. of Calderwood and his brother Harry be informed of this my earnest entreaty that they will befriend my wife and children in every way. Indeed I know they will. They will be like fathers to the fatherless!

The doctor had also prepared a list of nineteen other friends and relatives, among them his cousin John Borthwick, owner of the castle, as "guardians, protectors of my dear wife and children trusting that they will direct the widow and fatherless children.'' He had sent a copy of the will to each person enlisted to provide counsel and emotional support for his family. This document makes clear that Dr. George's former admonitions to his offspring regarding depth of character were sincere. His acute sense of the responsibility of fatherhood made a deep impression on both of his sons.[32]

While the widow was still recovering from the loss of her life companion, she suffered a second blow—the death of a child. She had safely nursed her little brood through the illnesses of childhood only to have her middle daughter, Catherine, now a young woman, contract a fatal illness. After Catherine's death, the bereaved mother could no longer bear to be in the family home. She moved her remaining four children to a house on Great Stuart Street next door to the Blackwoods, a well-known family of publishers.[33]

For three years, her two sons remained at home. Neither elected to attend the university, but John David continued his education on his own, emerging from his books only to draw and paint. Some art historians believe that he received further art instruction, perhaps from portrait painter Robert Innes, who lived within the neighborhood, and there were also seven drawing academies in Edinburgh where he might have studied.[34] At any rate, he soon earned the reputation of being ''a very clever water-colour painter.''[35]

THE CONTINENT

When each of her sons turned twenty-one, Janet Borthwick presented him with an inheritance from the father's estate in a fund to be drawn upon a bit at a time. Her sons were quick to take advantage of their financial independence, embarking on a few short sea voyages and wandering throughout England and France and as far south as Naples. After their travels, they returned to tiny Scotland believing themselves quite continental. Edinburgh was no longer large enough to contain them.

George was the first to go. In June 1846 he filed a power of attorney with his Uncle James Kinnear, the Writer to the

Signet, granting him control of his funds during his absence. In August he departed for Liverpool with plans to set himself up as a businessman. John David was not long in following his brother's example. In December he likewise granted his uncle power of attorney over his holdings and began making preparations for a lengthy trip. Apprehensive about leaving his mother and two sisters without a man in the house, he arranged for them to take two live-in servants. Though John David was attempting to assert his independence from George by striking out in his own direction, he selected as his destination the very New World country his older brother had already visited. It would not be the same as when he had entered the unknown, and therefore frightening, world of the Academy; George would not be with him this time. His bag packed with drawing materials, his mind stocked with historical facts, and his soul saturated with the romantic notions of Scott, Shelley, and Wordsworth, the gently reared young artist set sail for the wild new lands, alone.[36]

PART II

Adventures in the New World

CANADA

Like his brother before him, J. D., as he now preferred to be called, sailed first to Quebec. Though it had originally been colonized by the French— Champlain having founded a trading post on the site of the present-day city of Quebec in 1608—the British had gained control of the area at the close of the French and Indian War. To pacify French-speaking inhabitants, the British had granted them the right of retaining their native language and religion; however, one decade before J. D.'s arrival, French Canadian dissatisfaction with British-imposed government had resulted in an unsuccessful rebellion. At the time the British were establishing a more democratic form of government in the newly united Lower Canada (Quebec) and Upper Canada (Ontario), where in 1837 J. D.'s fellow countryman, W. L. Mackenzie, had led an uprising.

J. D. found things peaceable enough on his arrival in 1847, the only open hostility being an occasional "set-to" between a couple of French Canadians. "Shaking their fists within an inch of each other's faces," he observed, "they call each other all the names imaginable, beginning with *sacré* cochon, and going through a long series of still less complimentary epithets, till finally *sacré* astrologe caps the climax. This is a regular smasher; it is supposed to be such a comprehensive term as to exhaust the whole vocabulary; both parties then give in for want of ammunition, and the fight is over."[1]

J. D. spent several months wandering about Canada, visiting the places George had written about and discovering new sites of interest on his own. Wherever he traveled he was treated as a gentleman; he was naturally reserved and quiet, and his manners and education marked him as a young man worthy of respect. In addition he was handsome with rather delicate facial features, average height and weight, and a muscular, athletic build. It was only natural that the kind treatment he universally received would color his view of the New World.

After spending more than a year in Canada, he was ready to move on to the United States, the land touted by periodicals of the day as a mecca of democracy, an egalitarian utopia destined to fulfill Robert Burns's prophetic lines:

It's comin' for a' that,
That man to man, the world o'er,
Shall brothers be for a' that.[2]

NEW YORK CITY

Though many immigrants had come to the States to escape poverty at home, J. D. had come to examine and judge the new nation, now numbering about twenty-three million inhabitants. After traveling the entire length of the country, getting as far south as New Orleans, he returned to New York, where he took living quarters and commenced familiarizing himself with the city. Though no longer the nation's capital, New York City was a bustling center of commerce and, through efforts of Wall Street bankers, the leading financial center as well. As for culture, there were ten theaters that presented minstrel shows, an opera house, an art academy, and the studios of several painters of the Hudson River School. The city and its surrounding romantic landscape provided sufficient activity to keep a budding young artist occupied, but it was difficult to focus attention on the east coast when a feverish emigration was taking place to the western shore in search of gold. Offices of the steamship companies, he soon discovered, were "perfectly mobbed" for a day and night before tickets were put on sale. In the spring of 1850, J. D. later wrote, he was suddenly "seized with the California fever."[3] Though he was as eager as the next man for quick, easy wealth, he also recognized that the uncivilized goldfields would make a perfect testing ground of the principles for which the revolutions of the past century had been fought: liberty, equality, and fraternity. And being an introspective young man, he was aware that more than the new society would be on trial—he himself was untested. The comfort and security of his early years had not given him opportunity to test his endurance or his commitment to the ideals his forefathers championed. The adventures awaiting him would doubtless be fraught with danger and hardship, as well as the constant threat of failure. Success, however, could bring the greatest peril of all; in achieving a materialistic goal, he might well sacrifice his personal idealism. Thus in hope that, though he could not match his older brother's feats as a student, he might possibly surpass him as a world traveler, he commenced his quest for enlightenment and self-knowledge.

Rejecting the four- to six-month voyage around Cape Horn as too tedious, he joined the clamor for a ticket on a steamer bound for the Isthmus of Panama. But he was so caught up in the prevailing excitement and so gripped by the contagious urgency to get to the far coast before the gold ran out that he made a grave error, one that in the long run would cost him much more precious time than having waited. Rather than holding out until he could obtain passage on government-contracted steamers—commodious vessels designed specifically for conveying passengers and mail—he grasped at the first available opportunity to get to sea, a small, ill-equipped sailing craft, pressed into service to earn its owners a quick dollar from the sudden demand for transportation. He sailed in May 1850. (*Three Years in California* incorrectly states the year as 1851.)

Thus only a few days after deciding to become a gold seeker in the wilderness, he found himself crowded among sixty other imprudent zealots on a temporary deck slung over the ballast of a creaky little barque of only two hundred tons. It provided his first opportunity to participate in a venture conducted completely without distinction of social class. There was no separation of cabin and steerage passengers because there was not a single cabin. Three tiers of planks had been constructed around the edges of the makeshift deck as berths, and a crude table flanked by benches had been tacked together to serve as a common dining facility.

The passengers aboard formed a sort of microcosm—Americans, English, French, Swedes, and Germans, representing nearly every trade and occupation, and a group of "nondescript 'young men,' " the category into which J. D. himself fit. He was too happy to be on his way to the goldfields to feel repentant about his hasty choice or to be concerned that he had no passage from Panama to San Francisco. In fact he welcomed the uncomfortable living facilities as an opportunity to condition himself for what lay ahead: "For my own part, I knew that I should have to rough it in California, and felt that I might just as well begin at once as wait till I got there." He was cheerful about the voyage and optimistic about the opportunity awaiting at the mines, and a benevolent Nature seemed to reflect his mood: the first day out of New York brought fine weather, and on the second day a delightful breeze sprang up, freshening the air. Though the numerous "landlubbers" aboard were having difficulty in finding their sea legs, J. D. could take pride in his Kinnear instinct for the sea. That, combined with experience from past voyages, left him hale and hearty.[4]

On the second night, however, the breeze suddenly developed into a strong wind, and then into a full-scale gale that not only prevented forward progress, but also mercilessly pitched the small vessel. It was impossible to get any rest, with the luggage and casks of provisions "cruising about promiscuously" and threatening to bring down the flimsy framework on which they slept. "Those who were not too sick to be able to form an opinion on the subject, were frightened out of their wits," J.D. wrote, "being sure, every time the ship laid over, that she was never coming up again."[5] Since the steward and waiters were as sick as the rest and therefore unable to prepare any meals, J. D. was given additional opportunity to prepare for the rugged times ahead: "There were not more than half-a-dozen of us who could eat anything, or could even stand on deck; so we roughed it out on cold beef, hard bread, and brandy-and-water."[6]

On the following day the gale let up and the barque continued, but the steward, even after recovering from seasickness, turned out to be a "useless vagabond," so passengers were forced to choose three of their own number to assume his responsibilities. Provisions were so sparse it became necessary to supplement the diet by shooting dolphins and eating the liver. Yet despite the poor food and accommodations, spirits of those aboard were generally high. Showing an appreciation of life's little ironies, J. D. noted that "no one grumbled, excepting a few of the lowest class of men in the party, who had very likely never been used to such good living ashore."[7]

Spirits were lifted even more when the ship reached the trade winds. Cool night breezes now made for comfortable sleeping, and sunny days provided the perfect opportunity for daydreaming about the final destination. "The all-engrossing subject of conversation," J. D. recorded, "was of course California, and the heaps of gold we were all to find there." But the closer they got to Panama, the more mindful they became of their dilemma. Before their departure, all had heard rumors that thousands were already stranded on the Isthmus, vainly attempting to obtain passage of any kind to San Francisco. A highly respected journalist had dispatched an article about some stranded gold seekers who had set out from Panama in log canoes. After a harrowing forty-day voyage, a few had made it safely back to Panama, but the rest had never been heard from since.[8]

Realizing the report was undoubtedly reliable did little to dampen the passengers' optimism, but it did have the unhealthy effect of contributing to a selfish isolationism that J. D. deplored: "Everyone was perfectly confident that he at least would have no trouble in getting along, whatever might be the fate of the rest of the crowd."[9]

As they neared Chagres, excitement among the passengers reached a high pitch. Though as susceptible to the fever as the others, J. D. could not help being amused at the ridiculous picture the party presented, burdened down with "absurd and useless articles" they had been "humbugged" into buying in New York before departure: kettles, cups, knives, forks, spoons, pocket-filters to strain dirty drinking water, and India-rubber contrivances ranging from coats to lifeboats. "But how to carry them all," he commented, "or even how to use them, was the main difficulty, and would indeed have puzzled much cleverer men."[10] Final hours were spent in "firing off and reloading pistols: for a revolver and a bowie-knife were considered the first items in a California outfit. We soon assumed a warlike appearance, and though many of the party had probably never handled a pistol in their lives before, they tried to wear their weapons in a negligé style, as if they never had been used to go without them."[11]

Shore came into view at last, the two-thousand nautical miles having been covered in twenty days. At evening they dropped anchor a mile from shore in a bay bounded by high bluffs covered with lush, green foliage. But before small boats from shore could reach their ship a storm erupted—fierce thunder, flashes of jagged lightning, and bucketfuls of rain—and they realized they would be spending their first night in the tropics aboard ship.[12]

PANAMA

They had been warned that Chagres was a "sickly wretched place," and the small village of cane-and-mud huts and two wooden hotels kept by Americans lived up to their expectations. After disembarking, the passengers broke into small groups to negotiate with native boatmen for the trip up the Chagres River. J. D. joined a party of nine, who first ate a breakfast of ham and beans in one of the hotels and then engaged a boat owner. Since the boat had no crew, two sailors who had jumped ship to join in the Gold Rush offered their services. The passengers were not particularly apprehensive about the river trip. New York *Tribune* correspondent Bayard Taylor, who had gone West at the suggestion of his editor, Horace Greeley, had reported, in 1849, lolling under an umbrella and taking in the splendid scenery while a capable crew deftly navigated:

> The river, broad, with a swift current of the sweetest water I ever drank, winds between walls of foliage that rise from its very surface. From the rank jungle of canes and gigantic lilies, and the thickets of strange shrubs that line the water, rise the trunks of the mango, the ceiba, the cocoa, the sycamore and the superb palm. Plantains take root in the banks, hiding the soil with their leaves, shaken and split into immense plumes by the wind and rain. The zapote, with a fruit the size of a man's head, the gourd tree, and other vegetable wonders, attract the eye on all sides. Blossoms of crimson, purple and yellow, of a form and magnitude unknown in the North, are mingled with the leaves, and flocks of paroquets and brilliant butterflies circle through the air like blossoms blown away. Every turn of the stream only disclosed another and more magnificent vista of leaf, bough and blossom.[13]

Taylor concluded that in spite of the "many dolorous accounts which have been sent from the Isthmus, there is nothing, at the worst season, to deter any one from the journey."[14] But J. D. and the twelve others crowded into the small boat soon realized their experience was destined to differ from Taylor's description. The landscape was as beautiful as claimed, but for the second time the passengers had been unfortunate in their choice of a vessel. It was not only overcrowded, but the two sailors hired to row turned out to be gold seekers who had signed as seamen in New York only as an excuse to reach California and had no previous experience as crewmen. Weather alternated between blazing sun and deluges of rain, and after a few hours of pulling against the current, the sailors both gave out, stranding the party several miles from the nearest settlement, unable to land them on either rugged bank. The boat owner, whom J. D. considered a "useless encumbrance," took up space but refused to assume any responsibility. In fact he remained completely indifferent to the outcome of the matter, and passengers fell to quibbling among themselves, unable to agree on the best course of action.[15]

It was not a very auspicious beginning to the great experiment in democracy, but J. D. was not discouraged. Though not normally an assertive person, he realized someone must provide leadership to get them back on track, and he, after all, was a Borthwick, one "who leads." He therefore determined to set an example for the rest by taking over the oars. A fellow Scot offered to assist, and with a scorching sun bearing down overhead, the two volunteers began laboriously inching the heavily laden craft upstream. Though J. D. proved equal to the arduous task, by dark they still had not reached their intended destination. He tied the boat to a tree branch, trying to appear capable but all the while thinking to himself, "So here we are, thirteen of us, with a proportionate pile of baggage, cramped up in a small boat, in which we had spent the day, and were now doomed to pass the night, our miseries aggravated by torrents of rain, nothing to eat, and worse than that, nothing to drink, but worse than all, without even a dry match wherewith to light a pipe. If ever it is excusable to chew tobacco, it surely is on such an occasion as this."[16]

When the moon rose, they continued on, reaching a village on the bank about dawn. After a breakfast of ham, beans, and eggs at a canvas restaurant set amidst the native huts by an enterprising but sickly Yankee, they continued on upriver, the sailors once more at the oars. When they tired, J. D., assisted by the other Scot, again took over. After a few hours of exhausting work, he became "rather provoked" at watching the rest, "sitting doggedly under their umbrellas" and not lifting so much as a finger to help. Since his demonstration of the nobility in hard labor had proven fruitless, he now openly suggested each man do his "share of work for the common good." The responses that came back perplexed him: "Some protested they did not know how to pull, others pleaded bad health, and the rest very coolly said, that having paid their money to be taken to Cruces, they expected to be taken there, and would not pull a stroke.'' J. D. and his compatriot rowed on to the next stopping point.[17]

Though it was only a collection of three huts inhabited by a handful of natives, more than fifty passengers from other boats were already huddled under the rain-dripping shelters, trying to persuade the local women to prepare them a meal. The native women's ''lazy listless way of doing things did not suit the humor we were in at all,'' J. D. wrote. ''The invariable reply to all demands for something to eat and drink was *poco tiempo* (by-and-by), said in that sort of tone one would use to a troublesome child. . . . We succeeded at last in getting supper in installments—now a mouthful of ham, now an egg or a few beans, and then a cup of coffee, just as they would make up their minds to the violent exertion of getting these articles ready for us.''[18] For a few dollars the women agreed to vacate one hut for the travelers to use as sleeping quarters that night, and J. D. found himself a spot in a loft made of bamboos and reached by climbing a notched pole!

The next day the river current proved so strong that poling the boat became necessary, and at last the remainder of the passengers gave in and took a turn. They spent the night at another hut, crowded with drunken travelers apt any minute to, in Yankee lingo, ''kick up a muss'' with the natives and Negro boatmen. After pacifying the rowdier lot, the saner members of the company persuaded all present to lie down on the floor, ''packed like sardines in a box,'' to try to get some sleep, but ''if one man moved, he woke half-a-dozen others, who again in waking roused all the rest.''[19]

Two more such days and nights were spent on the river, eating and sleeping with the natives and making a few hard-earned miles each day, sometimes by stepping into the water and towing the boat over rapids. Occasionally they met a boat of gold hunters headed back in the opposite direction. On this same river Bayard Taylor had reported an encounter with a returning Californian who was carrying a box of gold dust worth $22,000 in one hand and a four-pound lump in the other. The sight of the gold had thrown the members of

Taylor's party into a frenzy to proceed.[20] But J. D. and companions experienced no such favorable omens; instead they met more boat loads of discouraged argonauts bound back to New York. Some were threatening to sue the steamship company for reneging on their promise to have a vessel waiting at Panama City for the second leg of the journey.[21]

At Cruces, J. D.'s group left the river. He had intended on hiring a mule for the overland portion of the trip, but on learning that his fellow travelers could not afford a mount, he abandoned the plan as unnecessary luxury and struck out on foot with the rest. Though he had anticipated a "pleasant" hike, he was soon "undeceived." The road abruptly degenerated into a rocky trail winding through gullies of dense jungle that held in suffocating heat but provided no protection from sudden downpours of rain. All day they looked forward to reaching the conveniences of the halfway house, but on arrival were disappointed to discover it was only a "miserable little tent."[22] Weary and rain soaked, they took a place in the line of wayfarers awaiting a turn at the use of the two plates and two sets of silverware the establishment owned. When finally obtained, supper was eaten under the envious eyes of those still hovering about in ankle-deep mud for their turn. J. D. persuaded his party that it would be wiser to leave the crowded tent and return to a native residence they had passed earlier. There they spent the night on "dried hides laid on the floor, as hard as so many sheets of iron, and full of bumps and hollows; but they were dry, which was all we cared about, for we thought of the poor devils sleeping in the mud in the half-way house."[23]

The road from that point onward ran through rolling countryside, but the jungle heat was still oppressive. Then at last a light breeze, smelling of the ocean, brushed their perspiring faces. By noon they could see the city of Panama, built on a low hill with two sides facing the sea. As they approached, they heard music—fifes, drums, and fiddles—and realized a fiesta was in progress. Streets were alive with gaily dressed celebrators of skin tones ranging from white to black, and "every intermediate shade of color." Some were setting off fireworks while others paid homage at gaudily decorated altars set up in the street. Chanting and singing emanated from open doors of dilapidated churches whose only remaining traces of their former grandeur were the lofty bell towers, still heavily ornamented with glistening oyster shell. Most of the houses were wooden, brightly painted, and with verandas on both stories, but the residences of the wealthy were made of stone or adobe brick, plastered over and painted.[24]

J. D. thought the native women in their frilly white dresses trimmed in colored ribbons "very handsome." At the neck they wore golden jewelry and in their dark hair flowers, but despite their charms, they had the strange habit of using their coiffure as a handbag. "It is not unusual," he noted, "to see the ends of three or four half-smoked cigars sticking out from the folds of their hair at the back of the head; for though they smoke a great deal, they never seem to finish a cigar at one smoking."[25]

Mingling in the carnival atmosphere were many a California-bound foreigner, noticeable by red flannel shirt and revolver and knife tucked into the belt. The principal businesses—hotels packed to overflowing and stores of every kind—had been taken over by "los Americanos," as all outsiders were called. An occasional enterprising native businessman had stuck up a shabby sign written in "very bad English" to the effect that he also had something to sell inside, but a buyer discovered the "energy was all theoretical, for on going into his store you would find him half asleep in his hammock, out of which he would not rouse himself if he could possibly avoid it. You were welcome to buy as much as you pleased; but he seemed to think it very hard that you could not do so without giving him at the same time the trouble of selling."[26]

Those who had been prudent and fortunate enough to have come to Chagres on the mail steamer found their continuation ship at anchor in the harbor, but the three thousand unfortunates played the waiting game, entertaining themselves by flocking to the main streets to join the gambling, drinking, and cockfight betting going on there, and quite frequently staging their own "rows and fights." It had become necessary to establish an American hospital complete with physicians from the States to treat the rampant diarrhea and fever spread by the "outrageously filthy state of the town." All that prevented the population from being "swallowed up" in the accumulation of its own waste, J. D. noted, was the heavy rainfall and ensuing runoff.[27]

By the Fourth of July he was still waiting. He watched the American celebration with a certain amount of amusement. A procession, led by a band playing "Yankee Doodle," filed into a canvas tent, recently vacated by a local circus, and solemnly listened to the reading of the Declaration of Independence. Then an impassioned orator took the stand and delivered "a flaming speech on the subject of George III and the Universal Yankee nation," after which the enthusiastic crowd dispersed to regroup at nearby bars. In the days following this ceremony, J. D. had ample time to contemplate the fervently nationalistic Fourth of July speech and attempt to reconcile its optimistic message with the disappointment he had been struggling to contain since leaving New York. He had fully expected to find a strong bond of brotherhood existing among the free men united in this common venture; instead, he was forced to admit that the principle of "every man for himself" predominated. Even the sick were regarded as encumbrances to be avoided since they were a "hindrance to one's own individual progress." He confessed he was truly disgusted with the "heartless selfishness" all about him.[28]

During the restless waiting period in Panama, J. D. met with a serious accident, though exactly what befell him remains an unsolved mystery. It is difficult to imagine any accident that a competent journalist, such as he turned out to be, would not capitalize on as representative of the perils of the journey, but for reasons unknown, J. D. chose to keep his misfortune a secret. Perhaps the details were so intimate it would have been indelicate to elaborate on them or, even worse, perhaps so much as admitting the incident would have proven embarrassing to his family at home. Such conjecture serves more to whet the appetite than to solve the riddle, but, for whatever motive, J. D. was tight lipped about the matter: "I met with an accident here which laid me up for several weeks.

I suffered a good deal, and passed a most weary time. All the books I could get hold of did not last me more than a few days, and I had then no other pastime than to watch the humming-birds buzzing about the flowers which grew around my window.''[29]

By the time he had recovered from his mysterious injury enough to be able to walk, he was very anxious to make up for lost time and therefore again settled for passage on one of the small sailing boats. They took as much as sixty days longer than the Pacific mail ships, but any spare tickets on these steamers were being disposed of among eager would-be passengers by means of lottery.[30] Though any of the ships departing for San Francisco would have been sorely overcrowded, J. D. was, for the third time, unfortunate in the vessel selected. It was supplied with provisions of a ``most inferior quality'' and in such limited quantity that in order to prevent starvation the ship had to make continual stops at ports along the way. But with the magic of California on their minds, J. D. and the other passengers accepted the ``hard fare'' gracefully. ``Every one,'' he wrote, ``was so confident of acquiring an immense fortune there, in an incredibly short time, that he was already making his plans for the future enjoyment of it, and present difficulties and hardships were not sufficiently appreciated.''[31]

Even against strong head winds, the mail steamers were reaching San Francisco in fourteen days, but after more than six weeks of battling raging gales and then waiting out endless calms, the little three-masted ship was still at sea. Finally, one September evening, carried on ``the first and only fair wind'' encountered on the entire voyage, it glided through the Golden Gate just at dusk. The glow of lights from the little city spread along the bay was a welcome sight to the passengers.[32]

SAN FRANCISCO

J. D. disembarked to discover a ``most motley collection'' of buildings jumbled together into a city: tents, multistoried brick businesses, corrugated iron shacks, ship hulls dragged ashore and converted into hotels, and wooden residences that had been sailed around the Horn in sections, assembled, and then painted white and trimmed with green shutters. The majority of buildings were not of any single material, but rather a "patchwork," consisting of wood, sheet iron, zinc, and canvas "indiscriminately" combined. In the central plaza stood a weathered adobe structure facing a row of handsome new gambling halls that continued the entire length of the street, blending into one blaze of light. Sidewalks piled high with goods of all sorts were the "scene of intense bustle and excitement." All were in a rush: Chinamen in purple-figured silk jackets, Mexicans with brightly striped serapes thrown gracefully across the left shoulders, Englishmen in shooting coats, Down-Easters in black suits, and New Yorkers and Frenchmen in the latest fashions from Paris. J. D. characterized the astounding sight before him as "life at high speed."[33]

His ears were "dinned with the discord of half-a-dozen brass bands, braying out different popular airs from as many different gambling saloons." Above the music and the babble of conversations in every imaginable tongue rang the shrill cries of newsboys advertising world events and steamship tooters "cracking up the superiority of their respective boatlines at the top of their lungs, somewhat in this style: 'One dollar to-night for Sacramento, by the splendid steamer Senator, the fastest boat that ever turned a wheel . . . with feather pillows and curled-hair mattresses, mahogany doors and silver hinges. She has got eight young-lady passengers to-night, that speak all the dead languages.' "[34] The incessant activity would occasionally be interrupted by the cry, "Hullo! there's a muss!" causing all in hearing distance to rush to the spot where some altercation had broken out. But, "if no one was killed," J. D. noted, "the mob would disperse, to resume their various occupations, just as quickly as they had collected."[35]

The interiors of the hotels, restaurants, and gambling halls were decorated in "most barbaric splendor," the "costliest French furniture, and a profusion of immense mirrors, gorgeous gilding, magnificent chandeliers, and gold and china ornaments." Their luxuriousness presented a strange contrast to some of the guests, for rubbing shoulders with the international set were those who had already visited the mines, "in all the glory of mining costume, jealous of every inch of their long hair and flowing beards, and of every bit of California mud which adhered to their ragged old shirts and patchwork pantaloons."[36]

While they were still reeling in amazement at their new surroundings, the passengers experienced a second shock: the cost of living was exorbitant. One new arrival wrote that he landed with ten dollars in his pocket, paid seven to have his trunks carried from the ship, ate a two-dollar meal, the cheapest he could find, and had one dollar left over—hardly enough to get to the mines.[37] Because the long delay in Panama had depleted the funds of many of the emigrants, they were forced to seek jobs in San Francisco to earn money for passage to the goldfields. J. D. was among those fortunate enough to be financially solvent, but because of the rainy weather, he decided to spend the winter becoming familiar with the city.

In his explorations he was not long in discovering a small adobe settlement two miles up the bay at Mission Dolores, a strong contrast to the noisy, bustling city. Land surrounding the little mission town was still planted to vegetables, as in the days of Franciscan padres; in fact the tiny village had changed little since that era. Being there was like stepping back a century and soaking up the atmosphere of pastoral life in the days of Spanish domination: "It had a look of antiquity and completeness, as if it had been finished long ago," he wrote, "and as if nothing more was ever likely to be done with it. As is the case with all Spanish American towns, the very style of the architecture communicated an oppressive feeling of stillness."[38]

The aura of dreamy timelessness hovering over the little adobe huts and heavy-walled church, with its Corinthian pillars and red-tiled roof, recalled history—how in the 1760s King Charles III had sent the Franciscans to California to deter Russians and English from gaining further foothold in the area. And in the very year the American colonies on the east coast were declaring their independence, members of the Anza expedition reached San Francisco Bay and constructed the original log-and-mud mission and a horseshoe-shaped fort. They named the pueblo that grew up nearby Yerba Buena, or Good Herb. Padres soon succeeded in rounding up the natives, converting them to Catholicism, and then teaching them to cultivate grapes, grains, and olives and tend herds of cattle, sheep, and swine. After Mexico achieved independence from Spain in 1821, secularization of the missions was gradually carried out. Thousands of mission acres were divided into huge ranchos, but the ranchero's pastoral society, in replacing the mission system, did not disturb the peace. Demoralized and subjugated Indians continued to work the fields and tend the immense herds of cattle grazing in the lush grass of the silent valleys and gentle hills, while owners of the vast estates supervised or entertained guests in the flowered courtyards of cool, thick-walled adobe ranch houses. Tallow, hides, and horns were exchanged with Yankee traders for the few luxuries essential to gracious living: shoes, cloth, jewelry, coffee, tobacco, and wines.

When, in 1841, American naval officer Charles Wilkes sailed into San Francisco Bay, he found that the port consisted of "a large frame house occupied by an agent of the Hudson's Bay Company; a store kept by an American; a billiard-room and bar; a poop-cabin of a ship, occupied as a dwelling by an Anglo-American captain; a blacksmith shop, and some outbuildings."[39] Five years later Sam Brannan's band of Mormons arrived, giving a spurt of growth to the town, not only by augmenting the population but also by providing it with civic leadership and its first newspaper, *The California Star.*

In 1848, however, Sam Brannan temporarily emptied the growing town of nearly all of its male population by riding through the streets and waving his hat while he shouted that gold had been discovered on the American River. To back up his allegation, he brandished a quinine bottle full of gold dust. The rush was on. An early resident has recorded for posterity the typical reaction to seeing a neighbor return from the mines with a pouch of gold:

> Out the metal tumbled; not in dust or scales, but in pieces ranging in size from that of a pea to hen's eggs; and, says he,

> "this is only what I picked out with a knife." I looked on for a moment; a frenzy seized my soul; unbidden my legs performed some entirely new movements of polka steps—I took several—houses were too small for me to stay in; I was soon in the street in search of necessary outfits; piles of gold rose up before me at every step; castles of marble, dazzling the eye with their rich appliances; thousands of slaves bowing to my beck and call; myriads of fair virgins contending with each other for my love, were among the fancies of my fevered imagination. The Rothschilds, Girards, and Astors appeared to me but poor people; in short, I had a very violent attack of the Gold Fever.
>
> One hour after I became thus affected, I was mounted on an old mule, armed with wash hand basin, fire shovel, a piece of square iron pointed at one end, a blanket, rifle, a few yards of jerked beef, and a bag of penola, and going at high-pressure speed for the "diggin's."[40]

Eagerly arriving forty-niners found the city on the bay looking like "a vast army encampment," the shore and surrounding hills "covered with tents." Along the beach, one argonaut reported, were scattered "a great number of trunks, chests, and valises of all sizes, and the most of them containing clothing of all descriptions, in many cases of value. These had all been thrown aside as useless encumbrances by their owners, who had started for the mines, being unable to pay the extra freight charged upon them."[41]

Because of the high cost of a hotel room, most disembarking passengers spent their first night on the beach, camped next to the bales of hides and piles of horns that rancheros had hopefully stacked there. But since gold-crazed sailors had jumped ship and headed for the mines, a large fleet of abandoned vessels lay in port, with no crew to load the waiting cargo.[42] One of the deserting seamen, a Britisher named William Shaw, wrote that the tent city was called "Happy Valley," though he thought "Sickly Valley" would have been a more appropriate name, because of the "filth of every description, and stagnant pools" encountered at every step. "Scenes of depravity, sickness, and wretchedness, shocked the moral sense, as much as filth and effluvia did the nerves," he wrote.[43]

At the time of J. D.'s arrival in September 1850, San Francisco was well on its way to becoming the metropolis of the West Coast. Though the young artist was proud of his familiarity with both London and Paris, the international community gathered in California offered him his first opportunity to observe a wide variety of cultures in interaction. Carefully observant of all about him, he strolled from quarter to quarter. In the French district he noted that even the letters of the signs had a "French look about them," but to court the American clientele, many French owners had given their restaurants names such as "Jackson House" or "Lafayette." Streets of the Mexican section were crowded with "lazy Mexicans lying about, wrapped up in their blankets, smoking cigaritas," and the German lager-beer cellars were so loud and smoky as to "deter any one but a German from venturing in." In the "curious pagoda-looking" Chinese theatres, performances went on day and night, but despite the "gorgeous dresses of the actors," the meaning of it all was "quite unintelligible to outside barbarians," like himself. In addition, the noise of the gongs and kettledrums became deafening after a few minutes.[44]

But wherever he wandered, he marveled at the immense "vitality" of the city. He concluded that the residents of San Francisco "lived more" in a week than the rest of the world did in a year: more hard work done, more speculative schemes conceived, more money made and lost, more crime committed, yet at the same time, "more solid advancement made by the people, as a body, in wealth, prosperity, and the refinements of civilization."[45]

J. D. possessed not only the eye of an artist, but also the intellect of a scholar, and he began making a series of comparisons between the Old World and the New. Here, he observed, "every man is his own servant." He also noted a fierce competition existing in each line of employment, every person striving to be of "foremost rank in his own sphere." He feared that many residents of the old countries lacked the vigor required to succeed. There was an oversupply of "young men of education, who had never dreamed of manual labor" and therefore found their services were not required here. In fact he believed that a "polished education," unless it also included an unusual amount of "democratic feeling," could result in an "extreme sensitiveness" that left a man unfit to take part in a "hand-to-hand struggle with his fellow-men."[46] Most interesting to him was a lack of community pressure that allowed the individual the freedom to be his true self, or human nature in its "bald and naked state," as he called it.[47]

Because of his political leanings, J. D. was most concerned with discovering the character of the Americans, but in order to be objective he realized he would first have to cast aside certain prejudices. At that time, relations between Great Britain and the United States were not the best. The American Revolution, the War of 1812, trade problems, and heated disputes over the boundary lines of Oregon and Maine had created deep-seated hostility on both sides. An English naval officer had expressed the mixed feelings the British typically felt for the rebellious colonists: "I don't like Americans; I never did, and never shall like them . . . I have no wish to eat with them, drink with them, deal with, or consort with them in any way; but let me tell the whole truth, nor fight with . . . an enemy so brave."[48]

A speech delivered on the floor of the House makes plain that many Americans harbored equally hard feelings against the parent country: "I hate the British government," Representative Owen Lovejoy of Illinois declared, weeping with anger. "I now here publicly avow and record my inextinguishable hatred . . . I mean to cherish it while I live and to bequeath it as a legacy to my children when I die. And if I am alive when war with England comes, as sooner or later it must . . . if I can carry a musket in that war I will carry it."[49]

Despite an awareness of past differences and a current feeling of repugnance for certain American crudities, J. D. felt genuine admiration for the new nation's dedication to personal freedom. "So long as he did not interfere with the rights of others," he wrote, a man "could follow his own course."[50] He also admired the Americans' "natural versatility" and "adaptability."[51] Observing the San Francisco cabs—lined with silk and ornate with silver—he discovered another national trait: "The Americans have a style and taste in driving peculiarly their own; they study neither grace nor comfort in their attitudes; speed is the only source of pleasure."[52] This tendency to "make the voyage through life under a full head of steam all the time," demanded recourse to stimulants, small doses of alcohol taken at regular intervals throughout the entire day. In fact, he considered drinking one of the peculiar institutions of the country—the habit of expressing courtesy to a friend by offering him a drink and his obligation to accept, the rapidity with which this common form of social intercourse was performed, and the enormous consumption of liquor without the expected accompanying vice of drunkenness.[53]

Though J. D. took pains never to write of his homesickness for Scotland, he spent his share of time in the long queues before the post office, hoping for a letter from his family:

> Closely packed together, the people were all in six strings, twisted up and down in all directions . . . Smoking and chewing tobacco were great aids in passing the time, and many came provided with books and newspapers . . . Many a poor fellow's face lengthened out into a doleful expression of disbelief and disappointment, as, scarcely had he uttered his name, when he was promptly told there was nothing for him. This was a sentence from which there was no appeal, however incredulous one might be; and every man was incredulous; for during the hour or two he had been waiting, he had become firmly convinced in his own mind that there must be a letter for him; . . . one would like to have had the post-office searched all over, and if without success, would still have thought there was something wrong. I was myself upon one occasion deeply impressed with this spirit of unbelief in the infallibility of the post-office oracle, and tried the effect of another application the next day, when my perseverance was crowned with success.[54]

Throughout the fall and winter he wandered about the rat-infested, mainly male-populated city, becoming familiar with every nook and cranny and the ways of those who inhabited them. He attended numerous masquerade balls, noting morosely that there were no more than six, at the most, female bodies beneath the costumes and masks. But since no weapons were admitted, it was always entertaining to stand by and watch the guests checking their pistols and knives. "If any man declared that he had no weapon," he wrote, "the statement was so incredible that he had to submit to be searched; an operation which was performed by the doorkeepers."[55] Occasionally, just for a brief respite from the dizzying pace of the Californians' "impetuous pursuit of wealth," he entered one of the "second-rate English drinking-shops, where John Bull could smoke his pipe and swig his ale coolly and calmly, without having to gulp it down and move off to make way for others, as at the bars of the American saloons."[56]

Throughout his various accounts of the Gold Rush, J. D. carefully represented himself as a journalist from Great Britain. However, a reader familiar with his Scottish heritage will notice an occasional poignant lapse that reveals the deep reverence he felt for that small piece of earth where he was born and reared. One such example is the winsome comment that the salmon of California may be as flavorful as those found in the Scottish rivers, but not quite as graceful in appearance.[57]

He spent days browsing in the colorful international shops surrounded outside by heaps of empty bottles, suggesting a "consumption of liquor which was truly awful"[58] Oriental bazaars, advertised by brilliantly painted signs lettered in artful characters and streaming with red ribbons, were jammed with customers. Among the display of copper cookware, fans, shawls, chess sets, dried fish, and preserved duck, were some "nasty-looking" eatables that wary Caucasians suspected of being rat pies.[59] From chic jewelry stores, emerged newly rich miners, sporting the peculiar combination of a dirty workshirt fastened with a diamond cluster.[60]

Feeling a need to escape from the city for a while, J. D. took the stage to San Jose, a town which like Mission Dolores "had a good deal of the California of other days" about it. The countryside was "smooth and open," yet "not so flat as to appear monotonous," and was "wooded with fine oaks."[61] Since San Jose was at that time serving as the state capital, several new streets of wooden houses had been added to the rows of adobe residences. A poplar-lined road led out of town toward Mission Santa Clara, the old path early inhabitants of the pueblo had followed to attend church.

It was but a five-hour ride back to the city, and, as usual at any hour of day or night, an auction was in progress. The auctioneer first rang a bell to attract an audience and then launched into his unintelligible spiel while a crowd gathered in the street.[62] Gambling halls were also "thronged day and night," large rooms "brilliantly lighted up by several very fine chandeliers, the walls decorated with ornamental painting and gilding, and hung with large mirrors and showy pictures, while in an elevated projecting orchestra half-a-dozen Germans were playing operatic music."[63] About the crowded tables, hazy with smoke and aromatic with brandy fumes, eager men of every race and rank elbowed their way to place a bet at a faro, monte, roulette, dice, or rouge-et-noir game. The professionals operating the tables were sharp dressers, but with a characteristic "haggard, careworn look," undoubtedly brought on by the constant pressure of accepting any loss or gain without the "slightest change in the expression of their face." The bettors struggled to appear equally unconcerned, but with them the effort was "often too plainly evident." Of all nationalities, the Mexicans "showed the most admirable impassibility."[64]

J. D. felt it necessary to make clear the distinction between a gambler and a bettor: "The gamblers were only the professionals, the men who laid out their banks in public rooms, and invited all and sundry to bet against them. They were a distinct and numerous class of the community, who followed their profession for the accommodation of the public; and any one who did business with them was no more a 'gambler' than a man who bought a pound of tea was a grocer."[65]

When the musicians in a gambling hall took a break, the place fell silent, except for the "slight hum of voices, and the constant clinking of money; for it was the fashion, while standing betting at a table, to have a lot of dollars in one's hands, and to keep shuffling them backwards and forwards like so many cards." During slack moments, the gambler would rise from the table and saunter about, leaving high stacks of gold and silver coin untended, "seemingly as little anxious" as if they were "under lock and key in an iron chest." Every gambling hall had a "long polished mahogany or marble" bar where twice a day a "sumptious lunch of soups, cold meats, fish," and other delectables was spread as a treat for guests. The wall behind this bar was completely covered with mirrors, gilding, gold clocks, and rows of ornamental bottles, before which "smart young" bartenders swirled together, "as if by magic," the ingredients for the "hundred and one" drinks offered.[66]

Despite the attraction of the cosmopolitan life, by spring J.D. was anxious to head north to the mines. Desirous of following the simple life of the manual laborer he was about to become, he determined to travel lightly. But his Scotch frugality would not allow him to discard his valuables, like the overstocked merchants who had dumped excess stoves, kegs of nails, and pianos in the mud as a boardwalk. Rather than imitate such wasteful behavior, he requested an acquaintance who was remaining in San Francisco to keep his baggage for him.[67]

On purchasing his ticket, he discovered that the steamer fare to Sacramento was slightly above the one dollar price advertised by tooters. When the first of the steamers, "long, white, two-story houses, floating apparently on nothing," had arrived in the harbor, after a slow, perilous, 17,000-mile voyage around the entire continent of South America, passengers had been forced to pay fifty dollars for a ticket to Sacramento,[68] but the keen competition between rival steamship companies had quickly lowered fares. In a state which had been admitted to the Union less than a year earlier, mass transportation was now available up the Sacramento, Feather, and San Joaquin rivers to the depot cities of Sacramento, Marysville, and Stockton.

Having spent six months in the seaport that had sprung into existence as quickly as if a wand had been waved, J. D. now set out for the interior. His first impressions of California distinguish him from traveling artists who had arrived before him; he had shown not only more depth of observation, but also more tolerance, open-mindedness, and good-natured acceptance. For example, John Woodhouse Audubon, son of the noted ornithologist, had fallen into deep depression at the hardships of the trip and had experienced moral outrage at the abounding vice in San Francisco. He deprecated gold as the evil that made the city a "hell-hole of crime and dissipation."[69]

J. D., though admitting that in this unusual society "a man was judged by the amount of money in his purse," had also pointed out the many benefits realized from the sudden wealth: charities, schools, theaters, and opera houses. Rather than becoming demoralized by the numerous excesses, he objectively recorded them. He made light of the inconveniences, referring to California as being "famous for three things—rats, fleas, and empty bottles." As an afterthought to the list, he tacked on "old clothes," since buyers hastily donned new outfits at the moment of purchase, carelessly dropping cast-off garments in the street outside the clothing store. Edinburgh merchants who survived by collecting discarded clothing and restoring it to shabby elegance, he mused, would have had a field day in the muddy streets of San Francisco.[70] But he was now leaving all that behind.

Wearing his own "worse suit of clothes" and with a blanket slung over his shoulder, J. D. leaned on the steamer railing and watched evening shadows fall across the green hills and fertile valleys they passed.[71] This same scene had proven restorative to the soul of the younger Audubon, who had also left the city at dusk: "Beautiful hills, smooth but steep, green and velvety to look upon, a few tall redwoods . . . The water was as smooth as a lake, and the moon rose on so calm a sheet that its reflection was a long straight line of light, almost as brilliant as itself, and I sat late on the deck to admire it, and to think of all at home, but at last went down to the filthy cabin."[72] When J. D. felt sleepy enough to go to the cabin, he discovered that passengers outnumbered berths by a wide margin and therefore wrapped himself in his blanket and curled up on the floor. He slept comfortably until three in the morning, when he was awakened by a blast of escaping steam.

The ship had arrived at the docks of the second largest city in California.

SACRAMENTO

The future capital sat on the river bank, only about six feet above water level, a short line of lighted buildings looming out of the mists. Stumbling along a boardwalk, where an earlier visitor had noted that rats "came out after dark in strong gangs,"[73] J. D. and the other passengers made their way to a nearby hotel for a short sleep. Promptly at 5:00 A.M. the entire house came to life, though it was still dark outside, and one hundred guests shared a candlelight breakfast and then hurried out to the staging area. Some made a brief stop at the bar for a quick drink, "fortifying themselves for their journey."[74]

The gray light of early dawn gave J. D. the opportunity to take a better look at the town. The broad Sacramento River, dissecting a vast plain, was lined for nearly a mile with vessels of every sort, many used as floating warehouses, and along the bank numerous auctions were already in progress. One early writer had recommended the auctioneers' wares because of their greatly reduced prices, despite the single drawback of "the damaged condition of most of the goods."[75] Beyond town lay the lagoon that had thrown John Woodhouse Audubon into a fit of gloom. He felt that the body of water gave the "country village" an "unhealthy" atmosphere, and throughout his stay lived in dread of contacting dysentery, malaria, or fever and ague.[76]

The town had been laid out at the landing of Sutter's Fort by John A. Sutter, Jr., but the nearby fort was now approaching decay. Sacramento had replaced it as a center of activity. Beyond the street fronting the river came parallel streets of First, Second, Third, and so on. Those at right angles were named by letters, thus making any address easy to locate. From the unpromising beginning in 1848 of one wooden residence, one log drinking saloon, and a dismantled ship used as a store, the landing had developed into a thriving trade center for miners from the surrounding area, city lots appreciating within only a few months from $250 to $3,000.[77] With the rapid increase in river traffic, businesses sprang up on the river bank like mushrooms after a rain. By the spring of 1849, the editor of the local paper went out on a limb by predicting the little river port would "become great." The editor supported his contention by praising the healthy climate and the many services offered, not the least of which was "the inauguration of the game of monte in the famous Stinking Tent, kept by James Lee."[78]

Upon J. D.'s arrival that spring of 1851, the editor's prophecy was already well on its way to being fulfilled. In addition to hotels, stores, and restaurants, housed in three-storied brick buildings that let out business space at the cost of $5,000 per month, there were printing offices, bowling alleys, a theater, and a racetrack complete with jockey club.[79] English artist and writer Frank Marryat, who had arrived in California only a few weeks before J. D., had reported attending a meeting of Sacramento's literary society. Though the members had a "tolerable collection of books and periodicals," Marryat wrote, they spent little time discussing them, or even reading them for that matter. The highlight of their meetings was a ceremony in which they spun a Chinese basket-hat marked with a black arrow. The unfortunate member pointed out by the hat was then obliged to treat the assemblage to drinks. The Chinese hat, Marryat stated, "was kept continually spinning by public acclamation."[80]

The broad-streeted business section, whose buildings were plastered with huge signs and crowned with fluttering American flags, extended to blocks of neat homes, most painted white and trimmed with green. The red dust that usually covered the streets had now been turned to gumbo by spring rains. The previous winter floods had made it necessary for residents to navigate these streets in small boats, or whatever else lay handy, such as a baker's trough or an India-rubber bed. One particularly heavy rainstorm had left the entire countryside a solid sheet of water, and, reportedly, a small steamer had proceeded up the street so passengers could enter a hotel at the second story window.[81] This great flood prompted city fathers to construct the present levee.

J. D. had but a brief time to ponder the surroundings; stages were already collected in front of the hotel and drivers were anxious for their passengers to board. Twenty-four vehicles, each drawn by four horses, were lined up four abreast in the wide street: an assortment of open wagon beds, light spring wagons covered with awnings, and several elegant, high-hung coaches. J. D. spotted a wagon with "Hangtown" painted on the side and began working his way toward it. "Pitching in my roll of blankets," he wrote, "I took my seat and lighted my pipe that I might the more fully enjoy the scene around me. And a scene it was, such as few parts of the world can now show:"

> The horses were restive, and pawing, and snorting, and kicking; and passengers were trying to navigate to their proper stages through the labyrinth of wheels and horses, and frequently climbing over half-a-dozen wagons to shorten their journey. Grooms were standing at the leaders' heads, trying to keep them quiet, and the drivers . . . were swearing at each other in a very shocking manner, as wheels got locked, and wagons were backed into the teams behind them, to the discomfiture of the passengers on the back-seats, who found horses' heads knocking the pipes out of their mouths. In the intervals of their little private battles, the drivers were shouting to the crowds of passengers who loitered about the front of the hotel; for there, as elsewhere, people will wait till the last moment; . . . "Runners" . . . were all mixed up with the crowd, and each was exerting his lungs to the utmost . . . Apparently, if a hundred men wanted to go anywhere, it required a hundred more to despatch them.[82]

When the runners had loaded every stage to overflowing, the grooms made a hasty retreat so as not to be trampled, and drivers gathered their reins and commenced to swear at the horses. The first row of teams moved out in a body, followed by the next row, and so on down the line. For half a mile they continued in formation, but on reaching the outskirts of town, each stage headed in its own direction at full run. J. D. suddenly found himself part of a small wagon community of various nationalities being pulled by "four splendid horses," who were "galloping over the plains like mad." He was exhilirated by at last being off for the mines. As the vast open space ahead gradually swallowed them up, he was reminded of the smallness of man in the great universe: "It was like going to sea," he thought, following "our own course over the wide world . . . The atmosphere was so soft and balmy . . . brushing over one's face like the finest floss silk. The sky was clear and cloudless, the bright sunshine warmed us . . . Our progress, rapid as it was, seemed hardly perceptible, unless measured by the fast disappearing chimney tops of the city, or by the occasional clumps of trees we left behind us. The scene all round us was magnificent, and impressed one as much with his own insignificance as though he beheld the countries of the earth from the summit of a high mountain."[83]

They sped over a grassy plain, dotted with masses of brilliant orange poppies and groves of oak. Behind them, the coastal mountains slowly receded, and before them rose glistening white peaks, "fading away in regular gradation till the most distant, though clearly defined." It seemed to J. D. that "the circumference of the earth had been lifted up to the utmost range of vision, and there melted into air."[84]

On they went, sweeping past cumbersome wagons drawn by plodding oxen and lines of sturdy little mules loaded with supplies for the miners. Occasionally they paused at a station, just long enough to hitch up a fresh team, and then raced across the level plain. Gradually they began to ascend, approaching low foothills sparsely covered with oak and pine. The horses slowed the pace, and finally the driver halted the team and asked passengers to step down and climb one particularly steep hill on foot. Afterwards, he made up for the lost time by galloping down the descending side at top speed. The road now became narrow, rutty, and strewn with large rocks and tree trunks, and passengers grew nervous that the wagon might turn over: "If there was safety in speed," J. D. wrote, "we were safe enough, and all sense of danger was lost in admiration of the coolness and dexterity of the driver as he circumvented every obstacle, but without going one inch farther than necessary out of his way to save us from perdition. He went through extraordinary bodily contortions, which would have shocked an English coachman out of his propriety . . . With his right foot he managed a brake, and, clawing at the reins with both hands, he swayed his body from side to side to preserve his equilibrium, as now on the right pair of wheels, now on the left, he cut the 'outside edge' round a stump or a rock.''[85]

Passengers suddenly had a first glimpse of actual gold digging: ''Four or five men were working in a ravine by the roadside, digging holes like so many grave-diggers.'' The sight jolted J. D. with the realization they might at that very instant ''be passing over huge masses of gold, only concealed from us by an inch or two of earth.''[86] But the stage hurried on, passing groups of miners, piles of rock, log cabins, and lumber shanties. Then the country once again became deserted, though there was still evidence all about of worked-out diggings—rows of grassy earth mounds and a sprinkling of deserted cabins. They had been on the road for eight hours and covered sixty miles when they descended a low hill and at last caught sight of a ''long straggling street of clapboard houses and log cabins, built in a hollow at the side of a creek.''[87] They had arrived at their destination.

HANGTOWN (NOW PLACERVILLE)

Hangtown was surrounded by steep hills covered with the stumps of huge pine trees that had been chopped down for building material. Along the entire length of the creek, parties of miners were digging with picks, bailing water out of excavations, and washing dirt in ''long toms.'' The creek had also been channeled into ditches, where numerous canvas hoses, ''looking like immensely long slimy sea-serpents,'' had been inserted to carry water to the ''toms.'' Since the area had already been worked for nearly three years, all ravines and flats had been converted to ''a confused mass of heaps of dirt and piles of stones lying around the innumerable holes, about six feet square and five or six feet deep.'' The only sounds to be heard were a continuous clatter of stones, the plop of a shovelful of mud, and the splash of water.[88]

J. D. dismounted from the wagon and sank into a street ''knee-deep in mud'' and ''plentifully strewed with old boots, hats, and shirts, old sardine-boxes, empty tins of preserved

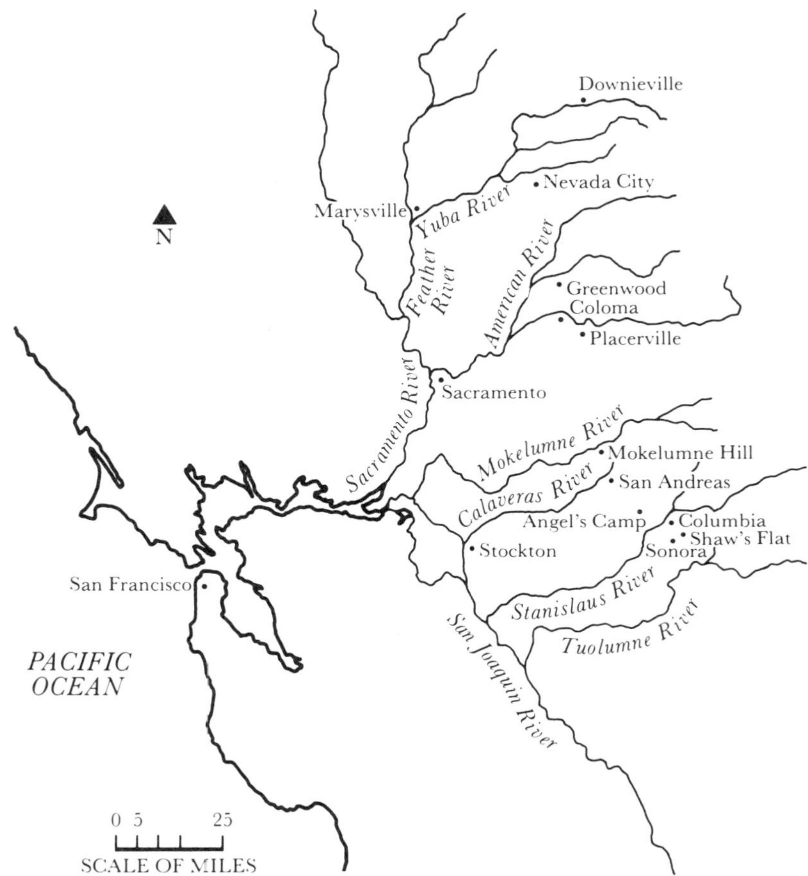

CALIFORNIA GOLD CAMPS

oysters, empty bottles, worn-out pots and kettles, old ham bones, broken picks and shovels, and other rubbish too various to particularize.'' Here and there appeared the head of a digger who had staked his claim in the middle of the single main thoroughfare and was busily engaged in excavating a six-foot square. Since it was two in the afternoon of a workday, the town was nearly empty, except for the mule teams and wagons weaving their way through the maze and then halting before the door of a store to unload cargo. Occasionally a lone miner wandered by. J. D. noted that the inhabitants had acquired ''a certain California air, which would have made them remarkable in whatever part of the world they came from:'' the brown faces, long beards, large muddy boots, and ''picturesquely'' ragged shirts and coarse trousers.[89]

He waded down main street, peering inquisitively into each place of business. There were several boardinghouses, with oilcloth-covered tables long enough to seat forty or fifty hungry miners, and several hotels, elevated to this more prestigious title because they used real cloth on the dining table. The largest buildings contained bars decorated with the same extravagances as those in San Francisco: mirrors, chandeliers, vases, and clocks. He also passed a triweekly newspaper office, a neat little Methodist church, and a butcher shop. The remainder of the stores were all of one variety, curious little places with no specialty. On entering one, he discovered the owner squatting on ''an empty keg at a rickety little table, playing 'seven up' for 'the liquor' with one of his customers.'' Behind the counter that doubled as a bar stood a row of tastefully arranged bottles and decanters, and above them were shelves displaying brightly labelled tins of sardines and vegetables, artfully interspersed with graceful, long-necked champagne bottles and squat, odd-shaped jars of ''exceedingly green pickles.'' Goods of every sort were also stowed away in every corner of the room.[90]

J. D. was fortunate enough to run into an acquaintance from San Francisco, a doctor who was now practicing in Hangtown who invited J. D. to move in with him. On reaching the doctor's cabin, J. D. was a little disappointed that his new accommodation was "merely six feet of the floor on which to spread my blankets." But on noticing that the host himself had no better bed, he could not feel offended. In the evening he learned the doctor also provided living quarters for four Australian miners, a piece of good luck for him. The Australians were looking for another hand to work the long tom, and J. D. eagerly volunteered.[91]

After a short night's rest on the ground floor, they awoke for breakfast and by dawn were hiking the two miles to the mine, carrying along a dinner of beefsteak and bread. Every hour of daylight was spent in back-breaking labor—shoveling dirt, sloshing buckets of water, and lifting out stones with a long-handled shovel—but J. D. kept up with the others. It was dark when they finally trudged back to the cabin in Hangtown. J. D. was exhausted and stiff, and disappointingly enough his first day at the mines had produced very little gold dust. Still he was determined to take his place beside the Australians the following day. The others were also a little discouraged, but explained that they intended to give the area a good try before abandoning it. Finding another claim was not as easy as in the early days, when men had pried chunks of gold out of rock crevices with a pocketknife.[92]

Rich deposits in the area had first been discovered in the summer of 1848 by a party of farmers who named their camp "Old Dry Diggings." In the winter an influx of Oregonians and Latin Americans joined the farmers and their Indian employees. Among the celebrities who had made a fortune in the area were J. M. Studebaker, future automobile manufacturer, who had gotten his start by building wheelbarrows for the miners at the price of ten dollars each. And Philip D. Armour's butcher shop had cleared $6,000, enough to open a meat-packing company back home in Chicago.[93] A third famous resident to strike it rich was James Mason Hutchings, later the editor of *California Magazine.* In addition to providing a fortune for the above mentioned, the camp had also gained notoriety as the site of the first mob lynching, after which its name was changed from Old Dry Diggings to Hangtown.

The joint lynching had taken place on the afternoon of January 20, 1849, under the following circumstances: A professional gambler named Lopez had retired for the night, his stock of coins stashed in a trunk, when about midnight five armed men entered the room, held a pistol to his temple, and then made off with his money. As soon as they had gone, he ran for help. An armed party rode after the robbers, caught them, and brought them back to town for punishment. The next day they were put on trial, and a jury composed of Old Dry Diggings residents sentenced the five suspects to a public flogging. How these prescribed floggings evolved into mob action has been described by Edward Gould Buffum, a veteran of the Mexican War who had recently been discharged from the army and who had stopped off at the goldfields on his way home:

> Never having witnessed a punishment inflicted by Lynch-law I went over to the dry diggings on a clear Sunday morning, and on my arrival, found a large crowd collected around an oak tree, to which was lashed a man with a bared back, while another was applying a raw cowhide to his already gored flesh. A guard of a dozen men, with loaded rifles pointed at the prisoners, stood ready to fire in case of an attempt being made to escape. After the whole had been flogged, some fresh charges were preferred against three of the men —two Frenchmen, named Barcia and Bissi, and a Chileno, named Manuel. These were charged with a robbery and attempt to murder, on the Stanislaus River, during the previous fall. The unhappy men were removed to a neighboring house, and being so weak from their punishment as to be unable to stand, were laid stretched upon the floor. As it was not possible for them to attend, they were tried in the open air, in their absence, by a crowd of some two hundred men, who had organized themselves into a jury, and appointed a pro tempore judge. The charges against them were well substantiated, but amounted to nothing more than an attempt at robbery and murder; no overt act being alleged. They were known to be bad men, however, and a general sentiment seemed to prevail in the crowd that they ought to be got rid of. At the close of the trial, which lasted some thirty minutes,

> the Judge put to vote the question whether they had been proved guilty. A universal affirmative was the response; and then the question, "What punishment shall be inflicted?" was asked. A brutal-looking fellow in the crowd, cried out, "Hang them." The proposition was seconded, and met with almost universal approbation. I mounted a stump, and in the name of God, humanity, and law, protested against such a course of proceeding; but the crowd, by this time excited by frequent and deep potations of liquor from a neighboring groggery, would listen to nothing contrary to their brutal desires, and even threatened to hang me if I did not immediately desist from any further remarks. Somewhat fearful that such might be my fate, and seeing the utter uselessness of further argument with them, I ceased, and prepared to witness the horrible tragedy. Thirty minutes only were allowed the unhappy victims to prepare themselves to enter on the scenes of eternity. Three ropes were procured, and attached to the limb of a tree. The prisoners were marched out, placed upon a wagon, and the ropes put round their necks. No time was given them for explanation. They vainly tried to speak, but none of them understanding English, they were obliged to employ their native tongues, which but few of those assembled understood. Vainly they called for an interpreter, for their cries were drowned by the yells of a now infuriated mob. A black handkerchief was bound around the eyes of each; their arms were pinioned, and at a given signal, without priest or prayer-book, the wagon was drawn from under them, and they were launched into eternity. Their graves were dug ready to receive them, and when life was entirely extinct, they were cut down and buried in their blankets. This was the first execution I ever witnessed.—God grant that it may be the last![94]

Reliable accounts, such as Buffum's, were not generally available in the camps where the mob action had taken place. The story passed down by those who participated, and heard by newcomers like J. D., depicted the impromptu juries as heroes of law and order. J. D. was particularly susceptible to accounts exonerating the lynch court because of his faith in the people's ability to rule themselves. And though the observations he made throughout his journey reveal a consistent attempt at open-mindedness and objectivity, he was unaware that members of the mass jury at Hangtown were drunk and that the defendants were absent and without representation at the trial. He also accepted the notion that the three hangings had, as claimed, brought peace and safety to the area. It is a rare instance in which his naivete damages his record's authenticity.

In spite of this consistent weakness for accepting a mob's justification, J. D. did make a significant contribution to an understanding of the law-and-order issue at the mines. Though several newspaper editors of the day blamed recurring acts of violence on the practice of going armed, J. D. pointed out that "the very prevalence of the custom of carrying arms" was "a cause of their being seldom used. They were never drawn out of bravado, for when a man once drew his pistol, he had to be prepared to use it, and to use it quickly." This understanding of the unwritten law governing the use of weapons sheds much light on the prevailing code for determining whether a killing had been in self-defense: "In the case of a row," he wrote, "it was not necessary to wait till a pistol was actually leveled at one's head—if a man made even a motion towards drawing a weapon, it was considered perfectly justifiable to shoot him first, if possible."[95]

To J. D.'s way of thinking, all was right in the democratic world of Hangtown, and proving himself worthy to be part of it by working in the mines had also set his personal world right. The disappointment he had experienced earlier over the selfish isolation of the individual gold seeker had vanished, now that he was here and had himself become a part of the international brotherhood. With pride in his own ideals and his physical stamina, he shared the austere living conditions, the rigorous manual labor, the long hours, and the common goal of the Australian miners who each night crowded in beside him on the floor of the doctor's small cabin. He thought the "earthen floor" was "quite as soft as any wooden board," and woke refreshed each morning, forgetful of his sore hands and aching muscles. He relished the crusty flour "dampers" his mates baked in the ashes of their "good hardwood fire," and rated the beefsteaks barbecued on a twisted iron hoop as a delicacy that "could not be beat anywhere."[96]

He was not even discouraged that the mine was not paying because they could always find a new one. "The claim did not prove rich enough to satisfy us," he blithely commented, "so we abandoned it, and went 'prospecting,' which means looking about for a more likely place."[97] After a few days searching, they staked a new claim about three miles from Hangtown, at a little settlement of a dozen cabins located in rolling hills cut by a small creek. Though the camp had one general store, they continued their nightly walks to the butcher shop in Hangtown, returning with steaks to accompany the hot, moist bread the Australians baked. "The Americans do not understand dampers," J. D. smugly noted. He scorned the bunks in the abandoned cabin they preempted at the new claim, preferring "the smooth earthen floor" as a "much more easy couch."[98]

A few miles from the new claim was a large Indian camp that J. D. soon visited. He made several sketches and notes, recording that the natives were fascinating but hopelessly "degraded." Some time later an Indian and his squaw returned the visit, and J. D.'s description of the incident reveals one of his less admirable traits, a tendency to view anything not beautiful as an object of amusement. The squaw, he wrote, "was such a particularly ugly specimen of human nature that I made her sit down, and proceeded to take a sketch of her, to the great delight of her dutiful husband, who looked over my shoulder and reported progress to her. I offered her the sketch when I had finished, but after admiring herself in the bottom of a new tin pannikin, the only substitute for a looking-glass which I could find, and comparing her own beautiful face with her portrait, she was by no means pleased, and would have nothing to do with it." J. D. did, however, concede there is no universal standard of beauty: "I suppose she thought I had not done her justice; which was very likely, for no doubt our ideas of female beauty must have differed very materially."[99]

A short time later, word reached camp that Indians had killed a white man, and J. D. attended the mass meeting in Hangtown to decide on a course of action. Miners flocked in from the hills and, with distinguished guests from the capital, crowded into a gambling hall. Most of those present were Americans, and a good share the gaunt, rifle-toting settlers who had traveled across the plains from recently settled states to the east, "with shaggy beards, their faces, hands, and arms as brown as mahogany, and with an expression about their eyes which boded no good to any Indian who should come within range of their rifles."[100]

But if J. D. was burdened with an Old World contempt for all that was less civilized than the Victorian society he had known at home, the speech made by a Kentucky doctor reveals that Americans had their prejudices as well. Particularly noticeable was the braggadocio J. D. had been doing his best to overlook or excuse since his arrival in New York. The Kentuckian spoke well, J. D. observed, "but from the fuss he made it might have been supposed that the whole country was in the hands of the enemy. The eyes of the thirty States of the Union, he said were upon them; and it was for them, the thirty-first, to avenge this insult to the Anglo-Saxon race, and to show the wily savage that the American nation, which could dictate terms of peace or war to every other nation on the face of the globe, was not to be trifled with."[101]

After the doctor had incited the assembled miners to a state of patriotic frenzy, Governor John McDougal stood up and shouted that he would pay any volunteers five dollars a day to "go and whip the Indians." Then those who wished to enlist were asked to gather on one side of the room, and nearly everyone "rushed eagerly forward" to enroll, everyone that is except J. D. and his Australian companions. Some time prior to the uproar they had decided the Indians were "quite peaceable." Therefore, the five of them returned to work. The Americans, however, spent two months pursuing the enemy through the surrounding hills in an attempt to teach the race "the respect due to white men."[102]

It was not such dangers alone that made J. D. conclude that gold hunting was an "exciting pursuit." The new claim of the Australian mining company was paying very well. Its owners enlisted additional partners and worked on throughout the summer until the creek went dry. Then, since they were unable to proceed without running water, they disbanded.[103]

The other members had claims elsewhere, but J. D. and a young Englishman were left adrift. Then one evening when they walked to Hangtown to purchase supplies, they heard news of a rich strike at nearby Coon Hollow. The next morning the two set out before daylight, but on their arrival at the Hollow saw that all of the land around the discovery site had been pegged off into thirty-foot squares and riddled with holes. They had arrived too late. They stayed on anyhow, idly observing the frantic activity in progress. As far as one could see, pairs of eager miners were sinking shafts into hillsides. While one man remained below ground and excavated, the second stayed at the surface and cranked up buckets of dirt on a crude windlass. Due to haste and lack of proper materials, cave-ins occurred with alarming frequency. This particular method of mining was referred to as "coyoting," and for the benefit of future readers who might be unfamiliar with the West, J. D. included in his notes a definition of coyote: it is a carnivorous animal that abounds on the plains and spends its nights howling "most dismally" at the moon; it is "half dog, half fox, and, as an Irishman might say, half wolf also."[104]

Fighting back envy, J. D. and his partner stood watching two Cornish miners who were pitching into their coyote hole with a will, all the while declaring gleefully that they would not accept $10,000 for their claim. J. D. and the Englishman consoled themselves by agreeing they had no "particular fancy" for the dangerous underground work, but feeling compelled to admit a certain amount of "sour grapes," J. D. added, "especially since we could not get a claim." A second consolation was the rich profits from his former mine, still heavy in his pocket. They hung around long enough to learn that the two blustery Cornishmen "could not get a cent" out of their claim and then moved on to a less crowded area.[105]

In Hangtown they had heard talk about good diggings on Weber Creek, some fifteen miles distant, and decided to give that area a try. Loading their food, pots, blankets, pick, shovel, hose, and long tom into a hired mule cart, they commenced the journey. The trail wound between thickly wooded hills spread with masses of white, yellow, and purple wildflowers, and J. D. was so overcome with the beauty and solitude that he had to pause for a moment to lie down in the "soft and delightful" flowers. Continuing on, they ascended steadily for more than six hours and finally came to the edge of a high mountain overlooking Weber Creek. The steep descent now had to be made in a series of "short tacks," steering for a tree each time, in case the cart got away from them. They reached bottom at last with the hired cart intact.

Rocky banks rising from both sides of the creek were sparsely dotted with cabins and tents, and there was one store. In the earlier venture, J. D. had worked with experienced miners, but he and his young friend now wished to prove they could survive on their own. The first order of business was to find shelter, and noting a small unoccupied tent, they entered the store to inquire about it. When the storekeeper replied that he owned the tent and they were welcome to use it, they moved in, quickly unloading the cookware, flour, ham, beans, and tea from the cart. Then, quite pleased with their new independence, they began prospecting for a good claim.

Within only a short time, they raised color and hastily assembled the long tom on the spot. After sinking their hose upstream, they began digging and soon had accumulated a heap of pay dirt large enough to commence washing. To their delight, the gold proved to be the most valuable kind, thin scales that floated on the surface of the water for an instant before settling to the bottom. Though such fine gold required very careful processing, the results were well worth the extra work. The two novices, rather than acknowledging beginner's luck, soon took on the air of old hands at the mines.

Though they were getting rich, the experience was no picnic. All day the summer sun burnt their faces and "crisped up" their hair, and at night a sudden downpour of rain would drench the tent, leaving "small pools of water in the folds" of their blankets. The roof leaked so badly everything inside became "soaking wet," and many mornings they were forced

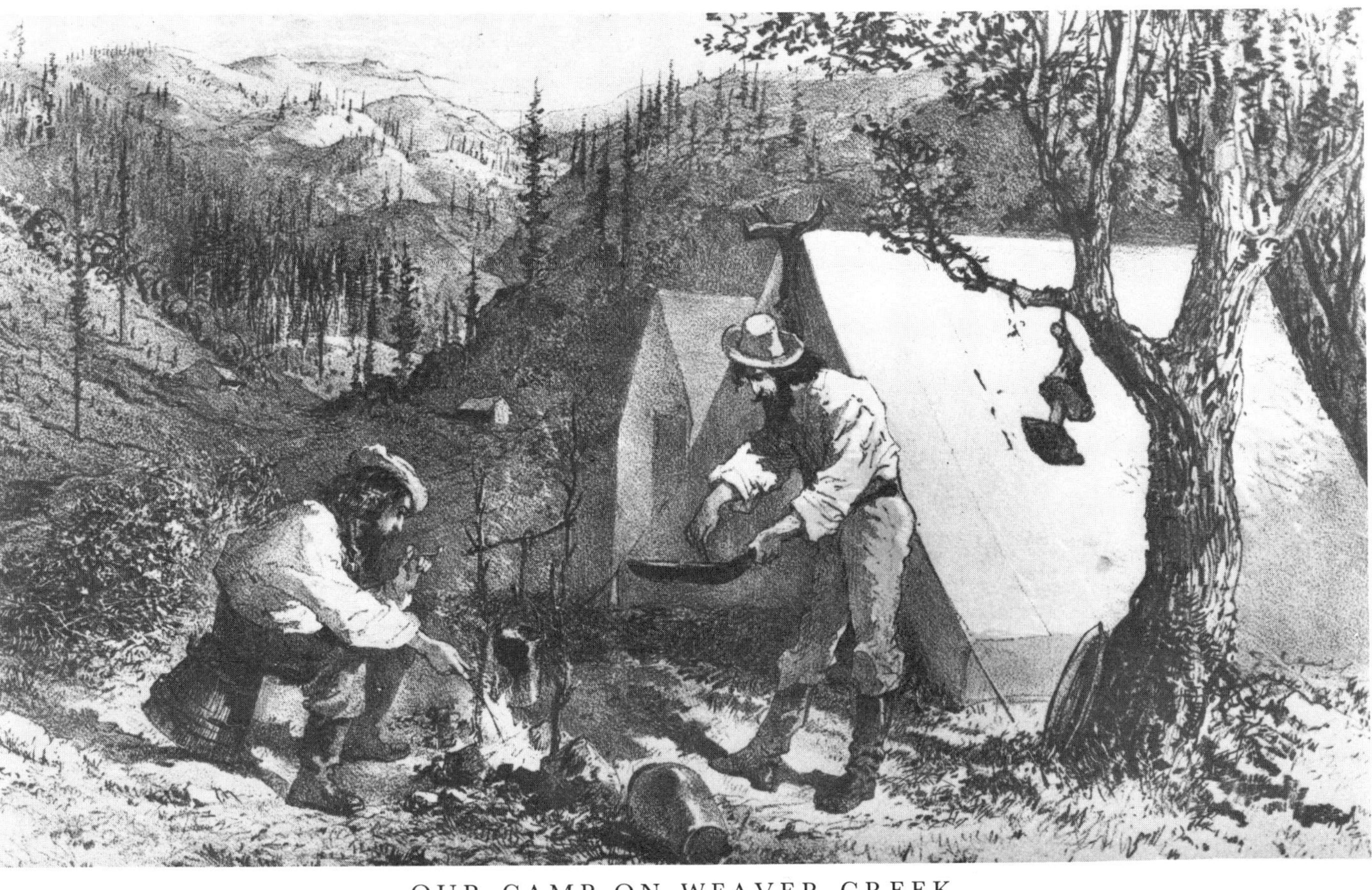

OUR CAMP ON WEAVER CREEK

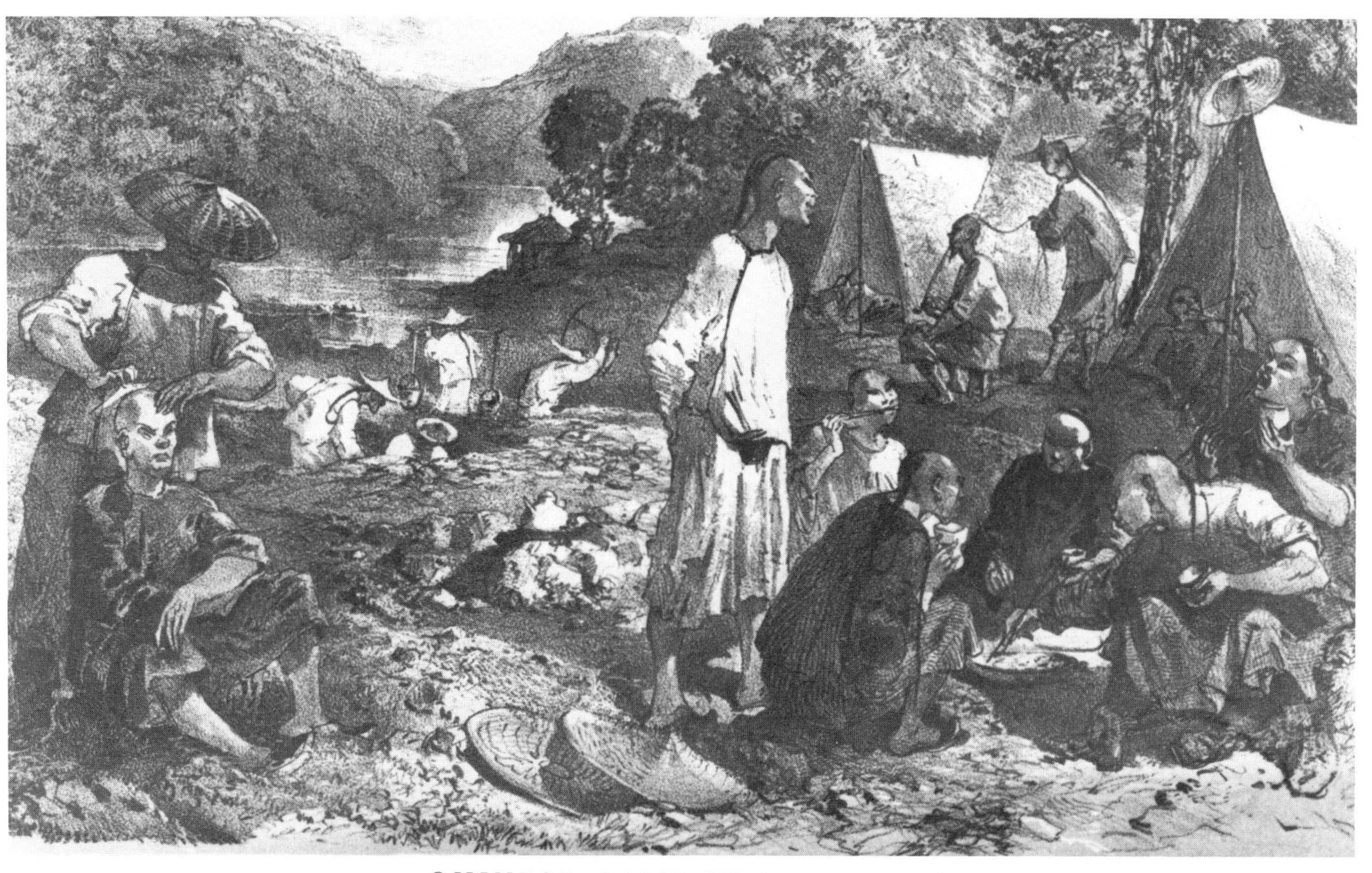

CHINESE CAMP IN THE MINES

to eat a cold breakfast of "raw ham, hard bread, and cold water." But after cheering themselves with "an extra pipe," they relieved their frustrations by "laying in fiercely with pick and shovel." Though J. D. still refused to admit homesickness, his writing reveals an overwhelming sensation of being "shut out from the rest of the world." He compensated by sticking to a rigorous work schedule, using any free time to sketch. One drawing of their camp pictured the artist himself as a shadowy, pensive figure seated before the fire, smoking a pipe and stirring the coals with a stick.[106]

For three weeks they worked the claim steadily, and with "very good success," but then suddenly the rich vein mysteriously disappeared, and they had to go prospecting again. A mile upstream they located another promising claim and, abandoning the storekeeper's tent, moved their possessions to a vacated log cabin nearer the site. Their new cloth-roofed home was perched on a rocky ledge overhanging the creek and proved to be so "intolerably hot" that they were forced to both cook and eat their noon meal under a tree. A second disadvantage of the new location was its proximity to a camp of Chinamen, who made quite a racket all night. The constant unintelligible chatter proved "rather tiresome" until they at last grew accustomed to the peculiar noise and began to sleep through it. Naturally J. D. visited the Chinese camp, making his usual notes and doing sketches. He found his new neighbors to be "inoffensive" and "industrious" people, though he noticed they did not possess the "same force or vigor" as American and European miners. Instead, they handled their tools "like so many women, as if they were afraid of hurting themselves." They were also "very averse to working in the water," and during the afternoon heat "assembled under the shade of a tree, where they sat fanning themselves, drinking tea, and saying 'too muchee hot.' "[107]

To the modern reader J. D. may appear bigoted and chauvanistic, but it is necessary to consider the climate of the times. Throughout the Gold Rush, the Chinese were allowed to work only those areas others believed of little value, and if they inadvertently stumbled across an abandoned claim which contained a rich lead, they were immediately driven out so others could reclaim the mine. And J. D.'s disparagingly comparing the race to "women" likewise shows him a man of his times. True, a more liberal attitude toward women was growing in the West; yet, ordinances passed in the camps reveal lingering male chauvanism. For example, it was not unusual for the all-male governing bodies to prescribe punishment for any woman daring to don men's clothing.[108] In reality, considering the Victorian society in which he had been reared, J. D.'s openness to the ways of the mining frontier was quite remarkable.

In addition to the Chinese at Weber Creek, there were several camps of Pike County Missourians whom J. D. found so fascinating that he devoted several journal pages to them.[109] He also observed the settlement of a mining dispute, a disagreement arising when one company of miners took out a claim in the creek bed and diverted water through a race that flooded the claims of other miners. Both parties to the dispute agreed to abide by the verdict of a miners' court and accordingly called a meeting. Though all present recognized that time was money, one hundred men had dropped pick and shovel and assembled to show their respect for "the laws of the diggings."[110]

At an opening ceremony, a coin was flipped to determine which side would have first turn at selecting a juror. After twelve had been selected, the chosen men "squatted themselves all together in an exalted position on a heap of stones and dirt" to listen to each side present its case. At the close of the evidence, the jurors "laid their shaggy heads together for a few minutes," and then announced the following decision: those whose claims would be flooded by the race were to be allowed six days working time before the water was turned in upon their mines. J. D. considered the verdict remarkably impartial and, though neither party to the dispute was particularly pleased with the outcome, all peacefully abided by the court's decision.[111] At the hearing held to settle the race dispute, someone had pointed out a need for revisions in the existing district laws, and a meeting was set on a following Sunday.

When, on the appointed date, nearly two hundred miners had gathered at the local store, those assembled selected a successful miner, James Mason Hutchings, to serve as chairman. Hutchings, by coincidence a neighbor of J. D.'s, then mounted an empty pork barrel and in a most dignified and orderly manner carried out the business at hand. J. D. could not help being impressed with the Americans' familiarality with the routines of public meetings. J. D. described Hutchings as a "very respectable-looking old chap," but at the time he had no way of knowing the chairman would one day be influential in his own career. Likewise, Hutchings was at the time unaware J. D. was a budding artist and writer.[112]

Two years after the above-mentioned meeting, Hutchings lost his Hangtown and Weber Creek fortune by depositing his wealth in a San Francisco bank that failed. He went on to earn a second fortune at the mines, however, this time by selling illustrated letter sheets. A third business venture was the establishment of the illustrated periodical *California Magazine*, and though this magazine maintained high literary standards, its profits for the entire five years of its publication amounted to only enough to buy Hutchings one suit of clothes. He was thus unable to pay contributors for their works. In one issue, Hutchings commented on the miners' meeting he chaired and one of the more celebrated personages in attendance: "We little thought when Mr. Borthwick was a blue-shirted fellow miner and neighbor of ours, on Weaver Creek in 1851, that although a countryman of Robert Burns, (a chiel's amang ye taken notes, and faith he'll print 'em,) or we might have conducted ourselves with more decorum as chairman (on a pork-barrel) of the miners meeting described in these pages. But how often is a man deceived by appearance—especially in California?"[113]

Hutchings and J. D. were not the only notables to reside on Weber Creek. The area was first mined by pioneer Charles Weber, founder of Stockton, who arrived at the confluence of

Weber and Hangtown creeks in June 1848 with a crew of Indian laborers. That December the camp was visited by Edward Gould Buffum, whose chronicle of the Hangtown lynchings was previously quoted. An account of life at the Weber Creek mines was also left by Sarah Royce, mother of philosopher Josiah Royce, who arrived with her husband and an infant child in October 1849 and stayed for two months.

While Buffum's chronicle provides impartial information about Hangtown events, Sarah Royce's account reveals the version of the lynching passed down by participants. That this version followed the usual pattern employed when justifying executions carried out without fair trial (the same used by apologists for the Montana Vigilantes) can be seen in the following quotations. Early histories preserve the rumors spread to convince the populace they were threatened by organized crime: "At that time there were organized bands of desperadoes, with signs, passwords and grips, and with chiefs and lieutenants, who lay in wait in and around the mining camps, ready for plunder and murder."[114] Anyone who has read Thomas Dimsdale's defense of the Montana Vigilantes cannot help being struck by the similarity of the argument. Mrs. Royce presents the second half of the standard argument—the contention that the lynchings eliminated further crime in the area, leaving all citizens secure: "I had heard the sad story (which, while it shocked, reassured us) of the summary punishment inflicted in a neighboring town upon three thieves, who had been tried by a committee of citizens and, upon conviction, all hung. The circumstances had given to the place the name of Hang-Town. We were assured that, since then, no case of stealing had occurred in the northern mines."[115] This presumption to an end to crime matches that made in Montana.

Shortly after the miners' meeting on Weber Creek, J. D.'s partner deserted him for another part of the mines, leaving him to look around for a new company. He had earlier thrown in his lot with fellow Britons, but he now felt he was ready to expand his experience. He therefore formed a partnership with two Americans. The three men abruptly bought a claim located six miles upstream, advertised by its former owners as "very rich," though the new company had not taken the trouble to prospect before the purchase. The three youthful members of the newly formed company had concluded that since the adjoining mines were producing well, theirs would also. As they commenced preparing the claim for excavation, however, they discovered it was going to require so much difficult labor—removal of rock and chaneling of water—four more laborers would have to be hired at a cost of five dollars per day per man. Even with the hired help, it took two weeks of hard work before they could get excavating and washing under way. Since there were no abandoned cabins or tents nearby, they also had to construct shelter, a wooden framework covered over by a "basketwork of brush," that required less than an hour to erect. Showing his usual positive attitude, J. D. commented that their new home made "a very comfortable kind of abode in summer."[116]

The old cabin at his previous claim J. D. generously donated to a young man who had just arrived at the mines, but on meeting the newcomer a few days later, J. D. was bombarded with complaints. The ungrateful inheritor reported that "the first night of his occupation he had not slept a wink, and had kept candles burning till daylight, being afraid to go to sleep on account of the rats."

"Rats, indeed! poor fellow!" J. D. wrote, "I should think there were a few rats. . . . Hardly was a cabin built in the most out-of-the-way part of the mountains, before a large family of rats made themselves at home in it, imparting a humanized and inhabited air to the place." While he had resided in the cabin, J. D. had each night stuffed his socks in his boots and hid his handkerchief in his pocket to prevent rodents from nesting in them and then allowed the little beasts to run at will. He concluded that those who disliked rats should "keep as far away from California as possible," since here they are given the same freedom as all others.[117] The long, difficult preparation of the new claim proved worthwhile in the end; the daily washings brought even a better return than expected. For the third time J. D. had been lucky at the mines. Week after week the three partners stuck to a rigorous regimen, spending every moment of daylight at the claim except each noon hour and all day Sunday. During his rest periods, J. D. regularly pulled out his sketch pad and settled down to capture the sights about him. After six weeks of continuous mining, the little American-British company was forced to bring its activities to a halt; the creek went dry. Since the partners were sure the claim still held an ample supply of gold that could be worked next season, J. D. had to decide whether he wished to continue following the lucrative occupation. The decision required a little soul-searching.

He had come to California to test himself in the rough, unsettled country, and he was quite pleased with the results. Without grumbling or bickering, he had participated in the international community, at first hand experiencing cooperation and brotherhood. His negative opinions of certain nationalities and races did not trouble him. For example, he considered the Indians "repulsive-looking wretches," who were nearly uncivilizable;[118] Mexicans were lazy; the Jewish merchants were "unwashed-looking" and "slipshod";[119] and Missourians wore the same "greasy-looking" clothes in which they had crossed the plains and would still be wearing on the trip home.[120] Still, he considered himself and the other inhabitants of California to be unprejudiced. It had not yet occurred to him that a lack of respect for any ethnic group swept away the basis of a true democracy. "It is a free country," he wrote, "as free to rats as to Chinamen."[121]

Confident that his education was now complete, he was ready to choose between becoming wealthy at the mines or following his natural bent and traveling about the country. Idealism won out over materialism: he decided on "throwing mining to the dogs." After selling his interest in the claim to his two American partners, he stuck a pistol and knife in his belt, tossed a blanket over his shoulder, and tucked a drawing pad under one arm. He was off for the greatest adventure he could imagine, wandering the mines completely on his own.

Each time he stopped to make a drawing, he discovered that he attracted an audience. It was the same wherever he went; men begged him to do a portrait or a sketch of their cabin and claim to send home. It soon became obvious he could make more with paper and pencil than he had with pick and shovel. Realizing his paper would soon run out, he sent an order to Sacramento at a cost of two and a half dollars per sheet and then continued moving from one diggings to another along Weber Creek, observing and drawing the "strange specimens of human nature to be found in them."[122]

He was elated at the sense of freedom and the constant discoveries made, but also at the novel idea that his fellow miners had now become his art patrons. After working his way back to Hangtown, he stopped to visit his doctor friend and found the cabin in "a pretty mess." The doctor had discovered that his dirt floor was rich in gold and had therefore hired six miners to excavate it. J. D. chatted with his friend and then, just as he had done at Weber Creek, walked the rest of the diggings. He noticed among the miners several masters and slaves from the Southeast, working claims side by side. In addition to this strange arrangement, he observed that in the boardinghouses and saloons, white men were serving slaves with no apparent resentment. J. D. admitted this democratic situation was probably more attributable to economics than notions of equality. The blacks were noted for being lucky at the mines, and when a full poke was stretched out, a merchant was not squeamish about the color of the hand extending it.[123]

After waiting around Hangtown long enough for the paper he had ordered from Sacramento and for letters from home to catch up to him, J. D. set out to explore new territory. His first scheduled stop was to be Coloma, the site that had started all of the excitement in the first place.

COLOMA

The town where gold had first been discovered was located on the south fork of the American River and was nestled at the base of a long range of mountains. Since by now the diggings in the area had been fairly well exhausted, J. D. found it the "dullest mining town in the whole country," nothing but a "few very neat well-painted houses."[124] He was already familiar with the history of the momentous event that had occurred here, but had he not been, he would have been instructed at the establishment where he dined. Any gathering place of the day had its storytellers, modern counterparts of the medieval minstrels who had gazed into the fire roaring on a hearth of Borthwick Castle, strumming and singing of heroic events of a shadowy but glorious past. Though the state of California was but one year old, it already had a wealth of lore to remind the tribes of restless miners of their traditions. There were tales of warning: a man had stolen gold dust from another's tent and in punishment had an ear cropped; another thief roamed the goldfields with a "T" branded on his chest. There were also tales to rekindle hope: at a nearby claim three partners had spent several weeks sifting out three tin cups of gold per day without so much as tiring themselves; another mining party had sunk a shallow shaft and then in only two hours panned out $2,500. Folk heroes most spoken of at Coloma were James Marshall and Captain Sutter. Marshall may have been an odd old codger, it was told, but the visionary Sutter was a gracious host, a little prone to drink, but very generous. A song popular in the mines paid his generosity a humorous tribute: "I went to eat some oysters, along with Captain Sutter, / And he reared up on the table, and sat down in the butter, / Tang de di, de ding, de dang; de diddle al de da."[125]

In 1834, John Augustus Sutter, plagued by insurmountable debt, had left his family behind in Switzerland and come to America with high hopes of eventually establishing a dynasty. In time, he joined a fur company and ended up at Fort Vancouver, from where he sailed to Hawaii. On returning to California, he brought with him a labor force of eight Kanakas and their wives to work the estate he hoped to acquire. He first became a Mexican citizen and then applied for a land grant of more than 47,000 acres. When awarded a grant in the then-unsettled Sacramento Valley, he sent for his own family. To his Hawaiian staff he added friendly local Indians, as well as any passing emigrant who wanted employment and then convinced a few capitalists to loan him funds for seed and livestock. Living out of a collection of grass shelters, the little community of workers commenced construction of a sturdy fort of adobe walls eighteen feet high and more than two feet thick. Hearing that the Russians intended to give up their post north of Bodega Bay, Sutter, in 1841, purchased the furnishings of Fort Ross on credit. The Russian cannons were then installed at Sutter's own fort to make it secure, and work commenced inside the walls on blacksmith and carpenter shops, a bakery, a distillery, and a blanket factory. Surrounding fields were sowed with wheat, peas, beans, and cotton, while nearby grasslands were stocked with herds of cattle, horse, mules, and sheep. Since the Mexican governor had appointed Sutter head of the troops at the fort, he literally ruled the valley. "I was everything," Sutter wrote, "patriarch, priest, father, and judge." He stated also that overland immigrants, weary, hungry, and often sick after crossing the mountains, were "allways hospitably received under my roof and all those who could or would not be employed, could stay with me as long as they liked."[126] Best known recipients of Sutter's munificence were the survivors of the Donner party. Sutter not only sent a rescue party to retrieve the eighty-nine emigrants, but also took in the forty-seven survivors. (Among the artifacts housed in the present-day museum at restored Fort Sutter is the doll little Patty Reed clung to throughout the ordeal). The discovery of gold at the sawmill Sutter and Marshall were building on the south fork of the American River was to bring an end to the empire of New Helvetia. Sutter's staff deserted him, and frantic forty-eighters swarmed in, staking claims on his land, trampling his crops, and killing his livestock like wild game.

An employee at Sutter's sawmill recorded Marshall's discovery of gold in his diary on January 24, 1848: "This day some kind of mettle was found in the tail of the race that looks like goald," Henry Bigler wrote. Bigler, a veteran of the Mexican War who had mustered out in the little pueblo of Los Angeles, had stopped off at Sutter's Fort on his way back to Salt Lake and, being short of funds, had hired on at the sawmill then under construction. In his daily logbook he recorded the event that was to transform a pastoral society of Latin-American, Catholic families (and the few foreigners who had intermarried with them and adopted their ways) into a churning mass of transient strangers, crazed for the gold embedded in the fertile soil. "Boys," Marshall told Bigler and the rest of the small crew, "by G-d I believe I have found a gold mine." Marshall, Bigler noticed, was holding his hat in his hand, and the crown of it was "knocked in a little" to hold about half an ounce of "the pure stuff"—thin flakes, little cubes, and kernels the size of wheat. "From that time," Bigler noted, "the fever set in and gold was on the brain."[127]

Though Sutter and Marshall asked their employees to refrain from giving outsiders any information about the discovery of gold, they did allow them to prospect on Sundays. Some of Bigler's friends worked their way down river about one mile to a small flat that came to be known as Mormon Island, and here, using such crude equipment as bread trays and cotton sheets, they washed out small amounts of gold at every opportunity. It was Sam Brannan who broke the news to the world. After watching his Mormon brethren washing out dust, he collected a sample, went back to San Francisco, and, as described by Bigler, "took his hat off and swung it, shouting aloud in the streets that gold was found. . . . The inhabitants of the place seemed to be panic-struck and so excited and in such a hurry to be off, that some of the mechanics left their work, not taking time even to take off their aprons. . . . The Californians began to come in thick and fast, having learned of the discovery in the *California Star*, and our little gulches were soon lined from end to end by gold diggers, who already began to dispute Marshall's claims to the land and commenced mining wherever they pleased."[128]

During the first two months of the rush, Sam Brannan's store at Sutter's Fort grossed $36,000.[129] As the influx continued, miners spread north from Coloma, following the several tributaries of the Sacramento, and also south along rivers and streams that flowed from the Sierra and emptied into the San Joaquin. Thus the goldfields were naturally divided into the Northern and Southern mines.

The "fever" written of by Bigler in his diary was real, its symptoms being a driving ambition for wealth accompanied by an excessive amount of optimism. There were also physical symptoms: when James Marshall had first spotted the shining pea in the bottom of the tailrace, and then another beside it, it had made his "heart thump."[130] The editor of the *New York Herald* referred to the fever as an "extraordinary mania" that prompted "poets, philosophers, lawyers, brokers, bankers, merchants, farmers, clergymen" to advertise their possessions for sale "in order to furnish them with means to reach that golden land."[131] One early visitor reported that the first arrivals, who were sometimes fortunate enough to pry out phenomenal amounts of gold from rock crevices with no tool save a pocket knife, "took care to show" their good luck. They swaggered into tent stores, purchased several expensive items with gold dust, seated themselves on the rough benches where all could see them, and then proceeded to break off the neck of a champagne bottle and wash down "sardines, turtle-soup, lobsters, fruits, and other luxuries, preserved in tins."[132]

The optimism that had brought the gold seekers to California from all parts of the world was not always justified, and many stayed on only because they did not have the money to return home. One disappointed forty-niner expressed himself in song, picked up by other miners because it rang true. The lines were sung to the tune of "Old Dog Tray."

> My happy days are past,
> The mines have failed at last,
> The cañons and gulches no longer pay,
> There's nothing left for me,
> I'll never, never see
> My happy, happy home far away.[133]

Apparently J. D.'s luck in picking three paying claims was not typical.

It was not by chance that he had selected Coloma, the site of discovery, as the starting point for his tour of the mines. With his strong sense of history, he needed to mentally recreate the adventures of the first gold hunters to arrive in the wilderness, partly for the thrill of experiencing their excitement for himself, but also to help him better understand the effect the flood of aliens had had on the environment and the effect the harsh but beautiful surroundings had had on them. To be-

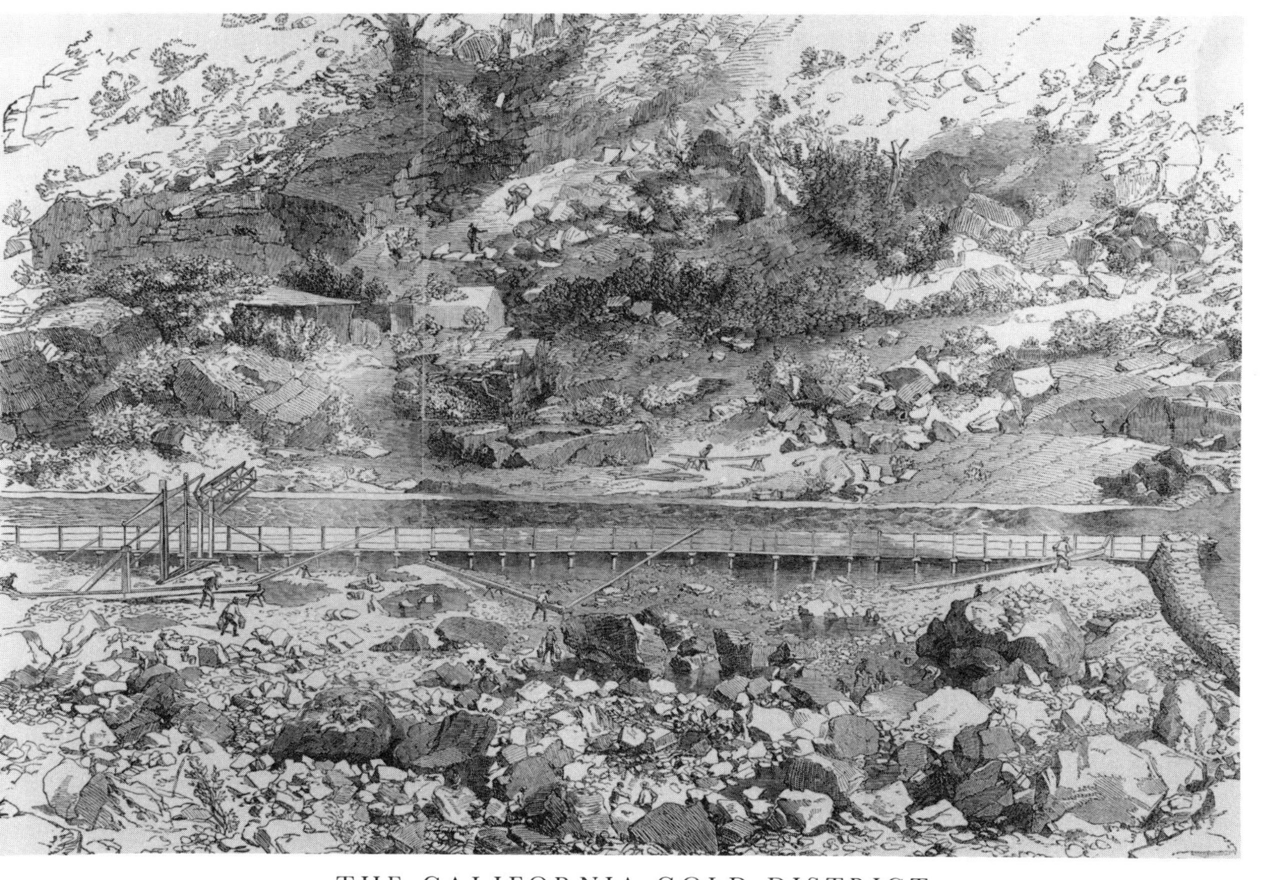

THE CALIFORNIA GOLD DISTRICT

come familiar with the land itself, he was determined to explore the goldfields on foot. He set out in the same direction as the first miners had, heading upstream.

The terrain he was to cross was rugged—"stiff hills" and rivers flowing through steep canyons—but the difficulty and danger only heightened his craving for the challenge.[134] Traveling alone added further peril. As he had realized when he inserted a pistol and knife under his belt, the area was not as safe as the mob at Hangtown would like others to believe. In one of the camps he had visited, a story was going around about a horrible atrocity: two miners had been found lying in a creek, "their heads cut open with a hatchet." Since the crime, motivated by no more than several hundred dollars, had been performed "in gloom of night," no clue as to who the culprits might have been was ever discovered.[135] With such madmen on the loose, J. D. charged himself with wariness at all times.

On crossing the range of mountains between the south and middle forks of the American River, he entered long, narrow Greenwood Valley and continued along the winding course of the creek for mile after mile. Though he met no other travelers, the banks of the creek and all of the ravines leading into it were heaped with piles of rock and upturned earth, and hillsides were sprinkled with abandoned cabins. He was suddenly struck by a sharp pang of loneliness. Seeing the "tenantless" cabins made the isolated valley appear even "more desolate than if its solitude had never been disturbed by man."[136]

At the very end of the canyon, he reached a small village and stopped to spend the night at the hotel. He was greatly surprised to find that the little establishment had a supply of the latest newspapers—the *New York Herald*, the *New Orleans Delta*, and the one most favored by miners, the *Illustrated London News*. It was the first opportunity he had had for months to catch up on "modern history." The London newspaper was quite familiar to him; it was a combination of travelogue, world news, general information, and satirical essay, intended for the rising middle class. Its literary and political editor was a young Scot named Charles McKay. J. D. noted that the editor was making a valiant attempt to cover events taking place on the American frontier, but the paper's correspondent had recently departed for England. He was suddenly taken with the idea of submitting one of his own drawings along with an article, offering at the same time to continue as a correspondent if the editor so desired. He had in mind sending a delicately detailed sketch he had made while in the Coloma area, and he sat down immediately and wrote an article to accompany it. "The place this Sketch represents," he wrote, "is situated on the South Fork of the American River, about 18 miles below Coloma, where gold was first discovered. The view shows a company of miners at work in the bed of the river, having turned the water by means of a dam from their natural channel into a wood flume or aqueduct laid on the rocks at the side of the river. The operation of working the bed of a river requires such an outlay of capital and labour before any of the precious metal can be extracted, that it is always undertaken by companies of from ten to twenty men." He next explained every detail of the washing-out process and the equipment used and then went on to the living accommodations of the miners.

> The company and the hands they employ, whom they also board, live on the side of the river, as seen in the Sketch. A chasm between two immense rocks is covered in with branches of trees, forming a sort of shanty, the end of which is constructed of an old tent, stitched on two or three uprights. Here there is a long table, with very primitive-looking benches; a cooking-stove; and a pile of provisions, consisting principally of hams and flour, the staple article of food in the mines. Here the miners take their meals. The little canvas shanty at the right of this is the residence of one of the company, whose wife has accompanied him to the scene of his labours.

He was excited at the prospects of having his first article published and, wanting to make it so interesting no editor could refuse it, added a paragraph to bring the scene in his sketch to life:

> At daybreak may be seen among the rocks, wherever a soft piece of ground offers a tempting resting-place, 'quite a smart sprinkling,' as a Yankee would say, of divers-coloured

> blankets—blue, red, green,—and, here and there, a buffalo-rug. Presently the cook comes out and beats a *reveillee* on his frying-pan with a carving knife. The blankets immediately begin to move, shaggy heads appear from under them, and, getting up and rubbing their eyes, the miners go down to the flume, where they go through their ablutions, and very frequently complete the toilet with the aid of a pocket-comb. By this time the cook is again beating furiously on the frying pan to summon them to breakfast. Not much time is devoted to this ceremony; the day's work begins by bailing out the holes, and is continued steadily till sunset, with the exception of an interval of about an hour at noon for dinner.[137]

J. D. felt that, between the intricate sketch and the written description, he had given a faithful picture of life at the mines, but he realized it would be necessary to convince the editor he was an expert on the subject. He therefore wrote a cover letter, explaining he had studied painting in Scotland, but had come to California as a miner and was therefore reporting from actual knowledge. Since he was fortunate enough to be at a location where mail could be dispatched, he bundled up his package and sent it on its way, fearful of rejection yet at the same time confident that his submission was a valuable piece. It would be months before he knew the fate the little parcel would meet, but his future reputation as well as his self-image were riding with it.

He left Greenwood and after half a day's walking through mountainous country sighted the middle fork of the American River below. "The scenery was very grand," he wrote. "Looking down on the river from the summit of the range, it seemed a mere thread winding along the deep chasm formed by the mountains, which were so steep that the pine trees clinging to their sides looked as though they would slip down into the river. The face of the mountain by which I descended was covered with a perfect trellis-work of zig-zag trails, so that I could work my way down by long or short tacks as I felt inclined. On the mountain on the opposite side I could see the faint line of the trail which I had to follow."[138]

After edging his way down the steep mountain and crossing the river in a canoe, he found himself in the little camp snuggled into a bend of the river. On all sides it was "honeycombed with the holes in which the miners were at work; all the trees had been cut down, and there was nothing but the red shirts of the miners to relieve the dazzling whiteness of the heaps of stones and gravel which reflected the fierce rays of the sun and made the extreme heat doubly severe."[139] The ragged "row of booths and tents" was called Spanish Bar by its inhabitants. J. D. made his way toward the largest canvas establishment, bedecked all along its front with a sign reading "United States Hotel." Since it was the noon hour, about seventy miners had already gathered in the bar for "cocktails," and others had pressed themselves in a huge knot against the door that opened onto the dining hall. At precisely twelve o'clock, the door was thrown open, revealing two tables loaded down with beef, pork, potatoes, beans, and pickles. A shout of joy at the sight and smell of the hot food was followed by a mass rush and a mad scramble for chairs. Half of the hungry men found a place on the benches surrounding the tables, and half did not. J. D., not wanting to resort to pushing and shoving, was among the latter. However, as he had lamented many times since his arrival, the Americans did not know how to enjoy a meal, but instead wolfed down their food as quickly as possible and then jumped up from the table. "In an incredibly short space of time," he noted, "the company began to return to the bar-room, some still masticating a mouthful of food, others picking their teeth with their fingers, or with sharp-pointed bowie-knives, and the rest, with a most provokingly complacent expression about their eyes, making horrible motions with their jaws, as if they were wiping out their mouths with their tongues, determined to enjoy the last lingering after-taste of the good things they had been eating—rather a disgusting process to a spectator at any time, but particularly aggravating to hungry men waiting for their dinner."[140]

The door was again shut while tables were being reset, and a second crowd formed before it. J. D. realized that if he were ever to reach the table he "must enter into the spirit of the thing," and accordingly "elbowed" his way forward, securing a place behind a tall Kentuckian who would be sure to clear a broad path. J. D. was worried that not knowing ''the lay of the tables, or whereabouts the joints were placed'' put him at a disadvantage, so the moment the doors were flung open, he spotted a platter of roast beef and ''made a desperate charge'' toward it. ''I was not so green,'' he avowed, ''as to lose time in trying to get my legs over the bench and sit down,'' but instead ''seized a knife and fork,'' and sunk them into the roast, at the same time ''occupying as much space as possible with my elbows'' and gradually eased down to the bench. After serving himself a cut of the hot beef, he joined the ''grab game.'' Though it was ''every man for himself,'' he was pleased to note that good humor prevailed: ''Conversation, of course, was out of the question; but if you asked a man to pass you a dish, he did so with pleasure.'' [141] After dinner, a smartly dressed young gambler set out a six-hundred-dollar bank at a table in the bar, and the miners entertained themselves at monte for a short spell before returning to their work.

Leaving Spanish Bar behind, J. D. hiked the twelve miles to the Grizzly-Bear House and spent the night there. The inn was a log cabin, whose front wall was covered by a bear skin so large it seemed to be ''taking the whole house into its embrace.'' He and four other guests seated themselves on two benches, flanking a table set in the center of the single room, and refreshed themselves from the decanters and kegs of liquor behind the bar. Meanwhile the chef had stepped out back to a stove covered by a canvas awning and was frying a large plate of steaks. The hot meat was served with nothing more than stale bread and a large pot of tea, but the five hungry men pitched in eagerly. After supper, two storytellers competed for the spotlight, one with tales of his adventures as a Mexican War hero and the other with his exploits as a grizzly bear hunter. ''At the conclusion of a bear story,'' J. D. and the other guests unrolled their blankets while the host swept out a corner of the cabin where they could sleep. After tucking boots under their heads for pillows, the entire party dropped off immediately. J. D. was soon in dreamland, where his adventures, even though imaginary, topped the phenomenal feats described so vividly around the fire earlier that night. He "went through the whole Mexican campaign, and killed more 'bars' than ever the hunter had seen in his life."[142]

NEVADA CITY

Being warned that several robberies had occurred in the area recently, J. D. joined two other travelers for the day's walk to Nevada City. About six that evening they strolled into the town that was on its way to becoming the third largest settlement in the state. It was spread out on several gentle hills rising above a meandering creek, but during the construction of the town, the magnificent pine forest had been reduced to nothing more than hundreds of stumps jutting out of the hillsides. The rolling streets were lined with "staring white frame houses, dingy old canvas booths, and log cabins" and walked by miners bespattered with white mud from the top of their hats to the soles of their boots.

J. D. parted with his companions to find a hotel for the night. He selected an establishment named the Hotel de Paris as being the most likely to serve a good supper and was not disappointed. He and the French miners gathered around the long table were first served soup, then *bouilli,* followed by *filet-de-boeuf*, cabbage, carrots, turnips, and onions. Next came the specialty of the house, a dish the owner called "god-dam rosbif," served with green peas. Dessert was a fresh cabbage salad and coffee laced with cognac. The meal was the "best-got-up thing" J. D. had tasted for months and he rose from the table "powerfully refreshed."[143]

After supper the Frenchmen offered to show J. D. the town, and together they spent the evening visiting the various gambling halls and listening to the bands. Since there were no rooms available at the Hotel de Paris, he had to sleep at a nearby boardinghouse, on one of the "canvas shelves" lining the walls of the sleeping room. He selected a top bunk, climbed up, removed his boots, and then stretched out, only to discover that he was lying with his ear against a thin wall next door to a theater. "They were playing Richard," he detected, "and I could hear every word as distinctly as if I had been in the stage-box. I could even fancy I saw King Dick rolling his eyes about like a man in a fit, when he shouted for 'A horse! a horse!' The fight between Richard and Richmond was a very tame affair; they hit hard while they were at it, but it was too soon over. It was one-two, one-two, a thrust, and down went Dick. I heard him fall, and could hear him afterwards gasping for breath and scuffling about on the stage in his dying agonies.'' At the final curtain two fiddles presented a number, and in the interlude of inaction the audience commenced ''hooting, yelling, whistling, and stamping their feet'' until the curtain again rose and the performance of *Bombastes Furioso* began. Though J. D. thought it was ''very creditably performed,'' he didn't find it nearly so humorous as the tragedy. When the theater closed, J. D. and the other six bunk occupants, who had been snoring throughout, were joined by several more guests. ''They had been at the theater,'' he told himself, ''but I am sure they had not enjoyed it so much as I did.''[144]

In the morning he left Nevada City, continuing on in the same northeasterly direction he had been following in his tour of the Northern Mines. He stuck to an old Indian trail for two days, but then inadvertently took a sidetrack and, not realizing his mistake, followed it to a point of extreme danger. When he was about halfway down a steep mountain, the soil became loose and large stones under his feet commenced giving way. He realized that if he took another step, he was apt to slide all the way to the bottom of the canyon, yet working his way back up the face of bare rock appeared nearly impossible. To make matters worse an unmerciful sun was beating down on him, the blankets slung over his shoulder kept snagging on projecting ledges, and his mouth and throat were parched. Taking a firm grip on himself, he put the vexations out of his mind and determined to work his way back up rather than risking a broken neck in descending any farther. At that instant, the spot where he was standing began to crumble, and quickly he snatched at a tree branch above him, latching onto it and attempting to pull himself up by mere strength of his arms. But each time he set his toes for a hold, rocks beneath his feet slipped away. He could hear them rolling, hurtling, and at last crashing in the canyon far below him. Without looking down, he took a firmer grasp on the slender branch in his hands and, drawing himself up, reached for a higher one. He continued inching upwards until he reached the line where the trees ended. From this point on he was forced to lock his fingers about crevices and ledges, hefting himself and then scrambling for a foothold. It was slow, exhausting work. His face was being scratched by the scrubby bushes sprouting from the rocks, and his shirt was nearly torn from his back. At last the grade of ascent flattened, and he was able to stand again and climb by strength of his legs alone. At the top, he turned and went back in the direction of the inn he had left that morning, impatiently counting off the miles to the spring he had passed earlier. As he walked, he "could not help thinking what a delightful thing a quart pot of Bass's pale ale would be, with a lump of ice in it." On second thought, he shifted to a sherry cobbler. "But I could not drink that fast enough," he mused, "and then it seemed that a quart pot of ale would not be enough, that I would like to drink it out of a bucket."[145]

It was late afternoon when he finally reached the inn he had left that morning. Since his trying experience on the mountainside had left him too tired to start out walking again, he decided to spend a second night there. In the evening he amused himself by sketching a pack train of mules camped nearby, and when other guests of the inn noticed him at work, they requested he do portraits of them. As each client sat down to pose, J. D. envisioned an image of the personality he wished to capture and drew that, rather than the man sitting before him. All of his sitters were "highly satisfied" with the way he had "pictur'd them off;" he wrote, "evidently they had no idea before that they were such good-looking fellows."[146]

The following morning he started for Foster's Bar and at evening reached the small camp, a collection of cabins sprawled along a river flat that had "the appearance of having slipped down off the face of the mountains."[147] There was but one hotel, and on entering it, he found that the entire front half was a barroom and the back half a dining hall. When he inquired about a room, the owner led him to a small hovel tacked on alongside the bar and motioned toward a cot. Since J. D. was weary from the day's walk, he retired at ten, but soon discovered he was not going to be able to sleep. The five monte tables in the hall were crowded with rowdies who had already been drinking for some time. He tossed and turned on the cot, confidently expecting the din to subside, but no letup occurred. It was obvious the halls of the camps were not conducted with the same decorum he had observed in San Francisco. "The uproar beat all my previous experience," he lamented, "drinking, quarreling, and kicking up a row generally." Then the individual quarrels seemed to merge into one outrageous brawl. "I half expected to see some of them pitched through the canvas into the sleeping apartment; or perhaps pistols might be used, in which case I should have had as good a chance of being shot as any one else." But as the ear-splitting noise continued, he eventually became immune to it and drifted off to sleep. When he woke at daylight, he discovered the revelry was only then coming to an end. He was told on getting up that during the night a miner had broken the monte bank, and the tumult had been caused by the winner treating the entire gathering to "an unlimited supply of brandy."[148]

J. D. concluded he did not "fancy such sleeping quarters," and began looking for a suitable place to camp. After a short search, he located a beautiful spot near a stream; purchased a coffee pot, tea, and sugar; and took up residence in his new outdoor quarters. That night he rolled himself in his blankets and when the morning sun woke him, got up and stretched his bedroll across tree limbs to form an awning that would shade him from the afternoon heat. "I found camping out a very pleasant way of living," he wrote. From the baker in Foster's Bar, he bought bread, and from the town butcher, steaks to be roasted on the embers of his campfire. Near his shelter grew huge masses of wild dahlias, so luxurious and sweet smelling that he could not resist picking an armful and spreading them out as a perfumed cushion to sleep on. Since he intended to remain at his little camp for several weeks, he

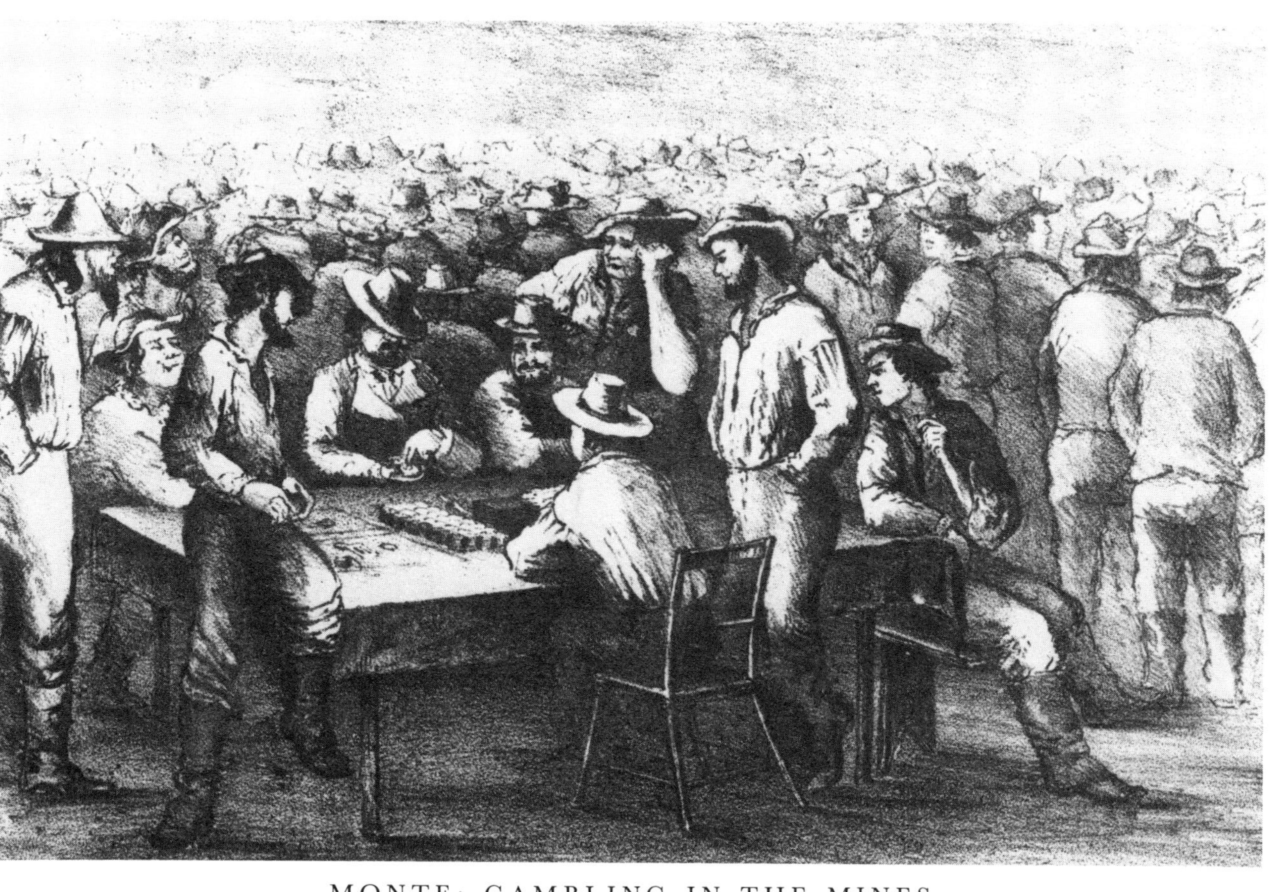

MONTE: GAMBLING IN THE MINES

ordered a new supply of paper from Sacramento and then commenced a series of excursions to surrounding diggings, making sketches of anything that caught his eye. Constantly at the back of his mind was the package he had sent to the *Illustrated London News*. He was worried it had not arrived safely, or that it had reached the editor's desk only to be tossed into a reject pile. Sometimes his mood swung the other way, and he was buoyed with the vision of one day purchasing a copy of the paper, flipping through the sheets, and, as if by miracle, coming across his carefully done drawing. After recovering from the joyful shock, he would sit down and savor every word of his article. Living alone gave him a great deal of time for such thoughts, and during the weeks of waiting to know whether his first piece had been accepted, it occurred to him that perhaps he ought to get off a second one, to a different paper of course. Then, even if the first were rejected, he could still keep hopes alive for the second. He was certain an editor would be most impressed with work that provided important information about mining and therefore decided to visit a picturesque spot a few miles distant where a company was constructing a flume almost half a mile long. He made several sketches of the flume project and on the return trip passed a "most romantic little bridge formed by two pine trees" in a heavily forested ravine.[149]

Unable to let such beauty go unrecorded, he seated himself among the bushes in a spot where the light fell at the precise angle he wanted. He realized it was not wise to remain for long in a position that might give the appearance he had concealed himself in the undergrowth so as to surprise and rob some passing traveler, but the little bridge had to be captured. He worked rapidly, ducking as low as he could so the top of his head would not be spotted, but before he could complete the task, a man and mule came ambling along the trail. He held perfectly still, hoping he would not be noticed, but just at the last moment the man's eyes darted in his direction and he "gave a start," but then quickly attempted to compose himself. "Good morning, Colonel," the rider said. "What are ye a-doin' of over there?" J. D. explained that he was drawing a picture, but the man appeared unconvinced; nevertheless, he made a second attempt to appear unsuspicious by making a comment on the weather as he goaded the mule to a higher speed.[150]

J. D. had been as alarmed as the rider and felt relieved no firing had been done. He had his own pistol lying on the ground in close reach of his hand and would not have hesitated to go for it had the stranger made the slightest motion toward his weapon. He was grateful he had not been forced into using it. After completing his drawing, J. D. walked back to town, but on entering the general store, happened upon the mule rider in the midst of a story about his close call by the bridge. He had been "awful skeered," he was telling his audience, and "had his pistol out, and was thinking of shooting all the time." J. D. felt obliged to preserve his own dignity by volunteering that he was the man in the bushes and that he had also had his pistol ready to "return the compliment." Instead of responding to J. D.'s remark, the storyteller strode outside and stuck a playing card to a tree. Then he backed up twenty paces and "put six balls into it one after another out of his heavy navy revolver." Realizing he was outclassed," J. D. chose not to carry the series of challenges any further. He made his purchase and left the store, "well pleased" that the stranger had not "taken it into his head" to make a target of him back at the bridge.[151]

To soothe his wounded pride, J. D. returned to his camp and sorted out the best of his drawings. It seemed to him that it would be safer to include several pictures this time so the editor could look through them and find something suitable. After selecting a nice variety, among them the sketch of the flume and one of the portraits he had kept, he wrote an accompanying article explaining the work being carried out in each picture. As for the portrait, he wrote,

> It is a likeness, and an honest one. . . . It is the head of one who . . . has become toil-worn, and embrowned by the combined action of the climate, who had been gold seeking to his heart's content, and who has saved something, hardly earned. He would give half he is worth to be at home now—home?

> How sweet a word to his ears; how musical the sound to him! . . . He looks shabby, his beard is unshorn; but the native fire is still in his eye, the warmth in his heart. His cheek had become attenuated, but his soul had enlarged; on him hardships have been as the refiner's fire, and have burned out the dross in his composition.[152]

J. D. was undoubtedly speaking of himself as much as of the miner portrayed.

The periodical he had selected as a second target for publication was *Gleason's Pictorial Drawing-Room Companion* of Boston. After carefully packaging his submission, he walked to the express company office in town. The company provided a variety of valuable services to the community, such as forwarding freight, maintaining a postal delivery independent of the U.S. government, and purchasing gold dust in exchange for drafts drawn on financial institutions in New York City. Because of the approaching rainy season, it was essential J. D. get his drawings and manuscript out of the area before heavy downpours made roads impassable. His visit to the express office was fraught with concerns: there was worry over the safety of his package, uneasiness that the unknown editor might not appreciate his work, and the added discomfort of being once more reminded of his humiliating experience at the general store, for the carrier charged with transporting his precious cargo back to civilization was none other then the sharpshooting mule rider who had toyed with the idea of blowing off his head as he sat sketching. J. D. felt he had had enough of Foster's Bar, and after paying the cost of mailing his package, collected the new supply of paper he had ordered, returned to the stream to break camp, and then headed out of town.[153]

DOWNIEVILLE

Mule train was the only form of transportation capable of reaching the little mountain town that served as depot for the mines along the north forks of the Yuba River. The pack trail led straight up a mountainside and then along the spine of a high range, thus providing a spectacular view. For the first

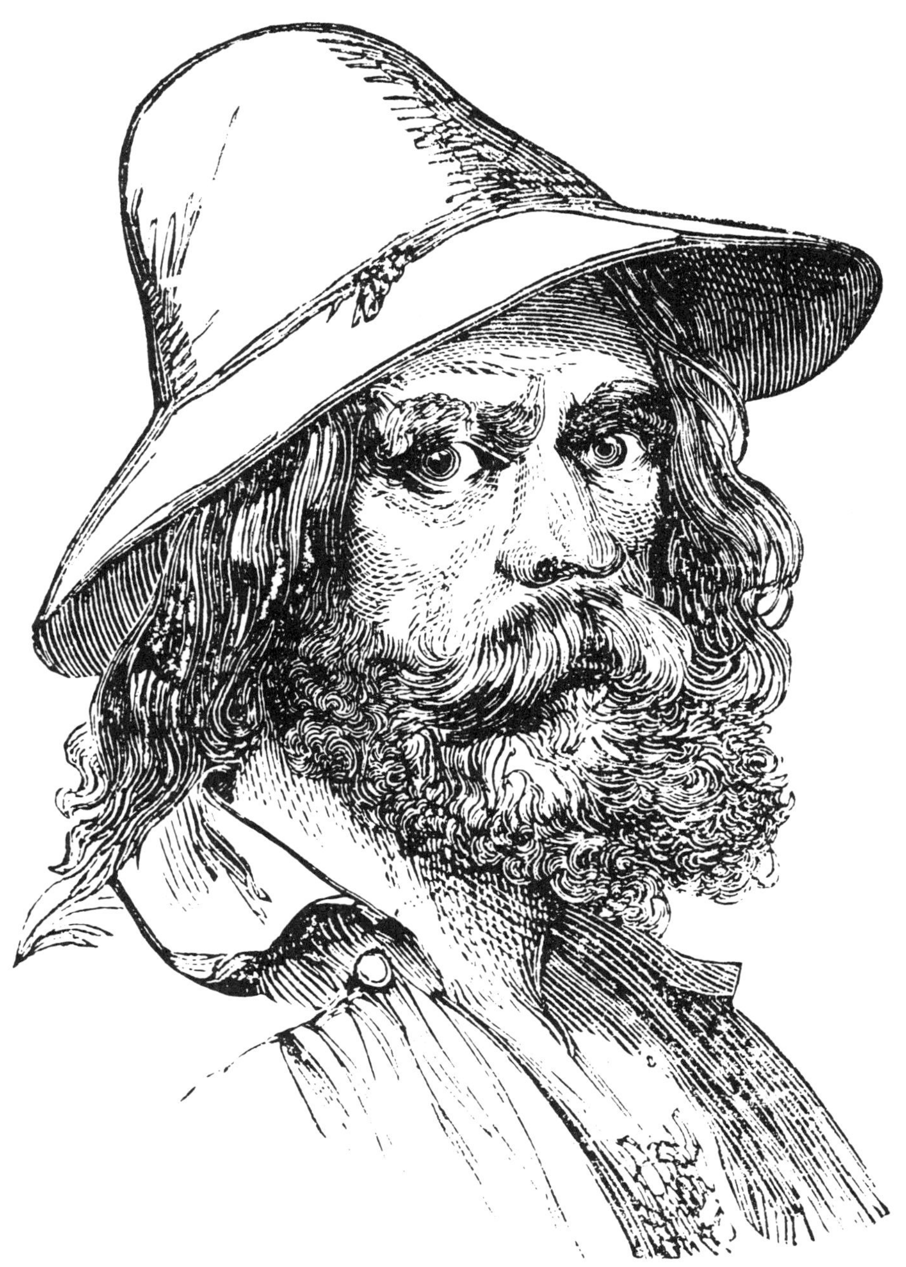

HEAD OF A CALIFORNIA EMIGRANT

half day, J. D. followed the winding, dipping path—trodden to fine red dust by hundreds of small hooves—without meeting another living soul. The solitude gave him the opportunity to restore his soul by soaking in the breathtaking beauty about him. To the west stretched mile upon mile of pine hills, indented with shadowy hollows and incised by streams flowing down to the vast, hazy plain below; and to the east rose ridge after ridge of forested mountains, fading into lofty white peaks that blended imperceptibly into the sky.

By noon he had reached the Slate Range House, where he dined and then proceeded on his journey. Thinking he had had his fill of solitude, he overtook another walker, an Englishman whose familiar accent sounded "very refreshing" to Scottish ears. The two men spent the night at a camp named Oak Valley, and the next morning after breakfast J. D. set out alone. Noticing a party of miners ahead, he caught up to them and traveled in their company the rest of the way. The dry heat was intense, but occasionally they came upon a spring of "deliciously cold water," where they could quench their thirst.[154]

J. D. was becoming anxious for a glimpse of the town that had generated so much talk in the other camps. It was of special interest to him because the original settlement had been founded by a fellow Scot, Major William Downie, who reported that a boyhood spent in the little country J. D. also called home had left him with a passion for exploring the world beyond the North Atlantic. Major Downie and his crew—an Irishman, an Indian, a Hawaiian named Jim Crow, and ten black sailors—had found the Yuba frozen over with a thin film of ice when they arrived at the forks in September 1849, but the early winter had not discouraged them from prospecting. Brushing off the light layer of snow, they washed out pans of dirt in icy water and discovered the area to be very rich in gold. Though Downie had the foresight to send a party, led by Jim Crow, back to the nearest camp for supplies, the men were unable to return until the following spring, finding Downie and the rest of his crew weak from starvation. Jim Crow's party was trailed by hundreds of restless miners who suspected good diggings had been located and therefore hastened to stake out claims and house lots.

There were the usual stories in circulation about fabulous strikes and an unusual one about a merchant, a woman restaurateur, who one day swept the trash off the dirt floor of her tent establishment as usual and noticed specks of gold glittering in it. Supposedly, that first dustpanful panned out five hundred dollars, and the businesswoman promptly folded up her tent, converting the eating house into a mine.[155]

The precipitous mountain trails had also spawned a number of tales—accounts of mules and men slipping off the path and hurtling to the rocks below, where the decaying corpses still remained as warning to others. A particularly hazardous spot in one trail had earned the name of Cape Horn, a precipice spanned by a pine log five inches in diameter. The trick was to rest one foot on the tree for a brief moment and brace the other foot against a rock ledge. In looking down to secure footing, "one saw far below, between his outstretched legs, the most uninviting jagged rocks, strongly suggestive of sudden death." Beneath the rocky jags wound the river, "clear and smooth, not a tree or a bush to save one if he happened to miss his footing." The most recent victim trying to make his way around the Horn was a Frenchman, "foolish" enough to set out for his camp after dark. Though he had provided himself with a candle and matches to light his way, "he was found dead on the rocks the next morning."[156]

Of course the most fascinating report to come out of Downieville was an unsubstantiated rumor that on the past Fourth of July a mob had lynched a woman. The editor of a San Francisco newspaper had reported hearing of the incident, but expressed "some doubt as to the genuineness."[157] A Sacramento editor, however, wrote that though he had at first "hoped that the story was fabricated," he had since located a witness to the "frightful scene" that had become a "blot upon the history of the state."[158] J. D. intended to confirm or deny the hanging.

As the trail left the backbone of the range and began its zigzag descent of the steep mountain slope, the party caught an "occasional view between the pine trees of the little town far down below, . . . so completely surrounded by mountains that it seemed to be at the bottom of an immense hole in the ground."[159] J. D. was disappointed, on reaching the floor of the narrow valley, to discover how small the town was—merely a single four-hundred-yard street wedged between the steep mountainside and the river. The main thoroughfare, however, was lined by "well-finished two-story houses, with columns and verandas in front," and the saloons were "fitted up in the usual style of showy extravagance, with the exception of mirrors." Because of the difficult mountain trail, there were no large mirrors in town, but "an extra number of smaller ones," J. D. noted, "made up for the deficiency."[160]

He took a room at a boardinghouse kept by a "pretty little Frenchwoman," who had given the place quite a civilized air. The tiny room, shared with another guest, seemed luxurious to a man used to "being stowed away on a shelf" along with twenty to thirty snoring roommates. Since "the *salle a manger* was underneath me," he wrote, "and as the floor was very thin, I had the full benefit of all the conversation of those who had indulged in late suppers, whilst next door was a ten-pin alley, in which they were banging away at the pins all night long; but such trifles did not much disturb my slumbers."[161]

Because of the extensive diggings in the area, the small town was able to support a theater, "laid out in the orthodox fashion, with boxes, pit, and gallery," where events ranging from Shakespearean tragedy to dog-and-badger fights were presented. The evening J. D. attended he viewed a play performed by the same company he had heard through the wall of his Nevada City hotel and an American glee club with a repertoire of songs of "decidedly national character." At the end of the performance, "a rough old miner stood up on his seat in the middle of the room, and after a few preliminary coughs, delivered himself of a very elaborate speech" to a lady who had sung some familiar ballads. He eloquently begged her to accept a purse of five hundred dollars in gold.[162]

J. D. was not long in inquiring of local residents about the hanging incident. They informed him that a Mexican woman had indeed been arrested and tried by an impartial jury, who had found her guilty of murder and sentenced her to death by hanging. As he had done before in Hangtown, J. D. naively accepted the version the perpetrators put forth. It was not until years later that the truth came out in various accounts published by eyewitnesses. One of the most informative accounts, from a legal standpoint, was written by David Barstow, who was seated on the stand throughout the extemporaneous trial, but more specific details are provided in other accounts.

The trial and execution had occurred the day after the previous Fourth of July celebration. On that day, Downieville citizens held a grand parade, followed by a "thrilling address" from John B. Weller, later to become governor of California. Since Weller had the reputation of an important politician and excellent orator, thousands of miners from outlying regions flocked to town to hear him. Throughout the day and evening, liquor flowed freely, resulting in a carnival atmosphere of revelry, "ribald song and laughter." By nightfall, some of the "rougher sort" were still amusing themselves, making the rounds of private residences, armed with bottle in hand, and breaking in doors to wake sleepers and invite them to a drink. The high-spirited crowd was led by young Fred Cannon, a popular, fun-loving Scot over six feet tall and of "herculean proportions."[163] It was rumored that this handsome blond had been attempting, though without success, to court a pretty Mexican woman named Juanita, so when he paused before the door of the clapboard shanty where Juanita and her "reputed" husband lived and gave it a few hard kicks, the other members of the party were not surprised.[164]

Juanita, who earned a living by taking in washing, was a "quiet, gentle creature,"[165] and she and her husband gave no response to the carousers. Cannon, however, was determined to see the woman and therefore continued kicking the door until it fell from its leather hinges. On seeing the damage he had done, friends quickly pulled Cannon away from the shanty and persuaded him to continue the game in another section of town. But early in the morning, as the members of the band were dispersing, Cannon returned alone to Juanita's house. His exact reason is not known. At the trial his friends maintained he had returned only to apologize and pay for repairs to the door. Yet the only witness to the killing reported that Cannon, on being greeted at the door by Juanita, first called her a prostitute and then stood blocking the doorway with his huge frame while he leaned inside and continued talking. Suddenly she lunged toward him and plunged a bowie knife into his heart. Though she was a "very small, slender woman," her "intense passion" apparently gave her unusual strength, and Cannon staggered, moaned, and fell to the ground, dead.[166]

News of the stabbing raced through nearby camps like a prairie fire. "The cry of 'murder!' came up the river," one camp resident reported. "Everybody was running towards town. At the scene of the action we found a vast throng surrounding a clapboard shanty, and, within, a miner was lying dead. We happened to be one of the few who crowded in. A broad stream of blood flowed from the breast of the slain man, as much as ten feet."[167] Those gathered at the cabin immediately began to cry out for the punishment of the murderer. "There were several reasons for this," the same participant stated. One was that Cannon had many friends; second, relations between the white miners and the Mexicans "lacked cordiality"; and third, Juanita's husband was a monte dealer, and "a robust ill-will" existed between "the roughly dressed miners and the usually flashy-dressed gamblers. . . . Thus it was that the general sentiment was that Juanita must die."[168]

As the assembled crowd grew angrier, Juanita ran from her home and took refuge in a nearby saloon, begging the owner to provide her protection. But the mob followed after her and surrounded the establishment, shouting in unison "Hang her! Hang her!" The alarmed saloon owner quickly handed the woman over to the "frenzied crowd," who roughly led her to the town plaza. Though the general intent was to lynch Juanita immediately, some of the more responsible residents persuaded the group to provide the frightened woman with a trial before hanging her.[169]

From those present, a twelve-man jury was selected, a prosecutor and defense lawyer appointed, and, with the corpse of "poor" Fred Cannon placed in a tent close by so everyone could "see his gaping wound," a trial was conducted on the same stand where Weller had delivered his patriotic oration the previous day. Cannon's many friends spoke out boldly of his good character and friendliness, but when the greenhorn appointed as defense attorney climbed upon a barrel to make himself heard, it was kicked from under him, his "hat going one way and spectacles another, while he was flung on the heads of the mob below, and carried a hundred yards before he touched the ground, receiving blows and kicks from all sides."[170] Then he was "driven across the river, and fled up the hill, leaving his hat and mule behind."[171]

Without further ado, the jury retired for a short time and returned with a verdict of guilty. "There was no surprise in the verdict," one witness admitted.[172] In a last-minute attempt to save the condemned woman, Dr. Cyrus Aiken jumped to the stand and shouted that the defendant was "with child," and the sentence should therefore be staid.[173] "A howl of incredulity" was raised, but the prosecutor, who had throughout the proceedings been attempting to calm the unruly mob and had found it necessary to restrain them from taking possession of the accused by erecting a cordon of ropes about her, insisted that a medical examination should be carried out. As a committee of diagnosis, the court appointed three doctors present, who escorted the woman to a nearby cabin and closed the door behind them. In a short time, they brought her back to the stand with a report that she was not pregnant. The disgruntled mob turned its wrath on Dr. Aiken, driving him out of town and declaring him in temporary exile for attempting to save the woman.[174]

The court then pronounced the sentence of death by hanging. Juanita was escorted back to her cabin and given one final hour of life. Rather than being allowed a priest, she was left to prepare for death in her own way. Her gambler husband, after having seen the treatment bestowed upon the defense attorney and Dr. Aiken, was afraid to make any appeals on behalf of his wife. She sat for the entire hour "unflinching," with the "angry crowd" surrounding her home. When her allotted time had expired, she was walked to a bridge, where a beam had been "swung out" over the water. Gracefully she stepped onto the plank and stood quietly surveying the sea of faces below her.[175] Then she calmly "adjusted the rope round her own neck, pulling out her braid of hair, and at the firing of a pistol, two men with hatchets, at each end, cut the rope which held the scantling, and down everything went, woman and all."[176] When she was judged to be dead, her corpse was cut down and taken to a hillside cemetery for burial. Cannon's body was then interred next to her grave.[177]

David Barstow, who later became an attorney, reported that the crowd assembled at Downieville on July 5, 1851, was the "hungriest, craziest, wildest mob" he had ever seen. In Barstow's opinion, "the hanging of the woman was murder. No jury in the world, on any principle of self-defense or protection of life and property, would ever have convicted the woman. She was roused from her sleep in the early morning by some ruffian pushing in her door, and unfortunately the knife was lying there, and in an instant it was in his heart, without time for reflection or thought. No jury or law in Christendom," he concluded, "would have held the woman guilty of murder."[178]

A witness interviewed by the *Sacramento Times & Transcript* expressed a similar opinion. John S. Fowler is quoted as saying, "The act for which the victim suffered, was one entirely justifiable under the provocation. She had stabbed a man who persisted in making a disturbance in her house, and had greatly outraged her rights."[179] John Weller, who was still in town when the trial was going on, was later accused of "pandering to the mob" by allowing them to proceed. Weller countered that "alone he could do nothing," adding that "there was considerable bad feeling toward Mexican gamblers and women generally, and there was no other way but to hang her."[180]

The consensus of the written accounts is that the hanging was indeed a racial issue. The editor of the *Sacramento Times & Transcript* referred to Juanita as a "friendless and unprotected foreigner" and concluded that the "perpetrators of the deed" had "shamed themselves and their race," but that the Mexican woman had "borne herself with the utmost fortitude and composure through the fearful ordeal."[181] Some twenty years later the editor of the Downieville paper had occasion to comment on the incident that had brought such notoriety to the little mining center: "In the old graveyard now being washed away lie the remains of Frederick Cannon, and close by those of the woman who was hung on Durgan Bridge for the killing. The following may be deciphered on the headboard of Cannon's grave: 'Sacred to the memory of Frederick Cannon, died July 5th, 1851, aged 25 years.' . . . The hanging was really the work of Cannon's friends, a lawless and dissipated set, and is now condemned by all as it deserves."[182]

But J. D. did not have access to any of the above-mentioned accounts, and he not only accepted the justness of the execution, but also, when he later wrote a book about his California experiences, included a chapter on the merits of "lynch law" as an "effectual preventive of crime."[183] However, throughout his wanderings in California, he never observed a lynching. Had he witnessed "from first to last the utter irresponsibility of mobs" as David Barstow did, J. D.'s thinking might have been different. The Downieville experience left young Barstow a changed man. "Since that time," he wrote, "I have had no sympathy with, nor confidence in mobs; I prefer the law for redress of grievances."[184]

J. D. remained in the Downieville area for several weeks, dividing his time between sketching the wild scenery while perched on some crag overlooking the river and enjoying the refinements of civilization. "Every village was a little city of itself," he wrote, "where one could live in comparative luxury. Even Downieville had its theater and concerts, its billiard-rooms and saloons of all sorts, a daily paper, warm baths, and restaurants where men in red flannel shirts, with bare arms, spread a napkin over their muddy knees, and studied the bill of fare for half an hour before they could make up their minds what to order for dinner.''[185]

Though J. D.'s intepretation of the Juanita affair may have been less than inspired, he did while in the Downieville area experience spiritual growth, a moment of rare self-insight, a sort of epiphany brought on by three unrelated events. The first was a chance visit to a claim operated by ''The Flying Dutchman,'' a German doctor directing a crew of two Americans, two Frenchmen, two Italians, and two Mexicans in constructing a wing-dam in the river. On J. D.'s arrival the eight men ''were all pulling in different directions at an immense unwieldly log,'' and at the same time cursing each other with ''most frightful oaths,'' but since each man spoke only his mother tongue, fortunately none could understand the others' insults. The German doctor ''was rushing about among them, and gesticulating wildly,'' shouting instructions in one language after another. Upon realizing that he had addressed a Frenchman in Spanish, or vice versa, he would curse ''his own stupidity in German, . . .blowing them all up collectively in a promiscuous jumble of national oaths.'' At one point, the work came to a complete standstill, and the Flying Dutchman gave up in despair. Soon he rallied again and spoke calmly to each in turn. After that, things ran smoothly, but only for a few minutes. Then the entire ''Tower-of-Babel scene'' was reenacted.[186]

J. D. was amused at the sight but, at the time, only made his usual comparisons about national characteristics, how the Germans were quite gregarious, but Frenchmen kept more to themselves, making little attempt to learn other languages and ways. Cooking was quite another matter, however; ''it was astonishing what a superior mess a Frenchman could get up'' with ''only the ordinary materials of flour, ham, and beef.''[187] Though J. D. left the claim with the strange image of the international crew firmly planted in his mind, he had not yet considered its profound significance.

The second event came about as a result of learning that a mountain thirty miles above Downieville was one of the highest in the mines. Since the view from its summit was reported to be one of the finest in California, J. D. grew eager to see it. The trail he would have to follow was rough and uncharted, and deciding to make the trip alone was not a wise one; over the past weeks he had heard tales of mule and human skeletons bleaching in the sun at the bottom of some deep gorge. There was also the memory of the strange accident he had suffered at Panama, but still he was determined to reach the summit of the sawtoothed peak and enjoy the magnificent view of the promised land he was exploring.

His motivation was partly a desire to be one with Nature, the same impulse that prompted medieval poet Li Po to lean into the water to embrace the reflection of the moon and in so doing fall out of the boat and drown. J. D. had given into this impulse on the way to Weaver Creek, when he had stopped to lie down in a patch of wildflowers beside the trail and again at Foster's Bar, when he slept on a bed of dahlias. But on this occasion it was more than his naturally romantic tendencies; he had fallen under the spell of the camp storytellers, spinning the epic of those who had raised themselves to the stature of heroes, whether by making a fabulous strike, losing a fortune on the turn of one monte card, enduring cold and starvation, or rounding Downieville's Cape Horn for such mundane purpose as buying a can of tobacco. The dangerous ascent of the highest mountain in the area would be a measure of his own stature and, if accomplished, a feat of heroism that would make the young artist a part of the legendary life at the mines, not a mere observer.

Right from the start, the venture turned out to be more difficult than anticipated. A miner had agreed to accompany J. D. on the first part of the journey, and as they wound along a rough, sinuous trail one hundred feet above the river, a keg of butter carried by a pack mule broke loose and went bounding down the hill, rolling all the way to the bottom of the gorge, then smashing to pieces and "buttering" a flat rock jutting out of the water. As J. D. watched in horror, the miner scrambled down into the canyon and scraped up what he could of the butter. Then he toted the patched-up keg back up the mountainside, loaded it back on the mule, and they proceeded on their way. About dusk, they reached the miner's cabin, where the host invited J. D. to spend the night. Worn out from the difficult trek and filled with warm supper, the two men stretched before the fire and "slept like a top."[188]

The following morning, J. D. continued alone, but the miner provided him with detailed instructions on how to keep to the trail. The going was even tougher than it had been on the previous day, and after many hours of steady uphill traveling, he had covered only four miles. Finding himself at a notch where a shelter and two arrastras had been erected, he decided to stop for the night. The lone occupant of the cabin graciously provided his guest with supper and they retired on the ground floor near the hearth. During the night, however, the fire burnt itself out and the bitter cold wakened J. D. "The log cabin was merely a log cage," he observed, "the chinks between the logs having never been filled up, and it had come on to blow a perfect hurricane." Gusts of wind passing between the cabin logs seemed strong enough to blow the entire structure off its perch. All night the gale raged on and continued without letup through the following two days, making J. D. a virtual prisoner. "The force of the wind was so great" he wrote, that one could scarcely stand outside, and the cold was so intense that the pools in the stream which ran past were covered with ice." When the trapped men tried to sit down to the table for a meal, the wind swept the tin plates to the floor, and when they tried to warm themselves at the fire, it howled down the chimney, filling the room with smoke and fragments of burning wood. But with the aid of his "pencil and two or three old novels," J. D. managed to weather the storm.[189]

The third day dawned "beautifully bright and clear," and he once more set out on his pilgrimage. Ore-car tracks led him to the top of the ridge, and he then began ascending stony ground "covered with wiry brushwood waist-high." His passage was lined with occasional bare spots of earth, invariably stamped with the imprint of a huge grizzly bear's foot.[190] He nervously recalled how the landlord of the Grizzly Bear House, where he had slept on his way to Nevada City, had warned that shooting a ball straight in the eye of "ursus horribilis'' only results in the beast's ''winking a great deal.'' To demonstrate his knowledge on the subject, the landlord had gone on to describe ''hair-breadth escapes'' and then pulled back clothing to point out scars, inflicted, he claimed, by the claws of various grizzlies.[191] J. D. was forced to admit that he had been forewarned. Keeping a sharp eye out for the reappearance of the fierce beast that had left the tracks, he climbed on, eventually reaching ground composed of ''long slides of loose sharp-cornered stones of all sizes.'' With each step forward there was a corresponding backsliding that seemed equal to two steps, followed by a minor avalanche of the sharp stones. J. D. crept upwards, scraping leather off his boots, barking his shins, resting on each ledge, and then tackling a new slide of loose rocks. After about an hour of discouragingly slow progress, he reached ''the immense wall of solid rock which crowned the summit.'' While he stood studying the barrier ahead of him to determine the best method of approaching it, he felt the stones suddenly giving way under his feet. He struggled for a foothold, still confused as to how to proceed. Obviously there was no choice but to go at it without a plan. Yet with one false step he would become part of the avalanche he was creating. ''After a pretty hard struggle,'' he wrote, ''I reached the top.'' But when he proudly looked about him, he discovered he was only ''between the teeth of the saw.'' Making it the rest of the way to the peak would require following a slanting ledge, about a foot wide, up the face of the rock, but that seemed mere child's play after what he had been through. Triumphantly he paced off the final steps and at last found himself at the top. He had successfully accomplished the mission he had set upon four days ago. ''I felt amply repaid for all the labor of the ascent,'' he commented ''by the vastness and grandeur of the panorama around me. I looked back for more than a hundred miles over the mountainous pine-clad region . . . I had visited. . . . On the other side . . . was a sheer precipice of about two hundred feet . . . and beyond . . . appeared the white peaks of the Sierra Nevada.''[192]

In spite of the bitter cold and fierce wind, J. D. sat at the peak for nearly an hour, contemplating the scenery and recalling his past experiences in the areas he could recognize below by outstanding landmarks. At a distance of nearly two hundred miles rose San Francisco's distinctively shaped Monte Diablo, as clear as if it were but a short distance away. Seeing the "vastness" from "such a lofty pinnacle," gave him the feeling of "being suspended in the air, and cut off from all communication with the world below."[193]

The image of the artist, seated on the rocky crag and taking in the beauty below, is reminiscent of Thomas Bewick's illustration of the *Traveller*. In all probability J. D. was well aware of the similarity between his present situation and that of the young man in Oliver Goldsmith's poem who sat atop an alpine peak and reflected on his experiences in the countries below. But J. D.'s thoughts on that day were far more cheerful than those of Goldsmith's melancholy hero. J. D. separated himself from the Romantic tradition not only by maintaining a firm basis in reality, but also by maintaining a consistently positive attitude. Fellow artist John Woodhouse Audubon had alternated between moods of deep depression and fits of ecstasy; on his arrival in California he became so depressed that he had to force-feed himself to stay alive, and despite the joy he experienced in observing the beauty of the wild landscape, he formed a negative opinion of the environment's influence on man. "California will for the present lower the moral tone of all who come here," Audubon wrote. "Men become coarse and profane in language, while the hard life does not improve the temper. . . . The sight of gold . . . makes them avaricious."[194] Audubon believed man's effect on the environment had been equally devastating. Though he admired the "solemnity and peace" of the unspoiled wilderness, he considered the mines to be "dreary."[195]

J. D.'s opinions present a decided contrast. He believed the Americans, rich beyond their age in wisdom, had had a salubrious effect on the wilderness, and he was hopeful over the possibilities for advancement opened up by the mining frontier. In settling California, the Americans had "imparted to it a good deal of their own nature, which knows no period of boyhood. The Americans spring at once from childhood, or almost from infancy, to manhood; and California, no less rapid in its growth, became a fullgrown State, while one-half the world still doubted its existence.'' Young as the new state was, he concluded, ''it was in one respect older than its parent country.''[196] Rather than deploring the miners' upheaval of the land in the valleys and mountains beneath him and agonizing over the toll the adverse labor had taken on men, J. D. applauded the ''energy and adaptive genius,'' that had ''immediately seized and improved every natural advantage which presented itself.'' He viewed the miner—exerting himself in manual labor, wading waist deep in a stream, and digging into the earth—as enjoying a sort of mystical union with Nature.[197]

The lofty mountain perch also provided J. D. an opportunity to reflect on his own accomplishment. In conquering the highest pinnacle of the Northern Mines, he had shown courage, self-discipline, and endurance—heroic virtues all. The risk had been great because he might have given up in failure. Instead, he had triumphed over all obstacles, proving both his manhood and his honor. Surely a man who could single-handedly scale such a mountain could also reach the top of whatever career he chose, even one notorious for bringing disappointment.

The solitude at the summit was a marked change from the chaotic atmosphere of the Flying Dutchman's claim, somewhere there below, and J. D.'s mood suddenly swung to the opposite pole. He was overwhelmed, as before in the Greenwood Valley, by loneliness, anxious to escape its oppressiveness. The descent was even more ''ticklish'' than the ascent had been. As he worked his way down, the ''loud report'' of rock he was dislodging was incessant in his ears. His hands and feet had become ''benumbed and chilled,'' and it took the remainder of the day to ease himself down the mountainside. Just before dark he reached the welcome cabin of his miner friend, who again invited him to spend the night.[198]

He returned to Downieville the next day. The chill in the air warned him of stormy weather ahead, and since he was anxious to be out of the mountains before the rainy season commenced, he did not tarry in town, but hurried on downriver. Though he was completely unaware, the third and final event in his spiritual metamorphosis was close at hand.

At Goodyear's Bar, the trail left the river and turned west, heading up a mountain slope. Darkness fell before he could reach the top, but fortunately he came upon a log cabin sitting on the banks of a stream. Since the place was decorated with a huge sign designating it the "Florida House," he entered to take a room. Inside, he found an Italian landlord, his Yankee wife, and their several children, but no other guests.

After sharing supper with the family, J. D. joined his host in front of the fire, where they sat for some time smoking their pipes. J. D. was not one to volunteer any information about himself, but the Italian began to relate his life story. He had spent the last few years farming in the United States, he said, and before that had lived in England and Scotland. As the man continued, J. D. became impressed by his abundant knowledge of European city life and tried to probe a little further into his background, but the Italian suddenly became reticent. J. D. began conjuring up all sorts of images in his head—"plaster-of-Paris busts of Napoleon, the Duke of Wellington, Sir Walter Scott, and other distinguished characters."[199] But the host would give no hints as to his origins, and J. D. allowed him his privacy. Finally, the man turned to his guest and asked if he would care to hear some music, "saying that he played a little on the Italian fiddle." J. D. was curious about the sort of instrument the man had in mind and replied he would be delighted. Then, to his great surprise and disappointment, the man arose and pulled down a small hurdy-gurdy, on which he commenced cranking out tune after tune. "At the first note, of course," J. D. wrote, the statues of dignitaries he had been contemplating immediately vanished and were replaced by "a vision of an unfortunate monkey in a red coat." His host's travels throughout Europe had been "very satisfactorily accounted for." J. D. even had the feeling that as a child he may have heard that very music box grinding out melodies on the streets of Edinburgh. He was suddenly flooded by an unexpected wave of sentimentality. The music "put me more in mind of home than anything I had heard for a long time," he wrote.[200]

After a while the sweet, bubbly, repetitious notes began to cloy, and when at last two strings snapped, J. D. was relieved. His host, however, was greatly disgusted at the bad luck; in the mountain wilderness, he had no way to repair his "Italian fiddle."

As J. D. lay in bed that night, the three salient events of the past days came together in his head like the pieces of a jigsaw puzzle: the Tower-of-Babel confusion at the Flying Dutchman's claim, the hour of reflection on the mountaintop, and the evening by the fire with the Italian organ-grinder. J. D. was ashamed to recall that at the revelation of his host's humble origins, he had suddenly viewed him as an object of derision. The young Scott could perceive quite clearly, perhaps for the first time, all the unattractiveness of his own prejudices and feelings of superiority. He had only been paying lip service to noble ideas of equality and universal brotherhood. In reality there was much to admire about the generous man who had offered his hearth, companionship, and music that evening: by his own efforts he had raised himself from a near beggar to being the owner of a crude frontier hotel, who dignified his little music box with the name of an instrument and brought it out on special occasions as an aesthetic treat for his guests. J. D. felt a strong surge of warmth for the man. "I only hope all the fraternity are like him," he thought, "and attain ultimately to such a respectable position in life." And then everything J. D. had experienced during his quest to the New World seemed to miraculously merge into a single significant insight: "Perhaps they are," he mused, "if only one knew them."[201]

PORT OF ENTRY

It would not be correct to imply that J. D. left Goodyear's Bar a new and perfect man, but he had had a new vista opened to him. For one brief moment he had realized man's potential for brotherhood. That evening he reached Oak Valley, where an incident occurred that, though minor, reinforced his discovery. He had walked the last few miles with a young man from the South, but at supper, the landlord, a Mr. Toots, noticed that the young Southerner was absent from the table. Suspecting it might be a matter of embarrassment over being "strapped," Toots sent J. D. to find his companion. "On going out and asking him why he did not come to supper," J. D. wrote, "he reluctantly admitted that the state of his finances would not admit of it. I told him, in the language of Mr. Toots, that it was of no consequence, and made him come in, when he was most unceremoniously lectured by the rest of the party, and by the landlord particularly, on the absurdity of his intention of going supperless to bed merely because he happened to be 'dead-broke,' getting at the same time some useful hints how to act under such circumstances in future from several of the men present, who related how, when they had found themselves in such a predicament, they had, on frankly stating the fact, been made welcome to everything."[202] The lecture was not wasted on J. D.

He left Oak Valley in the company of an American who invited him to pay a visit to his camp at Slate Range. The American's camp turned out to be the "least luxurious habitation, and in the most wild and rugged locality" J. D. had yet seen in the Northern Mines.

> On a rough board which rested on two stones were a number of tin plates, pannikins, and such articles of table furniture, while a few flat stones alongside answered the purpose of chairs. Scattered about, as was usual in all miners' camps, were quantities of empty tins of preserved meats, sardines, and oysters, empty bottles of all shapes and sizes, innumberable ham bones, old clothes, and other rubbish. Round the blackened spot which was evidently the kitchen were pots and frying-pans, sacks of flour and beans, and other provisions, together with a variety of cans and bottles, of which no one could tell the contents without inspection; for in the mines everything is perverted from its original purpose, butter being perhaps stowed away in a tin labeled "fresh lobsters," tea in a powder canister, and salt in a sardine-box.[203]

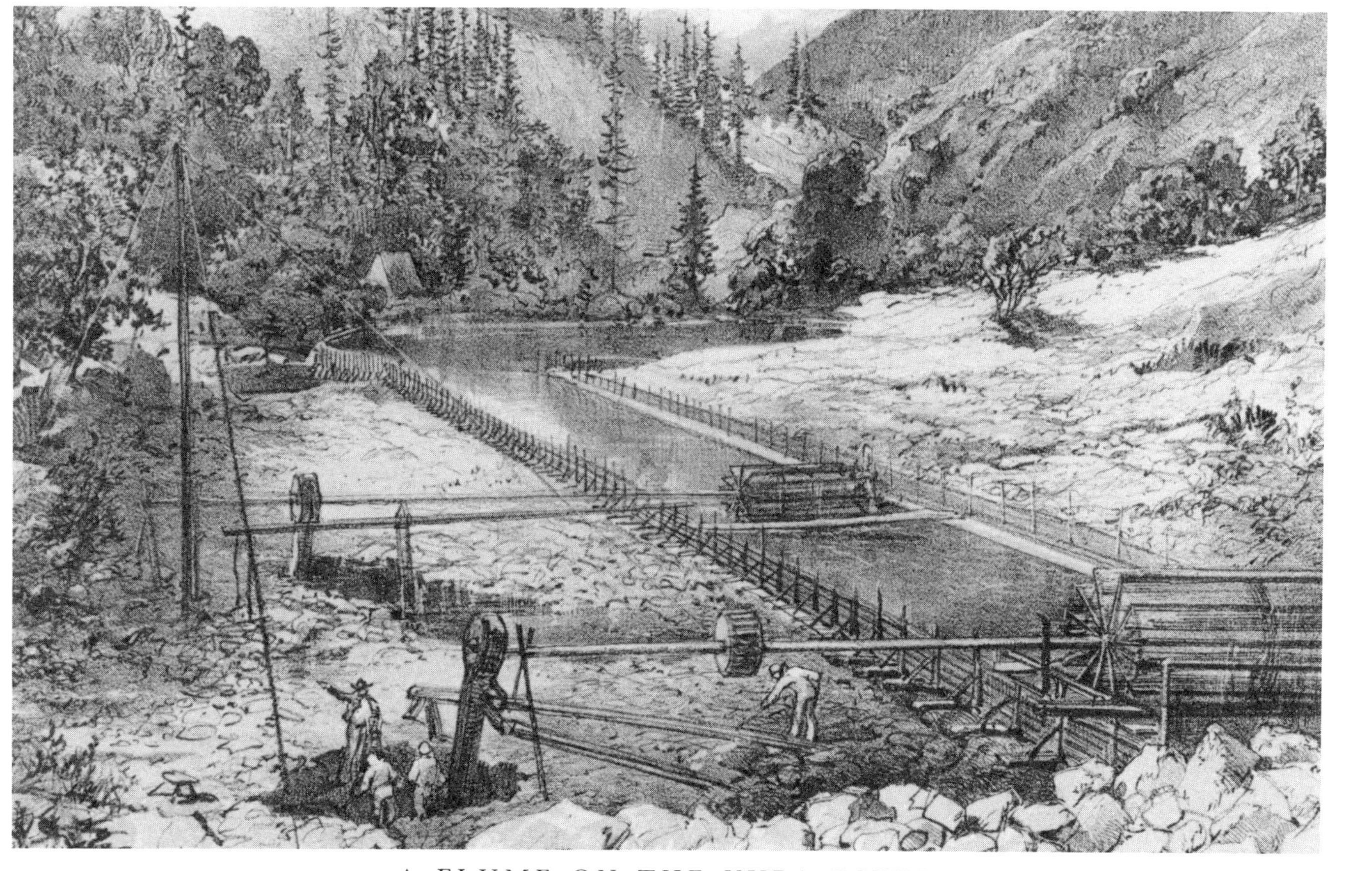

A FLUME ON THE YUBA RIVER

Just beyond the camp, the Americans had pushed the Yuba River out of its bed and into a new channel. During their labors, they were constantly scurrying across a slippery bridge, consisting of a slender pine tree sprayed by a revolving water-wheel.

After sketching the Yuba flume project, J. D. visited a nearby Chinese camp, where the storekeeper dozed on a floor mat in "the seventh heaven" from his opium pipe lying next to him. Next he walked to a little settlement called Wamba's Bar. At its single business, "half store, half boarding-house," he arranged for lodging, assuming it would be for but one night. But by dawn he realized he had delayed too long in leaving the mountains. As he was preparing to commence the day's journey, rain began to come down "in such torrents" that he was forced to stay inside. Rain fell all day and continued the next. J. D. and the other guests at the small inn sat by the stove and listened to fast-falling drops pounding against the roof of the clapboard shanty. Occasionally they wandered to the window to watch the swollen river rushing by "in a raging torrent, the waves rolling several feet high." Broken planks, shattered logs, and entire pine trees swept by, crashing into each other and rearing on end. J. D. thought it a "grand sight; the river seemed as if it had suddenly arisen to assert its independence, and take vengeance for all the restraints which had been placed upon it, by demolishing flumes, dams, and bridges, and carrying off everything within its reach."[204]

The inn, situated at the mouth of a creek, was one of the objects likely to be carried away by the flooding river. "The waters rose to within an inch or two of the floor," he wrote, "and as they carried logs and rocks along with them, we feared that the posts would be carried away, . . . slip off the rocks into the angry river a few feet below."[205] The host removed the pane of glass from the window in preparation for a hasty exit and then laid several axes next to the back wall, ready to slash through to freedom should the waters carry the inn from its foundation. There had been no easing of the downpour, and with the water level creeping closer to the inn's floor, those trapped inside did not dare fall asleep. They sat alert until daylight, when a few volunteers ventured outside and made their way along the river bank until they located the logjam that was acting as a dam. After breaking up the accumulation of logs and other debris, the drenched men returned to the cabin to wait out the storm.[206]

Even after the rains had stopped falling, it was two days before the river was safe to cross. On the third day, J. D. and a companion attempted the crossing in a rowboat and safely reached the opposite bank. They then clamored up the mountainside to drier land and followed the muddy ridge all the way to Nevada City, walking under a warm sun that was melting the few inches of snow that had fallen at the higher altitude. But immediately upon their arrival in the city, skies clouded over again and by the time they were situated at a hotel, a snowstorm had erupted. The bad weather lasted for three weeks, alternating between warm and freezing temperatures that accordingly left layers of frozen rain and snow. Deplorable road conditions caused a delay for supply trains, and within a short time a food crisis existed. From outlying camps, miners swarmed into the city, begging for food and shelter and relating woeful tales of the suffering inhabitants were undergoing in remote regions. Several men had frozen to death in deep snow, trying to make their escape, while those who had elected to stay were surviving on grain intended as mule fodder.[207]

Despite the adverse traveling conditions, J. D. was determined to reach San Francisco. His reason was too personal to be mentioned; he wrote only, "I had occasion to return to San Francisco at this time, and the journey was about the most unpleasant I ever performed. The roads had been getting worse all the time, and were quite impassable for stages or wagons."[208] The most logical explanation for his stubborn persistence in trying to pass over the "impassable" was a desire to be at the port of entry as the newspapers arrived. He had commented earlier that unless one was on hand at the precise moment the express arrived at the outlying camps, there was little chance of ever seeing a newspaper. And he was anxious to peruse every copy of the *Illustrated London News* and *Gleason's Pictorial.* The editors had had sufficient time to get his pictures and articles in print, and it would have been a shame to be a published writer and artist and not even be aware of it.

Though all trails were covered with snow and ice, J. D. found an acquaintance who knew the area and was willing to try to lead him out. The first day they covered twelve miles, at times tramping through snow as deep as four feet, and on the second day, they reached "the regions of mud and slush, and rain." Under steadily pouring skies, they waded in soupy mire, forded waist-high streams, and groped their way across log bridges completely submerged by swollen waters. In a small boat, too near the "size and shape of a coffin" to permit peace of mind, they were ferried across the flooding Yuba, waves lapping over the "flat-bottomed, straight-sided" little skiff and threatening to swamp it. The river current was so powerful that even the strongest swimmer could not have reached shore, and the crude ferry was carried nearly a half mile off course, just in crossing the one-hundred-yard distance. On landing, they found the town of Marysville flooded as high as the top story of the large brick businesses.[209]

From this depot city for the northeast mines, they caught a steamer for the remaining fifty-mile journey to Sacramento. The surrounding plains, J. D. wrote, now appeared as a "vast inland sea." Treetops along each submerged bank marked the regular river channel, and here and there a cabin roof jutted out of the water. J. D. was filled with pity at the sights they encountered. "On the tops of the cabins and sheds, on piles of firewood, or up on the trees, were fowls calmly waiting their doom; while pigs, cows and horses were all huddling up together, knee-deep in water, on any little rising ground which offered standing-room, dying by inches from inanition. The squatters themselves were busy removing in boats whatever property they could, and at those cabins whose occupants were not yet completely drowned out, a boat was made fast alongside as a means of escape. . . . We saw two men sitting resolutely on the top of their cabin, the water almost up to their feet; a boat was made fast to the chimney, to be used when the worst came to the worst, . . . They looked intensely miserable, though they would not own it, for they gave us a very feigned and uncheery hurrah as we steamed past.''[210]

The steamer passengers found Sacramento in a similarly ''wretched'' plight. The only point where land was still dry was atop the levee. ''The streets were all so many canals crowded with boats and barges,'' J. D. wrote. ''Gentlemen poled themselves about on rafts, or on extemporized boats made of empty boxes.'' In the higher sections of town where water in the street was not deep enough to navigate, ''horses were harnessed to large flat-bottomed boats, and numbers of these vehicles, carrying passengers or goods, were to be seen cruising about, now dashing through a foot or two of mud which the horses made to fly in all directions as they floundered through it, now grounding and bumping over some very dry spot, and again sailing gracefully along the top of the water, so deep as nearly to cover the horses' backs.''[211]

Because they had arrived too late to catch the steamer for San Francisco, the passengers were forced to spend the night in the flooded city. In spite of the threat of the levee breaking and admitting the river that rose several feet above the water level in town, residents proceeded as usual, hotels, theaters, and gambling houses doing record business. The one source of consolation J. D. could invoke was ''endeavoring to compute how many millions of rats would be drowned.''[212]

The next morning he took passage on the steamer to San Francisco. Disembarking at the port city was like entering an entirely different world—a clear, radiant sky and warm sunshine that made everything look ''bright and gay.'' There had been great change in the city during his nine-month absence: large brick buildings dominated the skyline, and planked sidewalks lifted pedestrians above the mud. The settlement had extended itself not only onto the surrounding hills, but also into the bay, so that where water had once stood now rose wide streets of stone-and-brick warehouses.[213]

J. D. took a room, preparing to stay as long as required to discover whether his work had been accepted or returned with a rejection notice. It was a restless period for him—waiting for each mail steamer to arrive, only to be informed at the post office that there was nothing for him. In spite of the balmy weather in the city, he heartily wished he were back at the mines. There was an occasional rain, but most mornings broke bright and warm; then in the afternoon the sea wind blew in, a biting breeze that chilled to the marrow of the bone. He continued purchasing each arriving copy of the *Illustrated London News*, but his picture was not to be found within the pages. He also continued waiting in line at the post office after the arrival of each steamer, but there were no packages or letters for him. Evidently his two submissions had not been rejected, at least as yet. Because of his worry over the fate of his drawings and articles, the cosmopolitan city had now lost its charm, and he wandered its streets forlorn and anxious.

For the entire winter he waited in vain. Then one bright day in early spring, a newsboy hallooed that the *Illustrated London News* had just arrived. As usual J. D. paid his dollar and began flipping through the pages. Suddenly he caught sight of his picture, every line vivid and clear—the miners united in working the riverbed and the little mule, bracing delicate legs against the steep mountain slope. On the following page was his article. He had not expected a by-line, but the editor had not only mentioned his name, but in addition given information about him:

> Of the many Illustrations of this new Gold Field which the obliging intelligence of Correspondents has enabled us, from time to time, to present to the readers of the ILLUSTRATED LONDON NEWS, the large view upon the preceding page presents the most practical picture. It has been sketched by Mr. John Borthwick, a clever water-colour painter, who first visited the locality as a goldseeker, but is now settled in the neighbourhood, and is actively engaged in his profession, by taking portraits of successful adventurers, chiefly to be sent to their friends at a distance. It will be seen that, besides presenting us with a picture, our ingenious Correspondent has sketched with equal minuteness the industrial economy of this extraordinary scene.[214]

He was at last published, and the editor had also referred to him as the paper's "Correspondent." He checked the date of the paper and noticed it was January 24, 1852. Undoubtedly his mother had seen the picture and article weeks ago. Janet Borthwick would be very proud of her second son.

Though the London editor's preface makes it clear J. D. was not, as formerly believed, the first artist-correspondent to cover America for a British newspaper, that fact did not lessen J. D.'s elation. The following month brought more good news —the arrival of *Gleason's Pictorial*, and in it, his article. Instead of selecting from the several pictures submitted, the Boston editor had included them all![215] This second publication seemed to confirm J. D.'s talent as both artist and writer. The spring of 1852 had indeed been a memorable season for him, but if he were to pursue the profession that now stood open for him, he could not rest on his laurels. He was in need of fresh material. Just as he had done the previous year, he donned his oldest shirt and trousers, tossed two blankets over his shoulder, grabbed a drawing pad, and set out for the mines. The great difference from his departure of 1851 was not visible: it was internal. John David Borthwick was no longer merely a wandering adventurer. He was an artist-correspondent, and every note jotted down was of consequence to world readers, every drawing made, another step toward a dream so daring he could scarcely acknowledge it even to himself.

MOKELUMNE HILL

Since J. D. had not visited the Southern Mines, he now decided to make an extensive tour of that area, hoping it would prove a fruitful source of subject matter. His route led him through the city of Stockton, located at the head of navigation of the San Joaquin River, and from there eastward. Spring rains had greened the countryside, and the "grandeur and beauty of the scenery" overwhelmed him. The same sights two years earlier had revived the flagging spirits of John Woodhouse Audubon. Though Audubon had become depressed on his arrival in California, his volatile emotions shot up on approaching the Southern Mines. It was a "most fairy-like country," Audubon recorded. "Every turn gives some vista of beauty in this Garden of Eden; the soft southerly breeze is perfumed with the delicate odor of millions of the smaller variety of prairie flowers, in some places so abundant as to color acres, whole hillsides, so thickly as to hide the ground. . . . One without home ties might well feel all his days could be passed in the beauties of these valleys, roseate, yellow and blue, so soft that the purest sky cannot surpass the color for delicacy. . . . And upon this exquisite vegetation always some view, wild and impressive, meets the eye.''[216]

Like Audubon, J. D. enjoyed the rare peacefulness of walking the green hills alone, but he was also comforted by an occasional glimpse of a red-shirted miner busily working a streambed. After two days of travel, he arrived at the Mokelumne River, crossed it, and followed a winding road to a mountain ledge overhanging the valley. The town of Mokelumne Hill lay in a ''sort of semicircular amphitheater of about a mile in diameter,'' and was composed of two or three wooden businesses and a collection of residences, mere ''skeletons clothed in dirty rags of canvas.''[217]

The town had first sprung up in the fall of 1848 as a trading post for French miners, who, as reported by the French consul at San Francisco, had coolly gathered up 138 pounds of gold in one of the gulches below. Though Irish miners tried to drive the Frenchmen from their rich camps, the consul came to their defense, and within a two-year period their numbers swelled to nearly eight thousand, sufficient to support a French newspaper. Highwayman Joaquin Murieta was credited with having committed a few robberies in the area, and as well, immortalizing a gambling saloon by paying it a visit. Local storytellers had a sizable repertoire of accounts of violent crime. It was said that until a vigilance committee took matters in hand, one killing at the very least took place each weekend for seventeen weeks running. On the opposite side were tales of fabulous wealth—$180,000 worth of gold dust extracted in but a few days.[218]

On J. D.'s arrival, buildings were plastered with announcements of an upcoming bull-and-bear fight. ''The celebrated Bull-killing Bear, GENERAL SCOTT,'' was to make his appearance in the local arena, the ads read, facing off against a ''perfectly wild'' bull, whose horns had *not* been "sawed off to prevent accidents." The following Sunday J. D. joined the throng crowding its way into the town arena to witness the "war" to be conducted by notorious General Scott, battle-scarred hero of numerous skirmishes. The occasion was as gay and colorful as a Fourth of July celebration—circled tiers of miners clad in red and blue, and Mexican women in "snowy-white dresses, puffing their cigaritas in delightful anticipation."[219]

The crowd hushed as General Scott, a grizzly of about twelve hundred pounds, was rolled into the arena in his cage and unceremoniously dumped onto the ground. While the disgruntled grizzly "floundered halfway round the ring at the length of his chain, and commenced to tear up the earth with his forepaws," a glossy-coated, sharp-horned bull, of "dark purple color marked with white," was prodded into making a spirited dash into the ring. After gazing steadily at the bear for a few moments, the bull "charged furiously." The wary grizzly "received him crouching down as low as he could, and though one could hear the bump of the bull's head and horns upon his ribs, he was quick enough to seize the bull by the nose before he could retreat." While the bear was shredding the bull's nose, the latter stomped his assailant with his hind feet. Then the two beasts broke apart momentarily to catch their breath, rested, and repeated the process, all to the spectators' squeals of delight.[220]

When either animal showed signs of wanting to withdraw from the conflict, ringmen goaded it into a fury, and the battle continued. Finally the bull became so weak from loss of blood he could not remain on his feet, and it became necessary to introduce a second bull. On seeing his fellow bull's entrance, the wounded animal rallied, and together the enraged beasts launched a fresh attack on the bear. "The poor General between the two did not know what to do," J. D. recounted, "but struck out blindly with his fore-paws with such a suppliant pitiable look that I thought this the most disgusting part of the whole exhibition."[221]

The joint assault continued, with the General gamely latching onto the muzzles of his huge attackers, tearing the flesh and letting blood until both bulls were unable to continue. Ringmen then shot them to put an end to their suffering, and General Scott was proclaimed the winner, to the gratification of all who had staked their savings on him. J. D. left the performance lamenting the "cruelty of the whole proceeding," labeling it "a scene which one would rather have prevented than witnessed."[222] The following day he returned to the deserted arena and made a series of sketches of the General, who all the while "growled most savagely, and stormed about his cage, even pulling at the iron bars" in an effort to get to the artist, whom he considered one of his tormentors. "I could not help thinking what a pretty mess he would have made of me," J. D. thought afterwards, "if he had succeeded" in breaking out of the cage.[223]

A few weeks later, General Scott fought again. As was his habit, he quickly clawed a trench for himself to crouch in as his opponent approached. But on the first charge, the bull was lucky enough to plant one horn between the General's ribs and in so doing struck a vital organ. Despite his fatal injury, the bear heroically fought on, but when ringmen saw the old warrior was not able to hold up his end of the combat, they were forced to put a rifle ball through his massive head. Heavy bettors suffered great losses that day; most had been convinced there was "nary bull in Calaforny as could whip that bar."[224]

Evidently heroism in the West was not limited to the miners. Throughout his travels, J. D. had seen women, such as the wife of the Italian organ-grinder, courageously making secure homes for their families in the wilderness, and at Downieville the condemned Juanita had shown a bravery and dignity that elevated her sex to a rare height. Even the beasts of the frontier showed unusual endurance—plodding, heavy-footed oxen and surefooted little mules who brought needed supplies to the most remote camps. And now to this list must be added the warring grizzly, who so gloriously defended life and honor in the Mokelumne Hill arena, right up to the moment of death.

In addition to the downfall of General Scott, J. D. witnessed a second marvel while at Mokelumne Hill: the construction of a fifty-mile canal to transport water to the dry diggings. He considered it a remarkable feat, typical of the

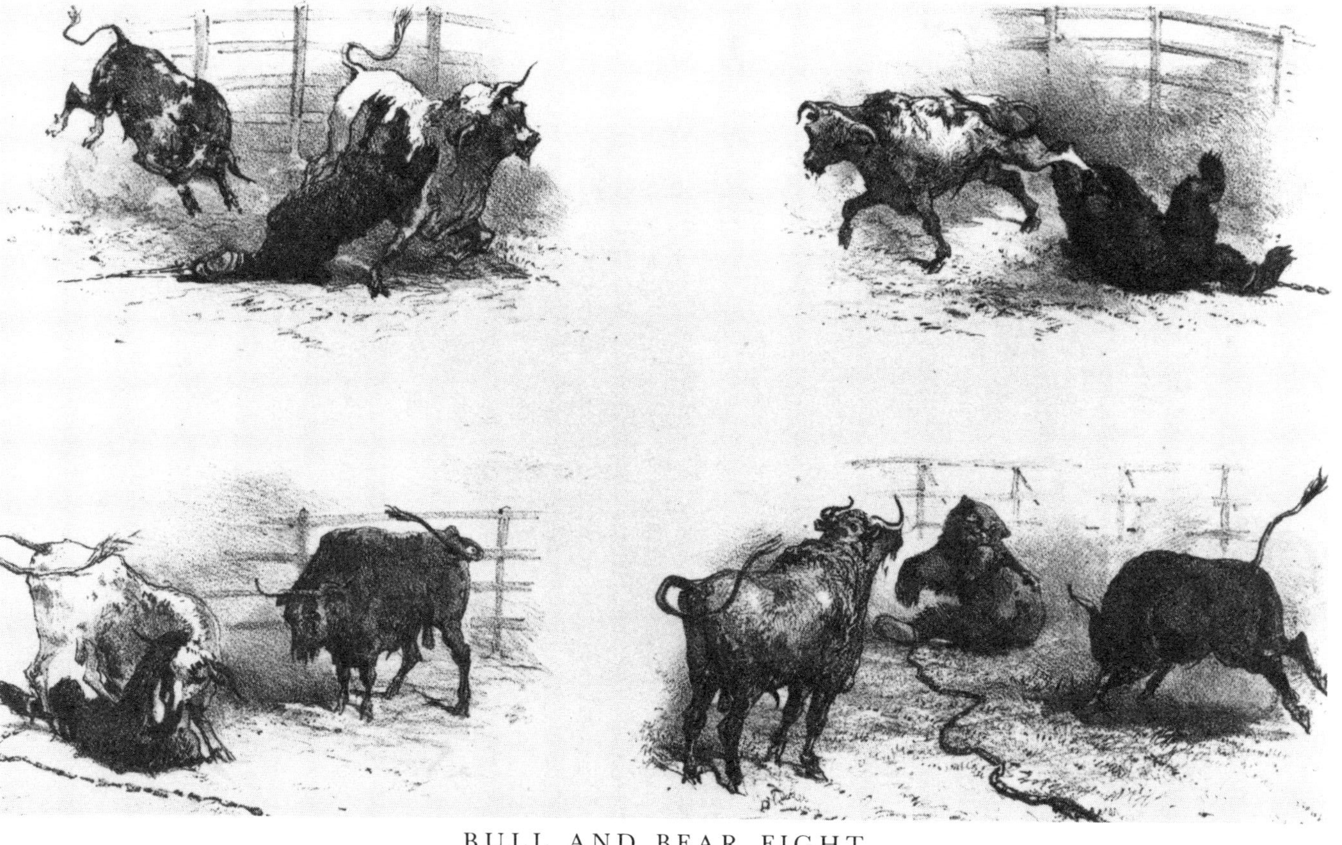

BULL AND BEAR FIGHT

ingenuity and energy displayed throughout the mines. The physical beauty of this engineering miracle, which allowed greater efficiency in obtaining the riches of the earth, was also admirable. "Hollows and valleys were spanned at a great height by aqueducts, supported on graceful scaffoldings of pine logs, and precipitous mountains were girded by wooden flumes projecting from their rock sides."[225] As a child in Edinburgh, J. D. had learned to reconcile opposites, blending a reverence for old ways with a zeal for the new; as a young adult he now consolidated the notions of the Romantic poets with theories of technical advancement. Men, it seemed, were capable of uniting to create wonders that matched those of Nature.

When J. D. gave up his room at the "holey old canvas hotel" in Mokelumne Hill, he headed for Volcano, about eighteen miles north. The area he passed was inhabited by Indians who seemed more prone to adopt the ways of the white man than other tribes he had encountered. They showed a particular fondness for the Mexican game of monte, resorting to digging for gold to support their habit. But despite their propensity for merging into the dominant culture, J. D. saw little hope for their survival. "As the country becomes more thickly settled," he wrote, "there will be no longer room for them . . . as they themselves cannot be turned to account, they must move off, and make way for their betters. This may not be very good morality, but it is the way of the world, and the aborigines of California are not likely to share a better fate than those of many another country. And though the people who drive them out may make the process as gradual as possible by the system of Indian grants and reservations, yet, as with wild cattle, so it is with Indians, so many head, . . . the result is certain though gradual extirpation."[226] Sadly enough, J. D.'s predictions were all too true. The Indian decimation commenced by the Spanish mission system continued throughout the era of American settlement.

As J. D. walked toward Volcano, he noted several differences between the Northern and Southern mines. For one thing the entire landscape was gentler and more rounded in the south—mountains had become hills and zigzagging rivers had turned to meandering streams. Here and there a solitary pine shot up along the rolling skyline, but the forests were mainly broad-branching oaks. The thin-scaled gold of the north had been replaced by round chunks of coarse ore, found mainly on the flats rather than along rivers. The log cabins and frame shanties of the northern camps were the exception in southern towns, composed mostly of canvas. This tame-looking countryside was inhabited by fewer solitary American backwoodsmen and more colonies of foreigners—entire settlements of Frenchmen, Mexicans, Chileans, or Chinese.[227]

At Volcano, he took time to descend into the most celebrated cave of the area. Lowering himself by rope, he dropped some twenty feet and then walked the slanted passage to a series of underground chambers. By candlelight, he wrote, "the effect was very fine; the stalactites, being tinged with pale blue, pink, and green, were grouped in all manner of grotesque forms, in one corner giving an exact representation of a small petrified waterfall."[228]

At the hotel that evening he encountered an unexpected reminder of civilization; several tables of miners—formerly lawyers and doctors by profession—were playing whist and chess, rather than poker and seven-up. The next morning he headed back south, bound for San Andreas, but on attempting to cross the Mokelumne River, found it too swollen with spring runoff. Noticing a small ferry resting on the opposite bank, he called out to the ferryman but received no response. Finally a miner working a nearby flat heard his calls and, laying down his tools, came to J. D.'s assistance. The miner's willingness to leave his own work to help an unknown traveler was to J. D. symbolic of "the obliging spirit universally met with in the mines." The flooded river was perilous to cross, but on reaching the bank in safety, the miner produced a bottle of brandy and asked his passenger if he would care "to liquor." J. D., with water "still gurgling and squeaking" in his boots, accepted the invitation "with a great deal of pleasure."[229]

As he traveled further, he noted a steep mountain ahead and, not wanting to tackle it so late in the day, decided to return to Mokelumne Hill for the night and make a fresh start by a different route.

The road he took the next day wound through green valleys bright with colorful flowers. At one point he was passed by a large party of Indian braves, carrying their squaws behind them. They were dressed in a haphazard conglomeration of native and white man's clothing—a man wearing the top of a suit, with a different fellow the trousers, and one young man wearing only one boot and a waistcoat that matched his neighbor's outfit. All sported brightly colored bandanas tied about their heads. As the strangely dressed party galloped past, J. D. wrote, "they looked down upon me with an air of patronizing condescension, saluting me with the usual 'wally wally,' in just such a tone that I could imagine them saying to themselves at the same time, 'Poor devil! he's only a white man.' "[230]

When he came to the Calaveras River, he found neither bridge nor ferry, but as before a Good Samaritan came to his aid. A Mexican, camped nearby to rest his mule train, offered use of one of his footsore animals, who pushed himself to all fours and solemnly carried J. D. across the wide stream.

SAN ANDREAS AND ANGEL'S CAMP

J. D. thought the tattered-canvas town of San Andreas to be "the most out-at-elbows and disorderly looking" camp he had visited. The two main streets, at right angles to each other, contained three gambling halls, each equipped with a Mexican band. Since the town was so small, the three different tunes being rendered by guitars, flutes, and harps could be heard at all times by residents, but J. D. found the blend of music "very pleasing."[231]

When he entered the San Andreas Hotel, the town's only wooden building, to ask for a room, he was told the main establishment was filled. There was, however, a room available in the annex. Then he was ceremoniously escorted across the street to a tent and assigned a vacant cot. Though the tent was wedged between two gambling halls, he did manage to fall asleep. Throughout the night he was intermittently awakened by either the strains of the competing bands or the "doleful" barrel organ music played during intermissions.[232]

On Sunday morning he attended service at the Catholic church, a canvas house with a small cross nailed above the door. The altar was fitted out in cotton print and "California candlesticks," candles stuck in the tops of empty champagne bottles. The small building was jammed with devoted Mexicans, as well as a few curious Americans, who out of respect kept to the back. But "two great hulking fellows," J. D. noticed, "came swaggering in, and jostled their way through the crowd of Mexicans, making it evident, from their demeanor, that their only object was to show their supreme contempt for the congregation, and for the whole proceedings. Presently, however, the entire congregation went down on their knees, leaving these two awkward louts standing in the middle of the church as sheepish-looking a pair of asses as one could wish to see. They were hemmed in by the crowd of kneeling Mexicans—there was no retreat for them, and it was extremely gratifying to see how quickly their bullying impudence was taken out of them."[233]

That afternoon a herd of wild cattle was driven through camp, treating spectators to a display of Mexican horsemanship. After watching them lasso a bull by the horns and then by the hind legs, J. D. concluded that "the Mexicans are unquestionably splendid horsemen, though they ride too long for English ideas, the knee being hardly bent at all."[234]

He spent only a few days in predominantly Mexican San Andreas and then walked south to Angel's Camp, whose mainly American residents had constructed a "civilized-looking place" of "well-built wooden houses." In the afternoon he visited a Chinese camp on the outskirts of town, where he was invited to a dinner. Though he refused the invitation to dine, he accepted "a pannikin full of brandy" and some cigaritas of very aromatic tobacco. "The Chinese," he later recorded, "invariably treated in the same hospitable manner any one who visited their camps, and seemed rather pleased than otherwise at the interest and curiosity excited by their domestic arrangements."[235]

That evening a ball was held at the hotel where he was staying, and J. D. attended, pad and pencil in hand. A flutist and a fiddler provided the music, the latter taking responsibility for calling the dances. "It was a strange sight," J. D. wrote, "to see a party of long-bearded men, in heavy boots and flannel shirts, going through all the steps and figures of the dance with so much spirit, and often with a great deal of grace, hearty enjoyment depicted on their dried-up sunburned faces, and revolvers and bowie-knives glancing in their belts; while a crowd of the same rough-looking customers stood around, cheering them on to greater efforts, and occasionally dancing a step or two quietly on their own account."[236]

He captured a scene of the miners performing "Lady's Chain," but ironically enough without any ladies. The lack was remedied "by a simple arrangement whereby it was understood that every gentlemen who had a patch on a certain part of his inexpressibles should be considered a lady for the time being. These patches were rather fashionable, and were usually large squares of canvas, showing brightly on a dark ground."[237] What J. D. portrayed in the drawing was how the miners danced "as they did everything else, with all their might."[238]

On leaving Angel's Camp, J. D. visited the mines along Carson's Creek. Most interesting was an American company that employed only Mexicans, because of their mining experience in their home country. This particular company's shafts attained a depth of two hundred feet, and the various galleries were reached by poles with notches cut in the sides. Mexicans descended the notched poles, gathered leather sacks of gold-bearing quartz, hoisted them over one shoulder, and ascended the succession of notches. Pack mules then carried the bags of ore down the winding trail to an arrastra operated on the river bank. As protection against the danger of underground work, wooden crosses were staked throughout the labyrinth of galleries and tunnels and each section of the mine named for the saint who was designated its protector.[239]

As J. D. had noted earlier in the Northern Mines, each camp "had its traditions of wonderful events which had oc-

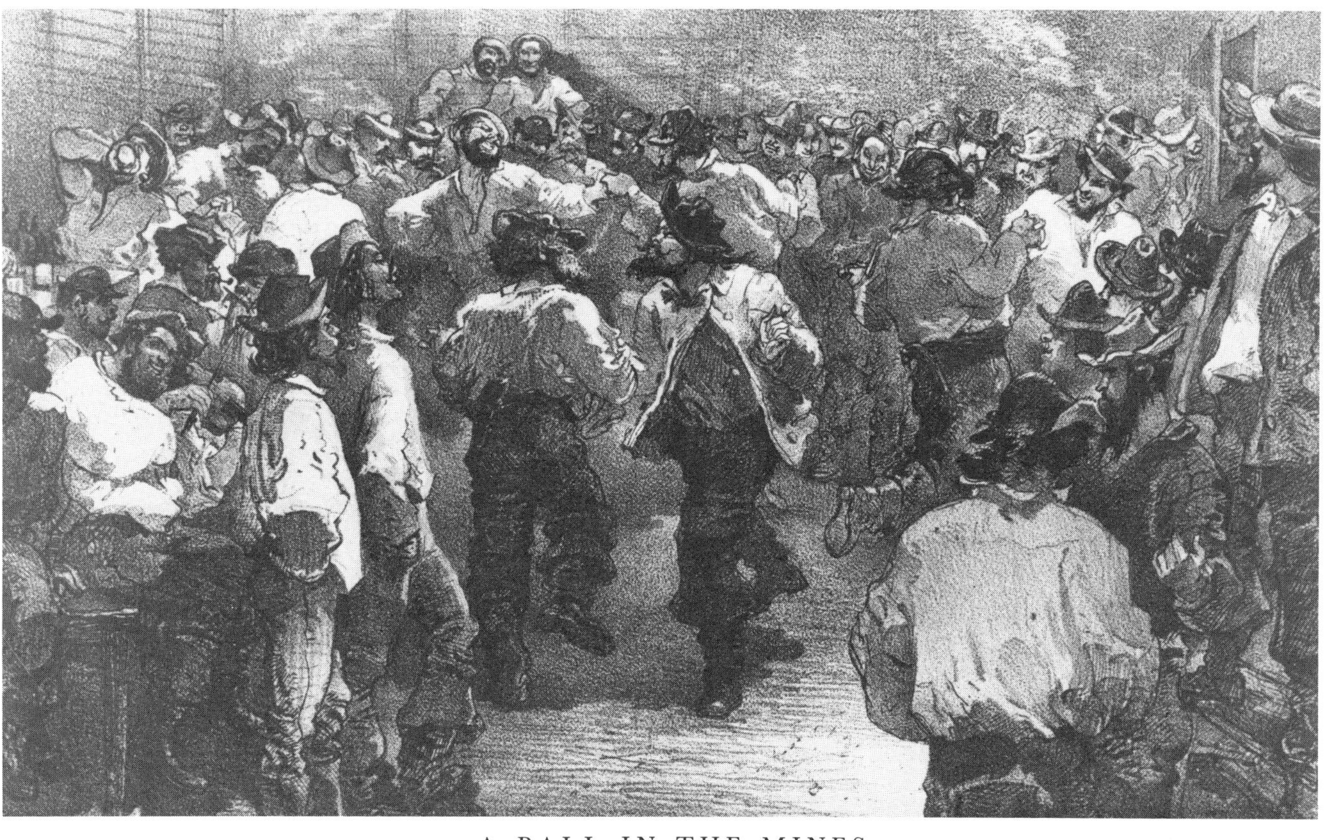

A BALL IN THE MINES

curred in the olden times; that is to say, as far back as '49—for three years in such a fast country were equal to a century.''[240] The unique tradition of the Carson Creek area was that the first miners to arrive had blasted out a rich deposit and after the explosion walked around with ''handbaskets'' to gather the pieces. J. D. believed ''this was only a slight exaggeration of the truth.''[241]

SONORA

After crossing the Stanislaus River on a ferry operated by three Englishmen, J. D. followed a well-maintained wagon road over the rolling countryside spread with massive, gnarly, branched oaks. Some of the hollows and gentler hills were surrounded by fences and placed under cultivation. Then appeared, stretching along a low valley for nearly a mile, the single street of the largest settlement of the Southern Mines—Sonora.

Flats in the area had first been mined by Indians, who in the early days traded gold dust ''weight for weight'' for calico, beads, matches, raisins, beef, and flour. Reportedly, one gullible brave exchanged $6,000 worth of dust for a string of beads that would have brought no more than $2.50 in a San Francisco store.[242] In 1848 a company of miners from Sonora, Mexico, who had brought their families with them, drove out the Indians and set up their own camp. They quickly made fortunes, showering their women with costly dresses and jewelry and decking out themselves in leather trousers, silver-ornamented jackets, and boots glittering silver spurs with rowels large as saucers. In the spring of 1849, the first Americans made their appearance, settling into a collection of brush shacks dignified by the name of Scott-town, after a half-Cherokee professional gambler who was the leading businessman in the area. Within only a few months the population increased to five thousand and Americans wrested control. The following year they discouraged nonwhite immigration by enforcing a ''foreign miners' tax'' of twenty dollars per month.[243]

Angry foreigners united, armed themselves, and prepared to go to war over the tax issue, but the Americans soon persuaded them to disband and get on with the process of making themselves rich. With peace restored, the process of civilization could continue. The first newspaper, *The Sonora Herald,* appeared on the Fourth of July, 1849. The most frequent news items concerned mining accidents, shootings, stabbings, and gunfights. The quarrels reported were often racial incidents, such as the following: "William Bowen, aged 22, from Rhode Island, stabbed to death by Mexicans, in a fandango house in Sonora. No arrests."[244]

The first town council met in November 1849 and voted to divide the town in lots. Profits from their sale were earmarked as funds to erect a hospital for scurvy patients. Town records show that a volunteer doctor had to pay five dollars for each bottle of lime juice needed to treat the rampant disease.[245] One member of this first town council, a young Canadian named William Perkins, left an account describing how he had come to Sonora to recover from a severe case of poison ivy. Of the grassy valley set between spurs of the lofty Sierra Nevada, he wrote, "I had never seen a more beautiful, a wilder or more romantic spot."[246]

Perkins found weekend shopping sprees in Sonora unmatched for excitement, like "brilliant bazaars of oriental countries"—gaudy silks, bright cotton prints, gold-embroidered shawls, silver-plated saddles, and embossed bridles spread out in colorful array for men who paid with "handfuls of gold dust."[247] With the arrival of miners from surrounding camps, the little town's streets became jammed solid with every race and nationality: Chinese in full, blue-cotton breeches; Hawaiians in bright print shirts and bare feet; Indians in military jackets but no trousers or drawers; Mexicans in leather jackets scalloped in fantastic red-and-blue patterns; Peruvians in white cotton shirts trimmed with colored bands; Chileans in black wool sarapes striped red, blue, and yellow; and Argentines sporting wide leather belts adorned with money pockets fastened by silver-dollar buttons.[248]

To the young Canadian the entire scene seemed "unreal and fairy-like." Tables were loaded with candies, cakes, dried fruits, pies, and tortillas stuffed with meat and chili peppers. Gambling tables had been set up in the streets—rough-hewn planks spread over with gold-embroidered scarlet cloth and piled high with silver dollars, gold doubloons, and pouches of gold dust. Darkness brought no letup. Business houses only lit their lamps, Perkins reported, and the streets as well were "strewn with lighted tapers." All night long "an infernal noise was kept up." Every gambling house had its band—guitars, harp, and clarinets—and street vendors, carrying pails of liquor iced with mountain snow, cried out continually in their "shrill falsetto voices," of their "agua fresca" for only "cuatro reales." Mission Indians gathered in circles, chanting "the most unearthly music, and keeping their throats moist by constant draughts of aguardiente," while Spanish American couples faced off to perform vigorous dances, the men "with perspiration streaming from every pore." From Saturday to Monday morning "the noise of drums, guitars, fiddles, lute, never for a moment ceased."[249]

Local histories reflect the oral tradition that early Sonorans were heroic men capable of great deeds:

> Still in the memories of present inhabitants are recollections of the streets so densely thronged that locomotion was impeded; stores filled to overflowing with men seeking to spend their accumulations of the week; on such days the number of people in town could not have been less than ten thousand! And these vast crowds consisted almost wholly of men;—men in the prime of life and of uncommon mental and physical vigor, as if they had been the picked men of their respective distant communities. And they were so in some sense, possessing the best qualities of daring, strength and determination that have left their impress that shall exist through all time.[250]

On J. D.'s arrival in 1852, the "Pride of the Southern Mines" had more than one hundred businesses: thirty-five hotels with restaurants, nine bakeries, (most kept by Frenchmen), eight butcher shops, four drugstores, three bath houses, two banks, two express offices, two stage lines, and an unspecified number of gambling saloons, all decorated with glittering chandeliers and showy mirrors.[251] "After cruising about the mountains among the small out-of-the-way camps," the town seemed "perfectly luxurious" to him. Here one could enjoy "most of the comforts and conveniences of ordinary life," he wrote, "even ice-creams and sherry-cobblers, . . . and no one took even a cocktail without its being iced."[252]

Still, it did not really hit home that he was once more in civilization until he saw a drunk who was "kicking up a row in the street," arrested and walked off to jail. For the first time in the mines, he had seen a man apprehended for drunkeness. "I was almost inclined to think it an infringement of the individual liberty," he wrote, "not to allow this hog of a fellow to sober himself in the gutter, or to drink himself into a state of quiescence if he felt so inclined."[253]

Most Sonoran businesses were of wood, some of adobe brick, and a few of canvas. J. D. was particularly impressed with the French- or Mexican-designed edifices, noticeable for being painted buff and trimmed in pale blue and for being ornamented with verandas on each story, outside staircases, and peaked, overhanging roofs. In stark contrast were the white, false-fronted, rectangular American houses standing next to them on main street.[254]

Only a year previously, artist Frank Marryat had been directed to a saloon, whose front wall advertised in bold, black letters a foot high and long, that it contained sleeping quarters on the second floor. Marryat ascended the stairs, paid his dollar, and then chalked his name on a slate opposite a vacant number. In the long, narrow, and dimly lit room, he could make out nearly a hundred crude cots, each marked with a numbered card and furnished with a dark-blue blanket and a bag-of-hay pillow. "Chinking of monte-bankers and calls for brandy-smashes" resounded from below, and wide chinks in the floor, revealed a blackened-faced minstrel "lolling out his tongue at the public," as he accompanied the chorus of "Charlestown Races" with the bones. "These wholesale human dormitories are also called corrals," Marryat explained, since like the rest of the world, they are conducted on the principle of "kick or get kicked."[255]

As proof of the continuously rapid change at the mines, J.D. only a short time later was able to take his pick of fine hotels. Following his usual preference, he selected a French establishment, settled in, and then had a look about town. He noticed that, in contrast to the Northern Mines, the fashion seemed to be to dress well, almost to the "degree of foppery." Most men wore no jacket, due to the heat, but instead a "rich silk handkerchief, scarlet, crimson, orange, or some bright hue, tied loosely across the breast, and hanging over one shoulder." Others had adorned their hats with "flowers, feathers, or squirrel's tails," and beards and hair were frequently "plaited and coiled up like a twist of tobacco" or divided into three tails hanging down to the waist." J. D. enjoyed seeing among the bizarre crowd several white-frocked Mexican women, their black eyes sparkling and dark hair gleaming. Completely out of place were the lone Easterners dressed in black suits and stovepipe hats. J. D. regarded these "forlorn individuals" as "birds of evil omen" among a "flock of such gay plumage."[256]

Marryat left a vivid description of a favored Sunday activity in Sonora. "No church bells here usher in the Sabbath," he wrote. It was instead the auction bell that aroused residents from slumber, summoning them to the spot where an entrepreneur had spread out his ware—kegs of butter, bags of dried apples, packs of Chinese sugar, jars of pickles, and bottles of "bad brandy." While the auctioneer, mounted on a centrally located barrel, goaded Germans, Frenchmen, Mexicans, and other nationalities to put in a bid in their native language, penniless loafers drifted about stabbing displayed samples with an open knife and wolfing them down. Since an adept auctioneer could easily work his audience to a pitch of near frenzy, competition among bidders was fierce. There was no keg of butter "so rancid," Marryat wryly commented, that it could not be "disposed of" at a Sunday Sonoran auction.[257]

J. D. had observed auctions in other towns, but in Sonora he encountered a form of entertainment he had never before witnessed. Though William Perkins and his fellow councilmen had banned bull-and-bear fights, they did permit bullfighting in the local arena each Sunday. J. D. was anxious to view the spectacle and attended at the first opportunity. Faithful to tradition, a brilliantly costumed troupe performed prescribed rituals with all the grace of a ballet company. J. D. made pages of notes on their artistry, yet the part he most enjoyed was the bull riding. He had never seen a horse make "such spasmodic bounds and leaps" as a bull did, but the expert rider, "thrown about so violently that it seemed enough to jerk the head off his body," remained aboard. When it came time to kill the bull, the matador thrust his sword into the back of the animal's neck with such speed and skill that the victim instantly fell dead. Appreciative spectators showered the arena with coins in show of their admiration for the magnificent performance. J. D. assuaged his guilt over enjoying the show by commenting that the bull had suffered less than cattle slaughtered by a butcher.[258]

Since the Southern Mines were obviously so different from the Northern, J. D. decided to remain in the Sonora area for several weeks. He had no way of knowing he had timed his visit, June 1852, to coincide with one of the city's worst tragedies. On returning late to his room one night, he had just stretched out on his bed when he heard an outcry coming from the street. Jumping up, he looked out the window to see the entire town "lighted up as bright as day." Across the way, one business house was "completely enveloped in flames," and people were running in all directions, attempting to empty buildings of their furnishings. J. D. rushed downstairs to assist his French landlady in saving her possessions, but found her in a near hysteria that left her incapable of action. Wanting to set an example of calmness, he began carrying the barroom trappings outside, and other guests joined him in the evacuation. Before they could get to any other rooms of the establishment, however, flames were lapping at the hotel walls. Though it was but a few minutes from the time of the original outbreak, the conflagration was general throughout a hundred-yard radius. In hopes of saving the rest of the town, residents frantically commenced tearing down a block of houses as a firebreak, but despite their united efforts, flying sparks ignited the newly accumulated rubble.[259]

For their own safety, inhabitants abandoned their rescue project and fled to the hills on either side of the valley. There, blackened and half-clad people sat down among "heaps of goods and furniture, confusedly thrown together, watching grimly the destruction of their houses." "The doomed city," J. D. wrote, "lay helplessly waiting its fate, for water there was none, and no resistance could be offered to the raging flames, which burned their way steadily up the street, throwing over the houses which still remained intact the flush of supernatural beauty which precedes dissolution, and leaving the ground already passed over covered with the gradually blackening and falling remains."[260]

The hillsides where the homeless huddled together were "lighted up as brightly as a well-lighted room, and the surrounding landscape was distinctly seen by the blaze of the burning town, the hills standing brightly out from the deep black of the horizon, while overhead the glare of the fire was reflected by the smoky atmosphere." Below, devouring flames roared on, and an occasional cache of gunpowder flashed into explosion. Glowing whirlwinds swept ignited clothing and blankets into the air for fifty feet, and then like fireworks the burning fabric burst into a "thousand sparkling atoms." Those watching on the hillsides had no way of knowing how many of their companions were trapped below. "It was a most magnificent sight," J. D. later recalled, "and, more than any fire I had ever witnessed, it impressed one with the awful power and fury of the destroying element."[261]

By 3:00 A.M., the conflagration had burned itself out and darkness once more fell over the hills. When a few hours later the sun rose, observers discovered by the faint light that "the whole city of Sonora had been removed from the face of the earth. The ground on which it had stood, now white with ashes, was covered with still smoldering fragments, and the only objects left standing were three large safes belonging to different banking and express companies, with a small remnant of the walls of an adobe house.''[262]

Though a few ''unprincipled vagabonds'' tried to stake mining claims on the burned area, businessmen quickly drove them away and began rebuilding. Rather than being ''cast down by their disaster,'' the ''hatless and shoeless'' citizens, set to work with an ''air of determined men,'' to reconstruct a bigger and better main street. By afternoon, ''the Phoenix began to rise.'' Lots were ''alive with men clearing away rubbish; others were in the woods cutting down trees and getting out posts and brushwood, or procuring canvas and other supplies from the neighboring camps. . . . On the blackened tract of ground which had been the street, posts began here and there to spring up; presently crosspieces connected them; and before one could look around, the framework was filled in with brushwood.''[263]

Among the ashes two bodies were found. One was burnt beyond recognition, but the other, ''merely the head and trunk'' of a man who had been unable to escape from a French hotel, was given a decent burial by several hundred Frenchmen. That night three thousand displaced residents shared the hillside as a sleeping apartment. ''Happy was the man who had saved his blankets,'' J. D. wrote, ''mine had gone.'' After a month of rebuilding, however, Sonora was ''in all respects a finer town than it had been before the fire.''[264]

Since by the Fourth of July, the town was still being restored, the entire countryside held a patriotic celebration in neighboring Columbia. Like Sonora, that area had first been settled by Mexicans, whose reports of rich diggings soon drew miners from other camps. The first tent-store opened for business served as both saloon and gambling hall. As the population increased, one pioneer businessman of Sonora also decided to relocate at the new camp. Along the creek bank, he built a corral for horses and sheep and nearby established a combination restaurant, dairy, and butcher shop. Services offered included delivering milk to a route of regular customers at the price of one dollar per whiskey bottle full.[265]

Wondrous stories were related of the fortunes made in Columbia in 1850, the year of its discovery. One indigent bummer, for example, stumbled across a seventy-two-pound nugget valued at $14,000.[266] To maintain order in the rapidly growing camp, citizens elected a constable, as well as an alcalde (mayor-judge), whose idea of justice was rather eccentric. Among his many peculiar decisions was the case of William Smith, who claimed that a Mexican had stolen a pair of leggings from him. After brief deliberation, Alcalde Sullivan fined the Mexican defendant three ounces of gold, but levied against the plaintiff, said William Smith, a fine of one ounce for having complained against a neighbor. A similarly unusual decision resulted from a case of mule thievery. When the convicted thief was ordered to return the animal to its rightful owner and pay a fine of four ounces of gold (one ounce for his crime and three ounces as court costs), he replied that he had no money. Stating that the court could not be expected to convene without collecting expenses, the alcalde therefore charged the plaintiff, "known to be in good circumstances," to pay the fine in behalf of the guilty man.[267]

Columbia's 1852 celebration of the Fourth of July was nearly identical to the holiday festivities J. D. had previously witnessed. Still, his description of the day is interesting for the insight it provides as to how Americans appear in the eyes of an outside observer. In the morning, those assembled for the program crowded into the bars and commenced "drinking success to the American eagle." The streets, fluttering with stars and stripes, were noisy with "a continual discharge of revolvers, and a vast expenditure of powder and squibs and crackers." Finally the opening parade got under way, led by a group of six female teachers and their pupils, who burst into hymn each time the brass band following them rested, having "blown themselves out of breath." Next came the Masons, decked out in "their aprons and other paraphernalia," followed by a struggling ragtag cavalry. "Whoever could get a four-legged animal to carry him, joined the ranks," J. D. wrote, "and horses, mules, and jackasses were all mixed up together." Following the equestrians were the volunteer fire companies, proudly trailing hooks and ladders behind them. Four hundred miners brought up the rear, some towing a wheelbarrow filled with pick, shovel, skillet, coffeepot, and mug, and behind that a long tom mounted on wheels, into which they continuously threw imaginary dirt. Others carried long-handled shovels over their shoulders, and "to make a show" wore ribbons tied about their slouch hats. J. D. realized there was meaning behind this "gorgeous pageant." The odd assortment of props were emblems of "the very rough style" of the miners' domestic life and of their "stout hearts and willing hands."[268]

After a few hours of marching about the streets, the procession turned into the bull arena, where a crowd had already gathered. As the miners made their appearance in the ring, the audience set up a mighty roar and the band commenced "playing 'Hail Columbia' most lustily." When the cheering had finally subsided, "a gentleman in a white neckcloth" read the Declaration of Independence, and the "orator of the day," a "pale-faced, chubby-cheeked young gentleman, with very white and extensive shirt-collars" delivered a rousing speech. The speaker, J. D. noted, "indulged in a great deal of buncombe about the Pilgrim Fathers, and Plymouth Rock." George III and his "red-coated minions" were mentioned as well, though in "not very flattering terms." The speech continued until the past had been completely "exhausted" and then became "prophetic of the future." Eventually some of the Americans seated near J. D. "seemed to think that the orator was piling up the agony a little too high," and began to shout, "Gaas, gaas!" A caged grizzly bear who shared the arena with the speaker expressed his opinion throughout the entire oration by "grunting and growling most savagely." As the speech concluded, hotel owners rang their dinner bells to summon boarders to table. After the meal, a bullfight brought an end to the day's festivities.[269]

During his tour of the mines, J. D. had frequently encountered former acquaintances, who, like himself, were extremely mobile. While at Sonora, for example, he met the Scottish gardner who had helped him row up the Chagres

River in Panama, and his countryman invited him to visit Shaw's Flat, a small camp still "wooded with oaks, and plentifully sprinkled over with miners' tents and shanties." The gardner was bringing a farm under cultivation and already had several acres of barley and oats to show for his efforts. Both Shaw's Flat and the farm sat atop Table Mountain, a long range that looked like a "colossal railway embankment," rising above mountain sides so steep as to be nearly perpendicular. "At the season of the year at which I was there," J. D. wrote, "it was a most beautiful sight, being thickly grown over with a pale-blue flower."[270] He made a sketch of the peaceful, wooded flat, showing two groups of miners united in work and a tiny mule-drawn cart disappearing into the distance.

STOCKTON

After spending another two months wandering the camps along the Tuolumne and Merced rivers, J. D. returned to Sonora and caught the stage bound for Stockton. They departed before dawn so that the "large open wagon, drawn by five horses, three leaders abreast," would reach its destination before the steamer pulled out for San Francisco. The first thirty miles of mountainous countryside was pleasant enough, but the final thirty crossed a hot, barren plain. "We moved along enveloped in a cloud of dust, which soaked into one's clothes and hair and skin as if it had been a liquid substance. On our arrival in Stockton we were of a uniform color all over —all identity of person was lost as much as in a party of chimneysweeps."[271]

Though J. D. had but one hour before boarding the steamer, he took time to wash off the layer of caked dust at a bathhouse; then he made two quick sketches of Main Street. The town, named for Commodore Robert Stockton, commander of the Pacific squadron during the Mexican War, was located on a slough near the head of navigation of the San Joaquin River. When in 1847 Charles Weber, pioneer settler of the San Joaquin Valley, had founded the first trading post in a marsh shrouded in bulrushes and infested with large mos-

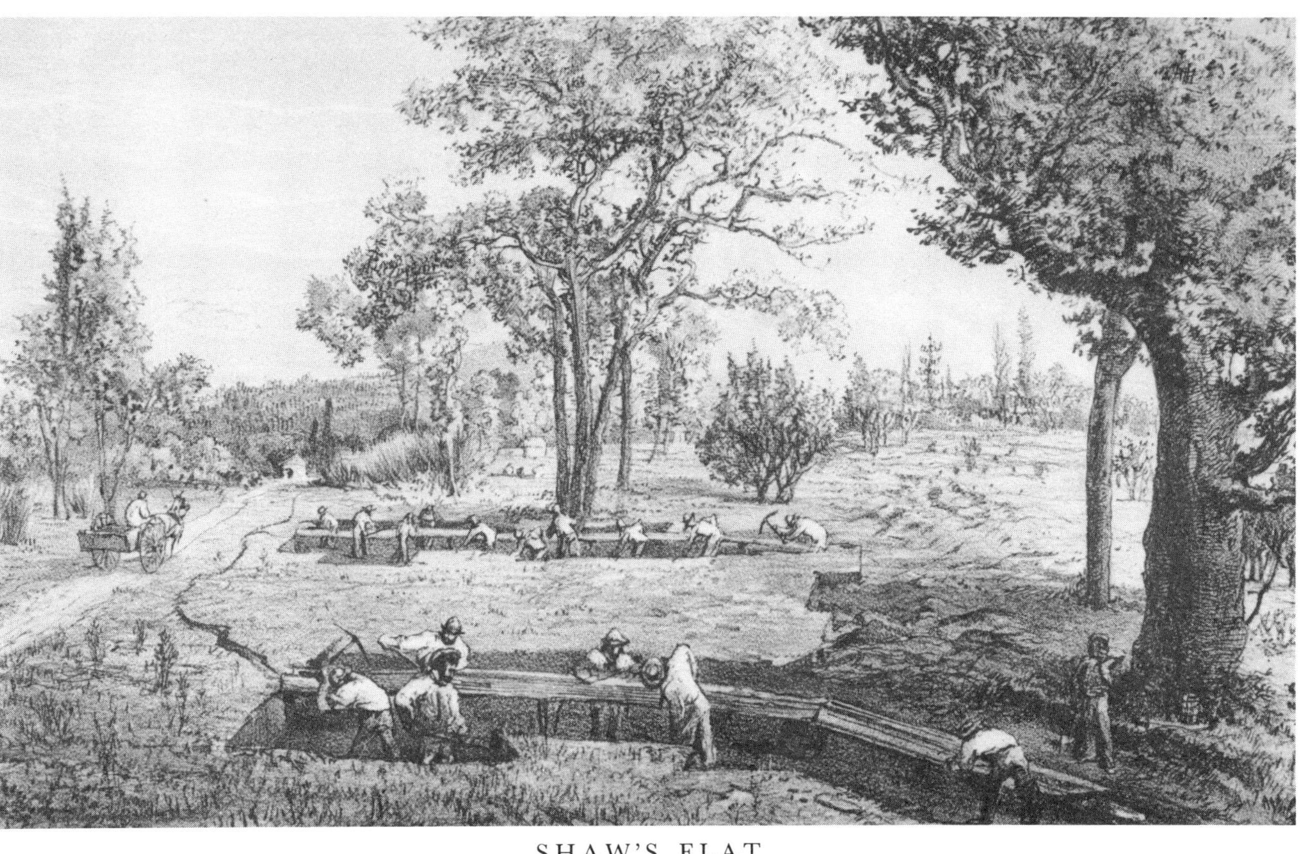

SHAW'S FLAT

quitos, he had aptly named the settlement Tuleburg. With the arrival of the forty-eighters, a tent city sprang up around Weber's lone wooden building and the several "tule" huts,[272] and on the arrival of journalist Bayard Taylor one year later, he found twenty-five ships at the little river port.[273]

In addition to the usual fires suffered by the easily combustible frontier towns, Stockton was subject to periodic flooding. Artist Marryat, in passing through on his way to the mines, reported the streets full of mudholes deep enough to submerge a horse to the saddle girth.[274]

John Woodhouse Audubon, who on his way to the Southern Mines stopped at Stockton, was struck with the "strangeness" of the environment. "A gallows is the chief object in the foreground," he wrote. "It was erected to execute a man for murder and robbery." In addition, as early as 1851, Stockton had been selected as the site for the state insane asylum. Since its inception, the town had served as winter quarters for miners of the surrounding areas, and there was always a large floating population hovering about the business section. But even the gaiety in the numerous gambling halls could not erase Audubon's impressions of fantastic unreality as he entered the popular Exchange Hotel:

> Such a crowd as the bar-room of this hotel presents nightly, cannot be found except where all nations meet. Cards were being played for stakes everywhere, and the crowd . . . is difficult to forget. The tall, raw-boned Westerner, bearded and moustached, like his Mexican neighbor beside him, the broad-headed German and sallow Spaniard, French, Irish, Scotch, I know not how many nationalities are here represented. I saw even two Chileans with their cold, indifferent air, all mixing together, each man on his guard against his fellowman. The tight fitting jacket and flowing sarape touch each other, all blending into weirdness in the dim light of a few candles.[275]

William Perkins, city father of Sonora, had also been awed by the scene Audubon reported, but rather than picking up on the mistrust and suspicion harbored within the minds of the gaming participants, Perkins had been overwhelmed by the mythic qualities of the first honest-to-goodness miners he had ever seen. "We began to smell the precious ores," Perkins related. "Here were even real live miners; men who had actually dug out the shining metal, and who had it in huge buckskin pouches in the pockets of their pantaloons. These men were awful objects of our curiosity. They were the demi-gods of the dominion of Plutus." Perkins examined them from head to toe: "Their long rough boots, red shirts, Mexican hats; their huge uncombed beards, covering half the face; the Colt's revolver attached to its belt behind, the *cuchillo* stuck into the leg of the boots—all these things were attributes belonging to another race of men . . . and we looked upon them with a certain degree of respect, and with a determination soon to present ourselves as little human-like in appearance as they were."[276]

The present stopover was J. D.'s second visit to Stockton, and he had long ago, in terms of California time, been initiated into the mining brotherhood. Freshly bathed and well acclimated to the wonders about him, he tucked the drawings of Main Street under his arm and boarded the steamer for the state's cultural and economic center.

SAN FRANCISCO

The 165-mile trip was made at the respectable speed of twenty miles per hour, and by ten o'clock that night the little steamer had reached its intended destination. The city bore little resemblance to its appearance in the fall of 1850, when J. D. had first set foot in California. "The barren sandhills which surrounded the city had been graded down to an even slope," he observed, "and were covered with streets of well-built houses, and skirted by populous suburbs. Four or five wide streets, more than a mile in length, built up with solid and uniform brick warehouses, stretched all along in front of the city, upon ground which had been reclaimed from the bay; and between these and the upper part of the city was the region of fashionable shops and hotels, banks and other public offices."[277]

Though the entire life-style of the city had changed—gambling halls and saloons being on the wane—"extravagant expenditure" was still "a marked feature." J. D. found no fault with extravagance, however, believing it was "more for the purpose of procuring tangible enjoyment than for the sake of show. Men spent their money in surrounding themselves with the best of everything, not so much for display as from due appreciation of its excellence; for there is so little provincialism; the inhabitants, generally, are eminently cosmopolitan in their character, and judge of merit by the highest standard."[278]

Other visitors noted specifics of the luxurious life being led in San Francisco during this time of prosperity. "Gorgeous decoration is characteristic," Marryat wrote. Ordinary businesses were ornamented with glittering chandeliers, gilt-edged mirrors, and glass columns; and walls were hung with French paintings. At a shaving salon, a customer sat on a crimson-velvet easy chair and rested his feet on a matching stool while from a marble washstand the barber lifted a gracefully designed bottle, screwed off the cap, and then massaged "eau de cologne" into a freshly shampooed head of hair and beard.[279]

During his rounds of the city, J. D. ran into James Mason Hutchings, his old acquaintance from Weber Creek. Hutchings reported that he had lost all his riches through the failure of the San Francisco bank where he had deposited his wealth. But rather than being downcast at his luck, he was planning a new line of business. He had composed a list of guides for newcomers to the mines, entitled "The Miners' Ten Commandments," and printed them on stationery in high hopes they would sell well in the isolated camps. He was, in addition, collecting drawings to be used as illustrations for his letter sheets. When J. D. quickly informed him that he had several available sketches, Hutchings agreed to purchase a few, among them one entitled "A View of Mokelumne Hill."[280]

Though city life offered a certain amount of excitement, there were rumblings in other parts of the New World. The January 24, 1852, issue of the *Illustrated London News* had devoted an entire column (right next to J. D.'s article) about gold discoveries in Australia that were "stimulating emigration to that distant but attractive quarter of the globe." In February 1853, a miner in Tuolumne City had written home about "the great number that is going to Australia." "The Australian excitement is about as great here," he added, "as the California fever was in 50 in the states."[281] Migration to Australia and California was simultaneous; incoming ships filled with Australians flocking to California's mining districts crossed paths at the Golden Gate with outgoing ships loaded down with Californian miners who were certain diggings would be even richer on the distant shore.

Throughout the winter J. D. grew increasingly restless; he had already spent three years in California. In early spring he collected his possessions, including those stored on his arrival in September 1850, and prepared to sail. It was difficult for him to leave America, knowing he would probably never return. Though he was still too close to the experience to evaluate it clearly, he sensed that his California days bore a special significance, both for him and the rest of the world. With his notebooks and drawing pads stowed carefully among his luggage, and a myriad of haunting images stored in his mind, he boarded ship, bound for the spot which seemed to offer the greatest promise of fresh excitement. Still, it was with mixed feelings that he watched the California mountains recede into the haze of memory.

PART III

Other Travel in the New World

AUSTRALIA

J. D. compiled no account of his Australian trip. Fortunately, others have left detailed descriptions of their experiences. The passage to Australia was long and monotonous. Most ships making the crossing were of the same caliber J. D. had encountered on his journey to San Francisco in 1850: small sailing vessels crammed with one to two hundred passengers and poorly stocked with inferior supplies. Various writers recorded the typical hardships endured throughout the voyage. American adventurer Charles Ferguson, for example, wrote that his twenty-two-year-old captain required passengers to take turns pumping out the leaky old barque in order to keep it afloat.[1]

But no matter what vessel a passenger selected, by two months at sea supplies were dangerously low. The equator-crossing ceremony temporarily relieved the doldrums brought on by an unrelenting diet of bean soup. Celebration commenced one day prior to reaching the invisible line when a crew member dressed as King Neptune made an appearance to ask for the names of the uninitiated. The following day, all gathered on deck about a barber chair set up to receive the new members of Neptune's kingdom. The man first in line was asked to step into the chair, but no sooner was he comfortably seated, than the chair was tilted over backwards, allowing its occupant to slip into a canvas tank filled with sea water. Crew members then wrestled the surprised man down, holding his head under water until he nearly drowned, letting him up for a breath of air, and then roughly shoving him under again. The rest looked on, cheering the enthusiastic sailors and laughing at the befuddled victim. Since it was J. D.'s first crossing of the equator, he was eligible for the ordeal. It can be presumed that he took his ducking with the same good humor he had shown when facing difficulties at the goldfields.[2]

Soon after the ceremony, they reached waters notorious for becalming ships for days on end. Passengers were left with nothing to do but mope about deck, accept their share of the rationed soup, pray for rain so there would be drinking water, and do laundry in saltwater. Ferguson wrote that during his ship's period of waiting at the equator, it became decorated from stem to stern with clothes lines draped with shirts and drawers.[3]

When a breeze finally sprang up, the released ship headed for Tahiti for food and water, taking ten days of steady sailing to reach the island. Canoes full of natives greeted the passengers, begging them to throw coins in the water so they could dive after them, and on shore a feast of roast pig, breadfruit, oranges, and pineapple awaited them. In addition to the natives, the island was inhabited by French military officers, an English consul, and a few convicts who had escaped from Norfolk. After a few days of recreation on the island, they again set sail, hoping to reach Sydney within a month.[4]

Their route took them directly by Norfolk, only five miles long and three wide and notorious as a "blood-curdlingly cruel" prison for Australian multiple offenders. Passing ships were usually required to moor in the harbor and keep all passengers and crew aboard while inhabitants rowed out with supplies, but Ferguson had been fortunate enough to be invited on land. "Never before or since have I had knowledge of such severe punishments," he had written after observing the treatment of the nine hundred prisoners sentenced to the island. Most horrifying was the "dumb cell," a form of solitary confinement in which a prisoner was lowered into an unlit dungeon being filled with water. The prisoner was forced "to pump for his life or drown." Such punishment was prescribed for minor infractions, while major infractions resulted in death. Each new day opened with a hanging ceremony at dawn. It was not uncommon for prisoners to awake to the sight of four or five corpses dangling from the beam across the prison's gate.[5]

From Norfolk it was but a few weeks' journey to Australia. On arrival, a pilot boat guided them into Sydney harbor, which was crowded with small barques like their own, massive freighters, and graceful clippers, each flying the flag of some distant nation. Both customs and health officials carried out thorough inspections and then allowed them entrance to the bustling city. Since Sydney was bounded by sand hills, on the land side its streets were very dusty. Despite this inconvenience, it was equipped with modern comforts. Convicts sent while England was still using the country as a penal colony (before 1830) had paved all main thoroughfares with stone, and buildings and streets were lit by gas. Because of their alleged mistreatment of Australian migrants to the California goldfields, Americans were not welcomed, but British visitors, such as J. D., were extended warm hospitality.[6]

He chose to visit New South Wales, the colony of Edward Hargraves's initial discovery. In late 1849, the California Rush had drawn Hargraves, and during his time in the mining districts he gradually came to the conclusion that the richest areas he visited bore a marked resemblance to certain areas beyond the Blue Mountains in New South Wales. Therefore, in February 1851 he returned home to commence a prospecting expedition. On discovering gold, Hargraves reported the sites to the colonial secretary and received in return a reward and an appointment. Since the British Crown owned mineral rights in the colonies, it was immediately announced that any would-be miner must first purchase a license, renewable monthly at a fee of thirty pounds, granting him the temporary lease of a small claim and ownership of whatever gold was recovered from it.

As news of Hargraves's astounding find at Ophir spread, surrounding towns quickly lost their male residents. New trails blazed across the wild land were plugged by trains of overloaded ox carts plodding toward the mines, and in the harbors, ships arrived daily from Melbourne, draining that city of its doctors, lawyers, clerks, and tradesmen. The great ranches that produced the colony's main product, wool, were left with no hands to tend the sheep. Then within a matter of weeks, strikes occurred in the Melbourne area. In anticipation of the expected rush, the new colony of Victoria was quickly created. The mines in Victoria—Ballarat, Bendigo, and Castlemaine—were easily worked and abounded in large nuggets of the precious metal.

Gold-laden ships were soon being emptied of their precious cargo in British ports. In response to newspaper reports of thirty-pound nuggets being unloaded, a worldwide rush commenced, every bit as exciting and feverish as California's had been two years earlier. The experienced Hargraves, and others who likewise had spent time in California, showed arriving novices how to operate a pan and cradle, and by J.D.'s arrival in late 1853, Victoria and New South Wales goldfields were surpassing those of California. Though Australia was indebted to California for its own gold discovery as well as for knowledge and experience brought to the country, relations between the British colony and the United States were strained.

One New York gold hunter wrote home upon his arrival in Australia, "Sydney is a city that I do not like. The inhabitants are very insulting to all Americans, so much so if you speak one word about the States, nine times out of ten it will create a row so that we must keep our mouths shut."[7] The editor of the Sydney *Empire* had clearly stated the existing hostile attitude toward "despicable Californians," so prone to lynch law: "Let no door be opened to receive the blood-stained wretches," he proclaimed.[8]

A rival editor expressed a fear brought on by America's expansionist tendencies: The "reckless and excitable Americans," he wrote, "might declare war on some country in order to expand their national boundary across the Pacific.''[9] To make the adverse Aussie opinion unanimous, a Melbourne paper added that Californians were ''ripe for anything, disorder and rapine, under the spacious pretext of serving the sacred cause of liberty.''[10]

Despite their unpopularity in the country, Californians and other Americans were prominent at both the Victoria and New South Wales mines. The Stars and Stripes fluttered over many a miner's tent, a gully was named California, and many businesses—stores, hotels, and express companies—were operated by Americans. And though most American immigrants tried to maintain low profiles, eventually they became deeply involved in the Australian colonists' struggle for rights at the mines.

A few Australians, however, already recognized that California had set an example they would do well to follow. Though individual citizens of the despised state might appear avaricious and bloodthirsty, as a group they had taken decisive and admirable action. One Australian, preferring anonymity, had written a letter to a San Francisco newspaper praising the political progress made during the California Rush: ''The Americans, accustomed to action, not whining and petitioning, have elected their governors, have accepted their constitution, without a moment's obstruction; and offered a practical lesson to these colonies which has produced a profound impression. . . . We cannot but feel mortified to contrast the spirit of that young nation with the still jealous restraints which fetter the enterprises of our own colonies, and the unwise reservations under the name of Crown rights.''[11]

As early as 1852 the working classes of Melbourne had been agitating for shorter hours and a better work environment, while other movements promoted universal education and internal improvements in the colonies, such as railways and bridges. It was only a matter of time until the problems created by the Australian licensing system at the mines were included as one of the demands for reform. Charles Ferguson's account of his experiences in the Victoria mines makes clear the miners objections to the ''onerous laws and official oppression'' of the British Crown.[12] Since the license must be obtained before digging could commence, a miner frequently ended up paying for ownership rights to gold he was never to uncover, and no matter what luck he had, he had to continue renewing his license monthly, or as the individual miner viewed it, paying for the right to go broke. Even more burdensome was the requirement that he carry his license on his person at all times, ready to show to any government official who so requested, even ''if it was twelve times a day.'' Since a cheap grade of paper was used for the license, it quickly disintegrated to shreds and tatters, and the miner had to hasten to town to buy another one. Punishment for mining without the license consisted of a fine and, since there were no jails in the gold camps, being chained to a tree for a specified period.[13] The international community of miners had no way of making their protests at the unfairness of the license requirements heard—no vote and no representative to speak for them.

Other than this source of conflict, J. D. found conditions at the New South Wales gold camps quite similar to California. A restriction on liquor sales at the Australian diggings resulted in only a slight decrease in the amount of rowdiness. Other minor differences were fewer log cabins and more tents of calico rather than canvas, but a striking similarity in the newly rich miners' enthusiasm for the theater. Charles Ferguson had earned the honor of sponsoring the first theatrical performance at the mines in his tent restaurant. Later, American actors and actresses such as Edwin Booth and Lola Montez had extended their gold-camp circuit to include Australia. One of the favorite skits—performed after a serious drama—involved a braggadocio California forty-niner, bawling about his new wealth, his readiness to resort to lynch law, and his country's unequaled democracy.[14]

Because of his California experience, activities at the Australian mines were too familiar to J. D., giving him the itch to move on after only a few months of excursions throughout New South Wales. In addition, he was growing increasingly homesick for Scotland and therefore decided in early 1854 to book passage on the first available outbound vessel. The voyage back to America provided time to contemplate the significance of the two gold rushes he had witnessed over the past four years. It was clear the new sources of wealth were bringing a needed boost to the world economy, but he believed that material progress had been matched by accompanying political and social advancements brought on by the conditions of forced equality. To his way of thinking, both gold rushes were inextricably intertwined with a universal movement toward increased democracy.[15]

It was some time before J. D. learned that his hasty departure from Australia had cost him the chance to witness one of the most exciting events of the decade. Had he tarried but a few months, he could have been present at the convention called in Bendigo to vent miners' grievances. Slogans displayed at that meeting, such as "Taxation Without Representation is Robbery," were reminiscent of the complaint American colonists made in the previous century. Those assembled in Bendigo sent a committee to Melbourne to present their petition demanding changes in the mining-license requirements. As a result, the license fee was reduced and the renewal period extended to three months.[16]

Though these concessions reduced tension temporarily, within a few weeks an inflammatory incident occurred at a mining camp on Reid's Creek. During a renewed attack to crack down on miners attempting to work an unlicensed claim, enforcement officers accidentally killed a man they were harrassing. Enraged at the death of a fellow miner, the others turned on the officers and drove them from camp. They then called a mass meeting, built a roaring bonfire, and burned their licenses. The following day the British military arrived on the scene to restore order, but, as reported by Charles Ferguson, "diggers made down on the troops with sticks and stones and drove them back."[17]

Realizing revolt was imminent, the governor called in police and British forces scattered throughout the Australian colonies and prepared to subdue the troublesome miners. "Americans tried to stay neutral at first," Ferguson wrote, but the threat of attack by the British soon necessitated their involvement. They joined other miners, on a hill where the Eureka Hotel had formerly stood, in constructing a breastwork of timbers, rocks, and parts from broken-down carts, and then hopefully ran up their banner, a Southern Cross formed of white stars embedded on a blue background. Messengers recruited supporters from surrounding camps and gathered weapons and ammunition as well. Camp merchants "gave all the powder they had free," Ferguson reported, and blacksmiths busied themselves in forging "Irish pikes," for close combat.[18]

The forces soon assembled were broken into units, frequently united by common nationality. Ferguson joined a group of sharpshooters called the California Rangers. When word reached the stockade that government troops, armed with a cannon, were marching from Melbourne, the miners made the mistake of sending several units to intercept them, thus leaving Eureka, as the hill fortress had been named, with less than two hundred defenders. Ferguson was among those who remained on the hill, and his account is one of the few left by participants. At 3:00 A.M. on Sunday, December 3, 1854, he wrote, "pickets came running in with information that the enemy were upon us." Quickly the "to arms" alarm was sounded and the defenders formed a line of defense. Then the first order rang out, "California Rangers to front!" Though the British forces, numbering 276, later claimed that they had only intended to read the miners the Riot Act, requesting them to disband or be fired upon, the California Rangers did not allow them the opportunity to carry out their plan. We "fired the first shot," Ferguson admitted, killing a British officer. The British quickly fired back and then commenced their charge. They "came down on us just as light of day was breaking;" Ferguson recalled, "splinters from the timbers of the breastwork were flying. . . . The soldiers were in among us, . . . discovered I was almost alone."[19]

Most of Ferguson's companions, untrained and poorly armed, had fled before the charging Redcoats. Finding himself abandoned, Ferguson whirled and vaulted over the wall of the stockade. He landed precisely at the feet of the enemy, who immediately arrested him. Looking about him, he noticed the soldiers searching and robbing the other prisoners. The hilltop ground about them was strewn with wounded rebels, and twenty-four others lay dead. "The morning sun was just rising and spreading its light over the forms of dead and wounded," Ferguson soberly observed, "in their long, last sleep and others moaning." Suddenly alarmed at his predicament, he turned to his captors and asked what punishment he and the other surviving rebels could expect. "Why, hung of course," a British soldier responded.[20]

The majority of the prisoners taken at the battle of the Eureka Stockade were later released, but thirteen were detained and charged with high treason. Charles Ferguson, having been one of the last defenders, was regarded a ringleader and therefore among those placed on trial. However, a sympathetic jury quickly aquitted him and the other twelve accused. A roar of approval from the court audience greeted each of the separate thirteen innocent verdicts, and at the close of the last trial, a mob of cheering miners escorted the freed defendants through the streets. Though a bitter memory for the rebels, the battle of the Eureka Stockade came to be recognized as a birth of Australian nationalism and a stunning victory for the ideals of democracy and liberty.[21]

By 1856 Australian colonists could boast amazingly rapid advancement in their struggle for self-government. The colonial governors and their appointed councils had been replaced first by a partially elected legislature granted limited power, and later by a bicameral parliament with fairly broad powers over domestic concerns. British capital provided many of the internal improvements demanded, and the continued outpouring of gold from the Victoria and New South Wales mines made residents of these colonies, with the possible exception of Canada, the wealthiest in the British Commonwealth. J. D. undoubtedly regretted he had missed the stirring events leading up to this progress.

NICARAGUA

For his homeward journey, J. D. chose not to follow the Panama route. He had seen all he cared to of the Chagres

River and of Panama City, where he had suffered his accident. Instead he took a ship bound for the new passage, developed in 1851 by Cornelius Vanderbilt, through Nicaragua. It not only shortened the distance to New York by 370 miles, but also provided an opportunity to travel through a country he had never seen.

Vanderbilt's charter granted him the exclusive privilege of transferring passengers from one ocean to another across Nicaragua, and "a large share of the California emigration," J.D. reported, were beginning to "stream though the country." After landing at the harbor of San Juan del Sur (on the Pacific side), passengers faced a twelve-mile trek on muleback, through "mountainous wilderness, the greater part covered by a dense tropical forest." During the five-month rainy season, the trail was "so bad that a mule would sink to his belly at every step; the twelve miles were not unfrequently a two days' journey and many a poor mule, after vainly struggling to extricate himself, succumbed to his fate, and was absorbed in the mud, leaving his rider to fight his own way through." "But," J.D. wrote, and he was speaking from experience, "such little difficulties were not thought much of by Californian emigrants in those days." On reaching Lake Nicaragua, travelers boarded a Vanderbilt steamer and navigated the lake to the source of the San Juan River, where they transferred to a steamer "peculiarly constructed" for surviving the numerous rapids of the San Juan. From that point it was a thrilling, white-water ride to San Juan del Norte, also known as Greytown. During the dry season, the entire trip could be made in only two days, but those hours allowed passing Americans sufficient time to admire the splendid greenery and ponder the titillating notion of making it the next state of their union.[22]

J. D. got no further than the first leg of the trip. His loss in Australia—missing the battle of the Eureka Stockade—had become his gain in Nicaragua. Obviously, in this strange New World, one magnificent event followed on the heels of another. He discovered that he had arrived in the tropical paradise only a few weeks after the outbreak of a civil war. The whole affair was made more ominous by American and British involvement. Covering a conflict of international importance was obviously a once in a lifetime opportunity. He must temporarily postpone his voyage home and remain in Nicaragua.

The American role in the small Central American state posed a serious moral dilemma for the young Scot. He had previously formed some strong opinions on the American national character, most of them favorable, but he was now forced to examine the motive of the United States injecting itself into Nicaraguan troubles. History repeats itself, Thucydides of Athens intimated in the fifth century B.C., because human nature is unchanging; therefore, world events have been and will continue to be motivated by such universal human passions as selfishness, pride, and greed. If his philosophy is correct, then modern readers with a clear idea of why Americans are involved in the Nicaraguan affairs during the 1980s will have an edge J. D. did not possess in understanding American involvement in the 1850s.

During his three years in California, he had concluded that the Americans had shown an admirable capacity for colonizing. "Thousands of men," he wrote, "were thrown suddenly together, unrestrained by conventional or domestic obligations, and all more intently bent than men usually are upon the one immediate object of acquiring wealth. It is to be wondered that chaos and anarchy were not at first the result of such a state of things; but such was never the case in any part of the country; and it is, no doubt, greatly owing to the large proportion of superior men among the early settlers, and to the capacity for self-government possessed by all classes of Americans."[23] Now in Nicaragua, J. D. saw a different side to the American character. In fact he was so concerned about the American passion for taking over the rest of the world that he could not focus his attention on the exotic landscape and the character and social customs of the inhabitants.

He did manage one half-hearted description of the country's beauty:

> The forests abound in rosewood, mahogany, and other beautiful woods, . . . the trees are completely covered with flowers, and the forests are a confused mass of luxuriant vegetation. There are several volcanic mountains in the country, . . . the finest is Ometepe, which rises out of the lake, in the shape of

> a perfect cone, to the height of many thousand feet. . . . The principal cities of Nicaragua are Granada, on the northern shore of the lake, and Leon, about a hundred and fifty miles to the north, and not far from the Pacific coast. They are both fine cities, built in the usual Spanish-American style, with narrow streets, and large houses of a single story, covering an immense area, and built in the form of a square, the centre being an open space, generally planted with trees and flowers, and all round which is a wide open corridor. The houses are very spacious and lofty, and admirably adapted to the climate.[24]

As for the citizens, "As long as a man has sufficient to supply his immediate wants, he cannot be induced to work, but will devote himself to the passive enjoyment of swinging in his hammock, and smoking a cigar. In this way they pass the greater part of their time, as very little labour is requisite to provide plantains, beans, and Indian corn, which are the principal articles of food." The chief entertainment consisted of gambling at cards and dice on weekdays, and on Sundays at the cockfights, "the great national sport." In spite of their lack of "ambition and energy," J. D. thought the Nicaraguans possessed "a great deal of grace." They are "extremely polite and formal in their manners," he wrote, "even the lower orders are remarkable for their gracefulness of gesture, and for their courteous phraseology."[25]

The brief space devoted to the landscape and native culture is understandable. J. D. was not a mere sightseer in the country; he was a serious reporter, attempting to grasp the intricacies of the internal situation so he could pass them on to the rest of the world. The revolution, he learned, had commenced in May 1854. Trouble had first erupted when President Chamorro, whose headquarters were in Granada, announced intentions of extending his term for an additional four years, but by decree rather than popular vote. In response, his critics formed the Democratic Party, under the able leadership of Francisco Castillon, a former minister to England. J. D. regarded Castillon as "a man of superior education, and with much more liberal and enlightened views than most of his countrymen." Democratic headquarters were in the city of

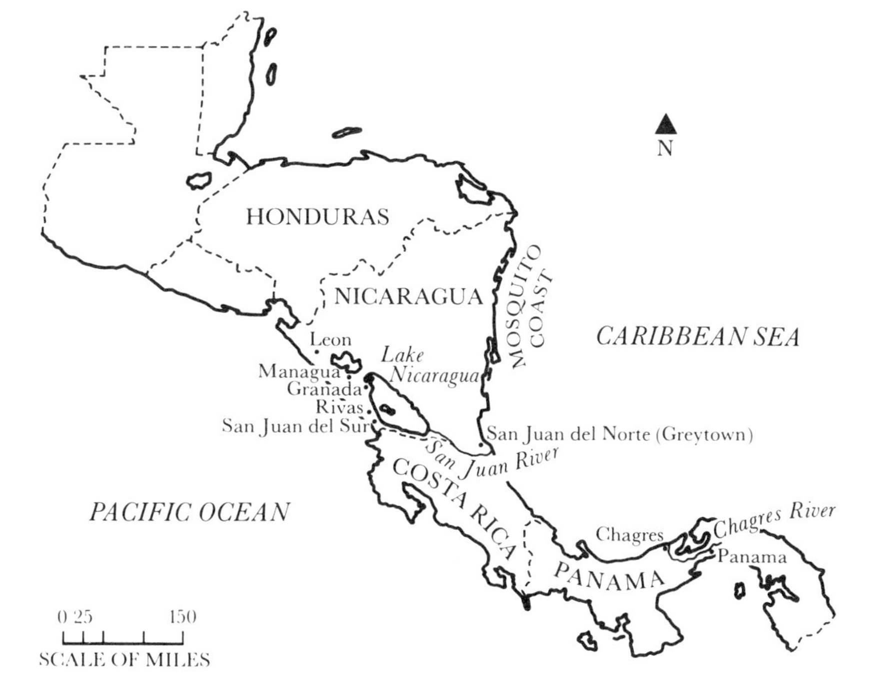

NICARAGUA AND PANAMA

Leon, the traditional rival of Granada. "Between the inhabitants of these two cities," J. D. explained, "there has always existed a bitter feeling of jealousy and enmity, and in most of their revolutions the opposing factions have been the Granadinos against the Leoneses."[26]

Before launching an attack on Granada, the Castillon forces in Leon had to raise an army. "The system adopted of recruiting is very simple indeed," J. D. wrote. "A few soldiers with fixed bayonets are sent out to bring in fresh men, or, to use their own expressive term, to 'catch' men. When the unfortunate recruit is 'caught,' a musket is put in his hands, and he becomes a soldier." The Democratic army next appropriated private residences as military barracks and proceeded to raise funds for equipment. "The mode of financing in time of revolution is equally simple with that of recruiting," J. D. stated. Citizens were asked "to fork out the dollars," and any who refused were "imprisoned and kept on a low diet," until they felt inclined to support the Democratic movement. Despite such flagrant violations of civil rights, Castillon's forces purported to be waging a war for the good of the individual citizens, and many Americans, convinced of the righteousness of the Democratic cause, joined the fight.[27]

Meanwhile in Granada, President Chamorro was preparing the city for the expected seige. Taking the central plaza as his fortress, he barricaded the narrow streets leading out from it with ten-foot-high barriers constructed of logs and adobe brick. Though opposing armies had met before in several small skirmishes in the villages, the expected assault on Granada was to be the first major confrontation. "The Democrats soon made their appearance," J. D. reported, "and taking possession of all that part of the city not enclosed in the barricades, they fixed their headquarters in an elevated situation, from which they could pop their cannon balls into any part of the Plaza."[28]

With a force of fifteen hundred, the Democrats then stormed the citadel erected in the Granada plaza. Since the entrenched forces of President Chamorro, who called themselves the Legitimists, numbered about one thousand, the match was nearly even. "Neither party were well provided with artillery," J. D. wrote. "They had each three or four guns, twelve and twenty-four pounders, with which they blazed away at each other for nearly a year, and between them managed to lay about three-fourths of the city in ruins." At one point the president's army appeared doomed to surrender for lack of ammunition, but a portion of the troops succeeded in breaking out of their stronghold and advancing all the way to the old fort at the source of the San Juan River. From here they purchased supplies from Jamaica and brought them back inside the plaza.[29]

By now the entire countryside lay in devastation; towns and villages had been ravished by each new invasion in the changing fortunes of the rival forces. J. D. was appalled at what he saw as he toured the countryside:

> One cannot but be struck with the ruin and desolation everywhere apparent, and with the remains of bygone wealth and grandeur, but little in accordance with the poverty and listless indolence in which the inhabitants are now contented to live.
>
> Their cities are half in ruins, and the churches, which, in their mode of warfare, they use as fortresses, have come in for their full share of destruction. Those which remain are peppered all over with cannon-balls. The ruins on the old indigo and cotton estates give one an idea of the different way in which the people once employed themselves.[30]

The seige of Granada lasted throughout the entire rainy season—July to December—a period in which "it rains in torrents for days at a time, and the roads become almost impassable." During the months of July and December, tropical fevers were rampant among soldiers in both camps. Then in February 1855, the Democrats abandoned their attack and retreated. The formerly beseiged Legitimists deserted their fortress and followed after them, suprising the enemy with an attack on the rear. "A bloody fight ensued," J. D. related, "the thickest of it took place in the church, in which some three hundred men were killed." After the fierce battle, the routed Democrats regrouped at Leon, leaving the Granada army in control of the southern half of the country. Believing their rebellion to be at a stalemate, disheartened Democrats made an impassioned plea for American aid.[31]

The Americans found themselves in an awkward position. They needed a convenient transportation route between their own east and west coasts, and the Nicaraguan passage had proven to be both easier and quicker than Panama's. Yet Great Britain, the leading maritime power of the world, had no intentions of allowing their former colony to gain exclusive control of an important trade route. The Union Jack already flew over the British protectorate of Mosquito Coast, provided for the Mosquito Indians residing on a forty-mile strip of land extending from the San Juan River to Honduras. And recently, the British had expanded this Mosquito base to include Greytown, the eastern terminus of Vanderbilt's crossing. Britain's flaunting of the Monroe Doctrine made America nervous, and in turn, Britain was apprehensive about America's espousal of "manifest destiny." A resolution to the threat of expansion by either party had come with the 1850 signing of the Clayton-Bulwer Treaty, requiring both countries to maintain strict neutrality over any future canals built across the isthmus.

Therefore, if Americans responded to the plea of the Democrats of Leon, they would be violating their promise of neutrality. As J. D. interpreted the matter, Americans were bent on seeking some way of attaining the country anyhow. "For the last five years an average of two thousand Americans per month have passed to and fro by this route," he wrote, "and, during the few days occupied in transit, have had ample time to admire and covet the splendid country through which they passed, to look with utter contempt on the natives, and to speculate on what a country it would be if it were only under the Stars and Stripes."[32]

The term commonly applied to the method Americans intended to make use of in expanding their territory to include the isthmus and the nearby island of Cuba was "filibusterism," a corruption of the word "freebooting." "It is a fixed idea with the American people," J. D. concluded, "that in due course of time they are to have the control of all the North

American continent, and of the Island of Cuba; they consider this their 'manifest destiny,' and any movement in that direction is looked on by them as a matter of course, and deserving of encouragement.''[33]

Nicaraguan Democrats were now offering just such encouragement. It was natural that all interested parties should turn for assistance to a man who had already distinguished himself as a professional filibuster, Tennessee lawyer William Walker. In 1853, Walker and a small band of confederates had sailed to La Paz, captured the governor of Baja California, and then declared this Mexican territory to be a free republic. Since Walker was one of the zealous Southerners who at the time were advocating the expansion of slavery in the United States through acquisition of new slave states, he wrote a clause into the new republic's constitution making slavery legal. Shortly after his victory, Walker lost his foothold in the country and was forced to flee.

He returned to San Francisco, only to be charged by his own countrymen of violating the nation's neutrality policy. General national support of his actions, however, brought about an acquittal. During the ensuing legal difficulties, Walker had earned the reputation of a courageous leader during his Mexican venture. With the encouragement of Secretary of War Jefferson Davis and shipping magnate Cornelius Vanderbilt, Walker was easily persuaded to join forces with the Nicaraguan Democrats.

After enlisting fifty-six Americans in his service, Colonel Walker sailed to Nicaragua. In May 1855 he landed in Realejo and marched his forces overland to Leon. The first campaign employing the united American and Nicaraguan troops was undertaken at Rivas near the end of June. By the time news of Walker's arrival reached Legitimist headquarters, rumor had swollen his forces from fifty-six to five hundred. The exaggerated report only served to rally opposition forces to protect their country from invading foreigners. Walker bravely led his men and two hundred native soldiers in the attack on Rivas, but at the first return of fire, the natives unanimously deserted their foreign commander, leaving him and his countrymen trapped in a house surrounded by Legitimist forces. For some time, the Americans bravely held the attackers at bay with rifle fire, but eventually ammunition ran out. When American rifles fell silent, the enemy at once realized the defender's predicament and quickly set fire to the house. As roof and walls caught fire, Walker boldly led his men from the burning building, cutting a path through the Nicaraguan soldiers at their weakest point, and fleeing all the way to San Juan del Sur. Here they took a schooner and sailed back to Realejo.

Despite this ill-fated entrance into Nicaragua's civil war, Colonel Walker was not discouraged. The next month he again challenged the enemy outside of Rivas, this time successfully driving a superior force into retreat and inflicting heavy casualties upon them, while losing only eight men himself. After the victory, he established headquarters at San Juan del Sur, where he could receive weapons and ammunition from California and as well recruit American passengers in transit across the isthmus. When he had augmented his troops to two hundred Americans and two hundred-fifty natives, he appropriated a Vanderbilt vessel and steamed to within a few miles of Granada. From that point, he prepared to march overland toward the Legitimist stronghold. Back in San Francisco, hundreds of adventurers were clamoring to board the *Uncle Sam*, a steamer laden with "crockery crates" full of arms stolen from the California state militia and intended for Walker's use. Though American officials made a show of conforming with the neutrality agreement, the ship was allowed to sail. "This is the way they do things in California," J. D. bitterly quipped in regards to the illegal shipment of arms.[34] Walker was "merely the practical exponent of a popular theory," a representative of America "as truly as" President Pierce and his cabinet.[35]

While Walker was sprucing up his forces, General Corral (chosen as commander after the death of President Chamorro) ordered a large part of his army to Rivas. Therefore, when Walker attacked Granada, he captured the garrison with little resistance. The people of Granada, just recovering from a severe epidemic of cholera, were terrified at finding themselves in American hands. But Walker was known for maintaining strict discipline over his troops, and he quickly restored peace to the city, thus making himself popular with citizens who remembered the acts of devastation and plunder carried out after previous victories. Since Castillon had died during the cholera epidemic, Democrats offered the office of president to Walker. He promptly declined the honor, stating that he preferred to remain in charge of the army. General Corral, on seeing the rising power of Walker's forces, declared a cease-fire and offered to negotiate an honorable peace. Walker and Corral then signed a treaty, uniting the warring factions into one government for the country. A formal ratification ceremony was carried out in a church, and afterwards the two armies were joined under Walker's command. As president the joint governing body selected a civilian, but named General Corral the new secretary of war. Delighted with the arrangement, America's resident minister quickly recognized the new government, and a period of peace and prosperity commenced. A brief interruption of the calm came about when General Corral attempted to organize an overthrow of the coalition government, but he was immediately arrested, convicted of treason, and executed.[36]

As Walker's reputation as an able military leader spread to neighboring countries, the president of Honduras paid him a visit, requesting aid in an expected attack from Guatemala. Walker, whose troops had recently been enlarged by the addition of seven hundred Americans, agreed to send half of his army to aid the neighboring government. "In Honduras, of course, the same game will be played as in Nicaragua," J. D. commented in the article he was preparing on the revolution. "In fighting for the people, the Americans will gain the ascendancy over them, and will keep it."[37]

Though convinced the Americans had violated their promise of neutrality to Great Britain, and therefore deeply concerned over this American greed for land and power, J. D. acknowledged Walker's leadership ability. "His followers hold him in the utmost esteem and admiration," he wrote, adding that Walker's conduct, since his accession to power in Nicaragua,'' had inspired ''confidence in his judgment and abilities.'' As for the general's personal appearance, J. D. thought he was ''not at all what one would suppose such a daring and successful filibuster to be, being an exceedingly quiet man, with a mild expression of face, and very decidedly Saxon features.''[38]

Historian Hubert Howe Bancroft was less diplomatic in his description of the curious little general. Walker, Bancroft wrote, was of ''puny stature,'' wore an ''ill-fitting coat,'' and had a heavily freckled face and pale-blond hair. His ''seemingly pupilless,'' large, gray eyes were ''half concealed by white eyebrows and eyelashes, at once repelling and fascinating with their strong, steady penetration.''[39] Still, Walker's bizarre physical appearance presented no detriment to his military career.

J. D. thought the ''Walker business in Nicaragua'' had been very ''cleverly managed'' by the United States. The Americans ''appear in the light of men who have'' come to this country ''at the request of a party which constituted the majority of the people,'' he lamented. ''They became citizens of the State, fought for it, and have risen to power.''[40] But, showing his usual optimism and acceptance of the world as it is, he concluded his article with the following observation:

> It cannot be doubted that the advantages to Nicaragua, in consequence of the introduction of American influence, will be very great. The constant fear of revolution being removed, the people will have more confidence in carrying on agricultural and commercial undertakings. The Americans will do away with all the antiquated absurdities of Spanish law, and amend a ridiculous tariff, whereby many of the commonest articles of civilized life have been virtually prohibited; foreign capital will be freely employed in the cultivation of sugar, rice, tobacco, indigo, and other valuable crops, in the production of which Nicaragua can compete with any country in the world; and the resources of the mining districts will be developed by energetic and experienced miners from California.[41]

J. D. had already noticed one such step toward improving the country.

> The power of the press is such an acknowledged fact in the United States and the establishment of a newspaper follows so closely on the advance of civilization, that wherever half-a-dozen Americans are settled together in the backwoods, one of them is sure to publish a newspaper for the edification of the rest.
>
> So in Granada one of the first things the Americans did was to bring out a weekly paper, called "*El Nicaraguense*"—"the Nicaraguan," half English, half Spanish. It is a very respectable sheet, with a good deal of its space devoted to the enlightenment of the public regarding the natural advantages of the country, its fertility, its delightful climate and great mineral wealth.[42]

Shortly after the return of peace to Nicaragua, J. D. wrote an article on the war and mailed it to *Blackwood's Magazine* in Edinburgh. Editor Blackwood published it upon receipt. As before, J. D.'s mother and sisters had the opportunity to see it before its author was aware of its acceptance. On reading the informative piece, Janet Borthwick had ample reason to be proud. Her older son, George, seemed destined to become a wealthy businessman, but John David was providing the thinking people of Great Britain with an account of a fantastic alien world and the even more fantastic events occurring there.

Though the American general seemed firmly entrenched in Latin America at the time J. D.'s article appeared, March 1856, the following year he lost control of the country. Reasons for American involvement in Nicaragua in the 1850s were not identical to those of the 1980s, but the basic motivation, as Thucydides contended, is the same. American passion for sharing democracy with the rest of the world by whatever means necessary is generally viewed askance by the rest of the world. Though the two Nicaraguan revolutions in question occurred more than one hundred years apart, numerous parallels exist. Both revolts were spearheaded by a supposedly liberal and progressive dissident, who accused the president in power of tyranny. During the ensuing conflicts, citizens suffered the usual horrors accompanying civil war: forced military service, casualties, interrupted home life and career, loss of property, and personal injury. Neighboring countries were also affected by the prolonged periods of strife, and outside sources were appealed to for aid. Though major powers claimed no involvement, both centuries had their scandals over strings pulled behind the scenes.

The final outcome of the 1980's conflict remains uncertain, but the peace instigated under General Walker did not endure. His advocacy of slavery did not sit well with the natives, and in addition he erred fatally in quarreling with his main supporter, Cornelius Vanderbilt. In 1857 Walker was ousted, and he returned to the United States in hopes of enlisting support for his cause. On his third attempt to gain a foothold in Central America, however, luck deserted him. In 1860 he was executed by a Honduran firing squad. The fickle American public, who now viewed the former hero as an incompetent, expressed little regret over his death.

J. D.'s coverage of the war in Latin American had broadened his perspective of the universal struggle for democracy and the role America was to play. But having endured two years in the strife-torn country, he was more than ready to return to Scotland. Throughout his travels he had represented himself as an ordinary British citizen, not once revealing his aristocratic background. He had been determined not to behave in the New World as one of those "detested" Europeans who boasted of their noble heritage. "Everybody who has travelled knows to which class they belong," Charles Ferguson wrote of such Europeans, though he "never knew anybody who wished to meet them again."[43] J. D. was not only ready to resume his identity as a patriotic Scot, he was ready to resume life as a genteel Borthwick. In the words he had used to describe the California immigrant "pictured off" back at the mines, the roving artist-correspondent would have given "half he is worth to be at home now—home? How sweet a word to his ears; how musical the sound to him!"[44]

PART IV

Return to the Old World

EDINBURGH

Though J. D. had spent the past decade "shifting his quarters with the readiness and resource of an Arab," on his arrival in Edinburgh in late 1856, he found his family at the same location he had left them—the house on Great Stuart Street. His two sisters were still living with his mother; Fearne, age thirty-one, appeared a confirmed spinster, but the youngest of the family, Janet, was in love with an army captain serving in Bombay and had plans to marry. The world traveler came bearing exotic gifts for the three women, certainly among them the "gorgeous Chinese shawl" that was "as necessary for the returning Californian as a revolver and bowie-knife for the California emigrant."[1]

Though J. D. had been gone for ten years, the most noticeable difference was only that his homeland seemed even smaller and more confining than he had remembered. Apparently the single great change during the decade of his absence had taken place within him; he had left Scotland a rather timorous, uncertain youth and returned a self-confident, successful man—a world-traveled journalist. Weekends provided the greatest contrast to California living. Whereas the mining-camp Sunday had been as boisterous as a country fair, the

Edinburgh Sabbath was "half-dead," residents venturing out only for "morning and evening services."[2]

Soon after his arrival home, J. D. began compiling the copious notes taken during his journeys. Then he organized them and commenced rewriting for publication. There was sufficient material for several periodical submissions, and as his first project he chose an article featuring his best drawings. The prestigious *Harper's Weekly* would be the target. His goal in the article was to cover the main aspects of daily life at the mines, reminiscing about early times and then updating to include recent changes. To depict the miners' entertainment he included a sketch of a ball, a monte game, and a faro table, and then composed paragraphs to describe each activity in detail. Gambling, he explained, was the prevalent pastime in early days, and an appropriate one since mining itself was nothing more than a gamble. Even after the California legislature banned this favored sport, he pointed out, the law was enforced only in the larger towns. In remote camps, games of chance continued seven days a week. "Swarthy, bearded men," armed with "silvered-hilted bowie-knives" and "heavy Colt revolvers," crowded into thirty-by-fifty halls, whose walls were swathed in "flashy calico" and whose ceilings were covered with "white cotton to resemble plastering as much as possible." Sunday was the busiest day, the oblong hall echoing with "the clanking of coin, loud voices, snatches of songs, curses, laughter, and the rattling of glasses at the bar."[3]

He also included a drawing of a Chinese camp, telling how these immigrants, on their arrival in San Francisco, "organize under the direction of a resident chief," who "contracts with the steamboat proprietors to transport an entire shipload at once to Sacramento or Stockton, whence they pass by squads into the mines," taking up abandoned claims and forming little villages. It was true, he admitted, that they were generally driven from any rich diggings, but the Americans presented an argument for this treatment: "It is urged that the Chinese are of no benefit . . . to the community: jealously hoarding every ounce of gold, and returning to China with it.

FARO

They buy no American clothing, generally bringing their own stock.'' This prejudice, he felt, had declined in later years: ''An immigration tax, amounting almost to prohibition, was once imposed, but was so repugnant to the views of many conscientious persons that it was not rigidly enforced, . . . The broad principle of universal toleration is the only one which can be consistently adopted in America.''[4]

The final drawing represented the early days of placer mining, but the text stated the current situation also.

> Instead of the solitary cabin and savage manner of living in isolated, miserable tents and huts . . . may now be seen permanently located families who have made California a home, and have introduced the comforts and pleasures of society. . . . Woman, too has not been unmindful of her mission in California, . . . hard-featured, harder-working Western woman, who boasts that she does more work than her laboring husband, and whose daily routine of household duties comprise a work-list that would appall any but a California woman. These are the real pride and hope of the country, and to their noble presence is due the thousands of comfortable cottages, or humble cabins, where the miner repairs with a light heart after the healthful labors of the day. These are the true homes of California, whence is springing up the finest and most robust generation of children on this continent.[5]

In the final paragraph, he commented on the coming loss of opportunity for the individual, the day when the rich mines would no longer be ''open to the whole world.'' ''The time, however, is approaching when, the surface diggings being exhausted, the great system of hydraulic mining and the consequent growth of companies will place the most available places under the control of capitalists. Thus the single adventurer will not enjoy the unbounded field.''[6]

As he mailed his package to *Harper's*, he felt more confident it would reach its destination than he had at the mines. He was also more confident it would be accepted, since it was coming from a writer who had already been published in three respected periodicals. His next project was to be a serial submission to James Mason Hutchings, the neighbor from Weber Creek who had purchased drawings to illustrate his stationery.

Hutchings was now publishing a periodical dedicated to singing the praises of the Golden State, and though the struggling editor would not be able to pay, J. D. was still anxious to have his account of his California experiences in print, especially in a magazine whose growing reputation compared favorably with *Harper's*.

J. D. commenced his story at the point where he had taken up mining, relating events in colorful detail, but focusing on the Gold Rush adventure rather than on himself. Though the reader would recognize the author as British, he would not suspect him to be a Scot. When he had completed several chapters, he mailed them to Hutchings, promising to provide further episodes at a later date. But, as mentioned previously, the Borthwicks lived next door to the publishing Blackwoods, who had already printed J. D.'s report of the revolution in Nicaragua. On learning of the projected serials on the California adventures, Editor Blackwood asked J. D. for permission to review the manuscript and was so impressed with its contents that he made an offer on the entire account. There was a stipulation, however; J. D. was not to send any more free chapters to *California Magazine*. Thrilled at the prospects of authoring a book illustrated with his own artwork, J. D. quickly signed a contract with Blackwood and Sons.[7]

Because of the timely subject matter, Blackwood insisted the book come off the press within only a few months. J. D. agreed, but he was not prepared for the struggle ahead in trying to meet deadlines. His past experiences had been with much shorter works, and he had not yet encountered the stiff resistance creative genius can put up against a self-imposed regimen of steady writing over an extended period. One point was in his favor, however; his natural tendency to periodically isolate himself from others so he could meditate now served him well. He had already ferreted out his personal ideas on the significance of the New World events in relation to the history of civilization. Sitting down and writing every day whether he felt creative or not proved difficult, but his will dominated.

In early 1857 Blackwood read the completed manuscript, pronounced it excellent, and rushed it into print. Then came hours of proofreading and finally J. D.'s first glimpse of the completed book. Holding in his hand the goldfield experiences, bound in a neat capsule, brought him a feeling of deep pride. Blackwood followed up the book's release with a review in the April issue of the family's periodical. This nearly ten-page review is entertaining reading in its own right, but only a few passages will be quoted in summary of the general reaction expressed to the book. The reviewer started out by admitting he might appear to be "a crabbed old gentleman, bilious from much port, and disgusted with the age" that had "left him so hopelessly behind." He found nothing more exasperating than being "obliged to feel insignificant in the presence of some beardless traveller . . . whom we know for an ass, as we did his father and grandfather before him," a man "without reverence, reading, or observant power." Yet, he wrote, "when we meet a traveller of the right stamp, nobody enjoys his talk or his writing more than we." In the following pages, it becomes obvious the reviewer regarded J. D. not as an ass, but as a traveller of the right stamp. The author of *Three Years in California* is characterized as a man with "a natural aptitude for dispensing with conventionalities, an open conciliatory temper, a habit of making the best of everything, a talent for roughing it, and a knack of detecting the significant features of new scenes, and graphically recording them."[8] Though J. D. had not intended to portray his own spiritual quest in the book, the reviewer had recognized the layer of meaning beneath the surface and therefore compared the work to John Bunyan's *Pilgirm's Progress.* "San Francisco," he commented, was "a city bearing so strong a resemblance to Bunyan's town of Vanity as fully to attest the strength and truth of the imagination of him who drew the allegorical picture."[9] J. D. was also credited with displaying "great power of comparison and analysis" in probing the national character of each group represented at the mines. As for J. D.'s own character, the reviewer thought the young author had shown "a degree of energy and self-reliance which would have done credit to the most acute of his Yankee fellow-travellers."[10]

Also, it was gratifying that "an educated and clever man like Mr. Borthwick" could pass through such an ordeal with increased respect for his species. The Pilgrim to the New World had obviously made spiritual progress, evidenced by the following passage from the book: "It is difficult," J. D. had written, "to believe that any one, after circulating much among the different types of mankind to be found in the mines, should not have a higher respect than before for the various classes which they represented." The review closed with a strong recommendation for the work, but just as meaningful to J. D. was the assessment of his own character. "In the mines," the reviewer had commented, "a man had nothing to trust to with confidence except his own honest exertions —and a man who can sufficiently rely on these to cast himself into such a struggle, amid such privation in so distant and strange a land, must necessarily have a great deal of good in him."[11] These words came at a time when J. D. was struggling with a difficult decision, and he evidently took them to heart.

Though it could be argued that the *Blackwood's* review must be discounted on grounds of conflict of interest, the praise it gives the book is actually quite objective. The reader cannot judge *Three Years in California* on the basis of the limited quotations included in the present volume, but anyone who has not read Borthwick's account is missing a rare treat. Borthwick's unique contribution to Gold Rush literature has been to place the era in its proper perspective in relation to world history and, as well, to offer the modern Californian a deeper awareness of the heritage that bears so heavily on current social conditions within the state. In fact it is surprising how many of Borthwick's comments about California society still apply equally well in the late twentieth century. The Scot's link to the past, often nonexistent in the modern American, enabled him to perceive the events of the 1850s in terms of everything that had preceded them; and his foresight allowed him to contemplate them in light of what would most likely follow.

He was qualified for this task by a natural artistic bent that caused him to view the entire panorama through a series of meaningful images. Like a photographer manipulating an adjustable lens, he moved in for a close shot to reveal an interesting human foible, or serious moral defect, and just as quickly slid out to the viewpoint where individual failings pale as life is observed from a higher plane of existence. He was especially gifted at merging the two opposing images into a single frame.

With both word and picture, he painted a transient society of restless, "go-ahead" adventurers, giddy at their new freedom from social restraints and exuberant in their hope of finding gold. He marveled at the vast natural wonderland, whose grandeur dwarfed the invading hordes, reminding the wary of their relative insignificance. He recorded gross abuses of this newly found freedom, as men dissipated themselves by self-indulgent excesses or destroyed others by permitting personal prejudice to erupt in violence. He observed the Old World shackles loosening before a forced leveling of social rank—doctors and lawyers grubbing in the dirt, and free men waiting on slaves. He recognized the California experience as a great catalyst of democracy, but out of requirements brought on by the unusual circumstances rather than through the propagation of feverishly patriotic ideas disseminated at a Fourth of July celebration. America's persistent attempt to convert the rest of the world to their religion of personal liberties seemed to result in hostility and distrust, but the great example, unknown in human history, had been the opening of the mineral lands to all comers. In no other country had the government relinquished its right to the gold in the earth. It was this opportunity offered to all at the California goldfields that had opened new vistas of democracy.

In fact, in the fertile mind of the young artist, the Gold Rush era became a study in democracy. In Nicaragua he had noted the phenomenon he called the "California education," an expansion of one's understanding of personal rights. Those arriving from New York on their way to the mines

> seemed to think that each man could do just as he pleased, without regard to the comfort of his neighbors. They showed no accommodating spirit, but grumbled at everything, and were rude and surly in their manners. . . . The same men, however, on their return from California, were perfect gentle-

> men in comparison. They were orderly in their behavior; though rough, they were not rude, and showed great consideration for others, submitting cheerfully to any personal inconvenience necessary for the common good, and showing by their conduct that they had acquired some notion of their duties to balance the very enlarged idea of their rights which they had formerly entertained."[12]

The admirable qualities most of the gold seekers displayed after their initiation into the brotherhood could be summarized as independence tempered by cooperativeness, avarice balanced by generosity. Borthwick's varied contacts in the New World brought him a new appreciation of the value and dignity of man. He viewed the gold hunters as a superior class of men, an elite gathered from all nations—heroic in their endurance, resilience, and courage, despite their incompleteness as individuals.

His thesis that the Gold Rush decade was equal to an entire century of experience in another time and place suggests that greater respect should be afforded the culture of a nation frequently belittled as too young to have produced anything of value. True, America's early attempts at the arts can be described as Yankee ingenuity superimposed on Old World material, symbolized so well by the amusing presentation of Richard III emanating through the flimsy wall in the Nevada City hotel. Yet in listing storytelling as one of the popular forms of entertainment on the mining frontier, Borthwick has elevated a yarn spun on the hearths of a crude hotel to the level of legend. The tales of miners' exploits—related as truth, though often an exaggeration of fact and an interpretation of character as either better or worse than in reality—were a refashioning of history to suit the popular imagination. Incidents of the discovery of a large nugget or of the lynching of a criminal take on the aura of fairy tales, expressing the common dream of a poor person becoming suddenly rich or of a world rid of all evil. In revealing the heart's desire of the common miner, they also lay open his secret heart.

Borthwick personally witnessed the emergence of our nation's developing character. America, he stated, was a country whose fundamental tendency was "to blow your own horn, and to make as much noise as possible with it;"[13] a country where "a man was judged by the amount of money in his purse;"[14] a country whose citizens were given to bragging; in short, a country of "ultra-democratic principles."[15] The individual American citizen was of "superior boldness, energy and perseverance."[16]

Yet, in J. D.'s opinion, the upstart nation was not godless. "The Americans," he concluded, "are often accused of boasting—perhaps deservedly so,"[17] yet "when we see a new country and a new home provided for our surplus population, at a time when it was most required—when a fresh supply of gold, now a necessary to civilization, is discovered, as we were evidently and notoriously becoming so urgently in want of it, we cannot but recognize the ruling hand of Providence. . . . We must indeed look upon this whole Golden Legend as one of the most wondrous episodes in the history of mankind."[18]

Thus, in the closing lines of his book, Borthwick has presented his personal philosophy as a framework to enclose the seemingly chaotic epic of the Gold Rush into the design of an orderly universe. In this final passage the author has at last dropped the mask of the professional journalist to express his most intimate belief, a belief nurtured by his parents throughout his childhood but now affirmed by his own experience: a faith that the universal brotherhood of man is bound together by the loving care of a Divine Power.

In August, James Mason Hutchings included the first chapters J. D. had sent him in *California Magazine,* closing with a notation the episodes would be continued in the next issue. From the material he had received he proceeded with the serials for six more issues, and though the seventh closed with the promise the account would go on, it was in reality the final one. Then in October of that same year, *Harper's Weekly* printed J. D.'s lengthy article, a ten-column spread illustrated with three eight-by-six and two twelve-by-six-inch drawings.[19]

These large pictures in *Harper's* show J. D.'s talent to better advantage than the smaller illustrations in his book, since one of the characteristics of his work is the use of extensive areas of intricate detail that add texture and therefore interest to the composition as a whole. Though the purpose of his drawings was to provide information about life at the mines, J. D. treated them as serious works of art. Each picture he created during his travels is carefully composed. Human figures show individuality, and occasionally a face seems recognizable, as if it had appeared in an earlier drawing, thus suggesting "the small world" of the miner, who during his wanderings anywhere between Panama and the furthest corner of the Northern Mines was constantly bumping into a friend he had traveled beside or dined and slept with in some small inn. As for the faces in "Chinese Camp in the Mines," their lines are distorted to an exaggerated angularity to express the artist's sense of strangeness for the men from a distant land.

Though the miner portraits were created under unfavorable circumstances—the sitter anxious to return to work at his claim and those waiting in line eager for a turn in the spotlight—the artist still attempted to suggest individual traits of character, such as independence, strength, and wariness. In fact nearly all of Borthwick's drawings depict scenes symbolic of the concepts basic to frontier life—highly self-reliant men cooperating in some vast project, or similar energy being exhibited at play. The gambling scenes not only depict the reckless gambling spirit of the miner, but also provide an apt metaphor for the occupation of mining, itself a gamble.[20]

Though "Chinese Camp" has what was later to be called an "expressionistic" quality, other drawings seem to anticipate the late nineteenth-century concern for capturing a fleeting moment in time, for recreating an impression left on the artist's receptive mind. For example, "A Ball"—alive with motion and hazy with atmosphere—bears a certain resemblance to ball paintings done later by Renoir, and "Shaw's Flat" brings to mind Van Gogh's orchards.

The "Shaw's Flat" motif of cart and driver disappearing in the distance also appears in the book, as partially quoted in the description of the stage trip to the mines: "The vastness of space . . . and our late neighbors, rapidly diminishing round us, and getting hull down on the horizon. . . . The scene all round us was magnificent and impressed one as much with his own insignificance, as though he beheld the countries of the earth from the summit of a high mountain.''[21] Thus one of the main themes of the book—the relative insignificance of the ordinary individual in the vast scheme of things, yet the individual's potential for elevating himself above the ordinary—is echoed in the drawings.

The profits from *Three Years in California* provided J. D. the opportunity to pursue the career he had desired, even from childhood, and that his travels throughout the world had only reinforced. Though he enjoyed expressing himself through the medium of words, his real love was painting. To become a renowned painter was his most private and cherished dream—not merely a painter who lived by his brushes, but a true artist who would contribute great paintings for the edification and enjoyment of humanity. It was such a daring venture that for many years he had postponed making the decision. The risk was obvious: he might come to realize one day that he did not after all have the talent and inner vision to become a great painter. Such knowledge would be devastating. Still, his previous successes with the book and the articles gave him great hope. Just as the *Blackwood's* reviewer had pointed out, his experiences in the New World when put down in words, clearly revealed his own character, the character he had set out to test a decade earlier. Throughout his travels he had kept his longing for home and family under tight wraps, rarely permitting himself the luxury of indulging in memories that might prove painful. Occasionally some minor detail had momentarily ''put him in mind of home,'' but he had never allowed his homesickness to make him ''turn tail and run,'' as he had seen others do. He had endured what Audubon termed ''unending loneliness,''[22] and he had consistently shown courage and strength, whether it be in rowing a boat upcurrent, climbing a mountain, or rescuing a distraught woman's furniture from fire. Certainly the accomplishments recorded in his writings proved he was a man who could unflinchingly face the ultimate challenge, the quest for immortality through art. It was not a decision to be made in haste, however, because it would entail leaving home again. Edinburgh had its galleries, but still he believed London to be the only city in which a serious painter should embark upon a career. Deep in his heart, he had always known that he must pursue this dream or lose respect for himself. The decision waiting to be made then was not so much if he should go to London, but when. For the time being he felt a need to bask for just a little longer in the sunshine of familial love. His father had written in his will that London was "far away," and J. D. was well acquainted with what it meant to be "far away" from Scotland. Besides, his older brother George, who was enjoying considerable success as a bill broker in Liverpool, had written that he would soon be returning to Scotland to marry his sweetheart. The event would be an opportunity for the family to be at home together once more, if only for a fleetingly brief time.

The wedding took place on February 8, 1859. George, now thirty-six, had like his father waited to marry until he could support a family in style. The bride was Mary Macdonald, age twenty-three, who had grown up in nearby St. Andrew's Parish. J. D. acted as a witness to the ceremony and afterwards added his signature to the record book. After a short visit in Edinburgh, the happy couple left for Liverpool, where they would set up housekeeping. Being with his older brother again spurred J. D. on toward the accomplishment of his own goal, but whether the motivating factor was brotherly encouragement or sibling rivalry is unknown. At any rate, shortly after the wedding J. D. packed his bags and once more bid his mother and sisters farewell.[23]

LONDON

When J. D. finally decided to dedicate the remaining years of his life to painting, he was already thirty-four. He arrived in the capital city alone, but with sufficient money from the proceeds of his book to get by until he could commence selling his works. When his book royalties were used up, he would have to survive on his modest inheritance. The main concern in finding permanent living quarters was that the place be suitable for painting; the neighborhood was not nearly so important as having a well-lit studio. He was forced to settle for a single room in a residence located off Sussex Street, a few blocks from the university. Though there was a business next door, four buildings occupied by a silk mercer, there were also two other artists on the street, another painter and a sculptor.

His landlord, William Thorogood, was a forty-year-old native of nearby Hertfordshire, who supported his family by operating a billiards room on the same premises as his residence, 22 Tottenham Court Road. Thorogood and his wife, Eliza, had two small children: Katie, seven, and George, five. In addition to J. D., the family kept a second lodger, a widow from Belgium, who had a teenage daughter. Though these seven residents shared a house, they retained their privacy by living as three separate households. Because of the congeniality of the landlord and his family, the situation was tolerable.[24]

J. D. commenced work immediately. During the prior decade, he had recorded the most exciting and important events taking place in the world, but these years of restless wandering had given him a rare appreciation for the values associated with home life. It was these often unrecognized values, the more precious to him for being so far from the home of his childhood, that he now chose to portray. By the following year, 1860, he had completed two oil paintings that he felt were worthy of exhibition: "Too Many Cooks" and "The Man at the Wheel." He placed both at the Royal Society of British Artists, pricing each at twenty pounds. He did not become a member of the Society, nor any other brotherhood for that matter, preferring instead to remain a "solitary" individual, one completely on his "own hook."[25] Records of the Royal Society of British Artists do not show whether his works sold, but the painting started immediately after the exhibit provides a rather ominous clue: he entitled the work "Dead Broke."[26]

The following year presented a second happy occasion for the Borthwick family to assemble in Edinburgh, the wedding of Janet, now age thirty-one. George and Mary arrived from Liverpool, and on September 17, 1861, Janet and Captain J.

T. Nicholson, age forty-one, were united in marriage, the first for both. Since the captain was still assigned to Bombay, the newly married couple would make their home there. The widow Borthwick, now in her sixties, had but two unmarried children left. Fearne seemed content to devote her life to serving as a companion to her mother, and John David seemed to be turning into a recluse.[27]

Of course J. D. could not think of marrying. He could not support a wife and children. His entire world revolved around his painting, at which he must work alone. Fortunately, his natural temperament suited the life a struggling artist must lead. He did, however, have a great deal of love to offer and was therefore mindful of the sacrifice he was making. His sole sustenance was his dream and the fierce pride he took in pursuing it. Before leaving Edinburgh, he had committed himself, and in writing so it could not be retracted, to the difficult London years. His experiences in the New World had convinced him that he, like the Americans, had that "spirit of individual self-reliance which impels" a man to "enter alone into the wildest enterprise, so long as he himself thinks it feasible." He was bent on "disengaging himself for the time being from all communication with his fellowmen, to plunge into the wilderness, and there to labor steadily, uncheered by any passing pleasure, and with nothing to sustain him in his determination but his own confidence in his ability ultimately to attain his object."[28]

After his sister's wedding, J. D. returned to the foggy, cheerless capital inhabited by a "wilderness" of disinterested strangers and "labored steadily." His confidence was still unshaken. In his early years, he had adopted the motto stated on the Kinnear coat of arms as his own: "I live in hope." He was as mindful of his "bold" and "hopeful" ancestors as he had been on the day he sailed to the New World. Yet the following year he produced but one painting that was exhibited: "Dead Broke." This work was shown at the Royal Academy of Arts, but again there is no record of sale. It was three years before he had more suitable works ready; in 1865 he completed "In Hertfordshire," inspired by a scene from his landlord's native countryside. It also was shown at the Royal Academy of Arts.[29]

Searching for fresh motivation, he recalled his earlier successes, all associated with his travel experiences. In the New World he had survived hardships with flying colors, and also prevailed by publishing the accounts and drawings. He hopefully returned to his California subjects. From a sketch made while in the goldfields, he painted "The Miner's Grave, California," and exhibited for the first time at the Royal Academy's rival, the British Institution.[30] Since he personally believed the California-inspired painting was far superior to anything he had done previously, he put a price of seventy-five pounds on it. His two final exhibitions came in 1867, at the newly opened Dudley Gallery.[31]

No record exists of the number of paintings J. D. actually sold, if indeed he sold any at all during his lifetime. But of course a failure to sell paintings is not necessarily a reflection of an artist's talent. Being saleless would have placed J. D. in good company; his contemporary, Vincent Van Gogh, had sold but one work at his death.

The late 1860s brought two important changes for the Borthwick family. To make ends meet, J. D.'s mother and Fearne were forced to take a gentleman boarder into their home, a French teacher named Dr. Dubuc, and George and Mary moved to London. George continued in the same occupation, a bill broker, setting up his business with a partner at 11 Clements Lane. Residing in the same city gave the two brothers opportunity to spend time together, and it must have been tempting for J. D., because of the trials he was enduring, to resume his childhood dependency on George. He could have moved into the more comfortable residence of his older brother, where domestic needs would be handled by his sister-in-law, and not only save money, but also be surrounded by family again. Instead, he staunchly maintained his independence, believing such a dependency would compromise his creative genius.

Though by 1871 he had not exhibited for several years, the aging artist was still working steadily, and still residing with the Thorogood family on Tottenham Court Road. His situation remained the same, but there had been changes in the two households with whom he shared the residence. Little George Thorogood had died and, as a companion for Katie, the family had taken in a niece. The Belgian widow and her daughter had moved, and their room was now occupied by a bachelor bank manager.[32]

Within a few years, however, the three-family household was to dissolve. Mr. Thorogood gave up the billiards room and moved his family to another part of the city, thus forcing his lodgers to seek new quarters. Again, it would have been easy for J. D. to simply move in with George's family, but he was still determined to be self-reliant. In St. Peter's Parish, he found a room in a residence located at 92 Elgin Road, the home of Mrs. Bella Albu. The widow Albu had four children: three teenagers who attended school and a daughter, age twenty-five, who taught music.[33]

The year 1876 brought another reunion for the Borthwick's, but this time a sorrowful one, the death of their mother. Janet had used up the last of the fund left her by her husband and therefore had nothing to leave her children other than the memory of her devotion to them. It was with good reason that J. D. returned to London in a state of depression. Not only was he mourning the loss of his mother, but also he had reached the point in his life when he must admit that his creativity was gone forever. He had dedicated himself wholly to his painting, giving up the opportunity for marriage and a family of his own, but in spite of all, he had failed to achieve the artistic success he had been working for during the past twenty years. He had learned a most painful lesson, for he now realized that despite dedication, hard work, sacrifice, and faith, cherished dreams do not necessarily come true. This lesson was difficult to reconcile with his natural optimism, but he must now undergo the initiation rites he had somehow evaded since childhood. Despite the manliness he had consistently displayed, as far as optimism was concerned he had remained a veritable child. The difficult London years at last brought on John David's long-delayed loss of innocence.[34]

During these final years of his life in the Old World, J. D.'s experiences in the New World were often on his mind. He remembered California as "that land of promise" that had realized the ideal of "perfect social equality."[35] Another Gold Rush artist, frequently mentioned in this volume, had experienced in his declining years the same phenomenon. John Woodhouse Audubon's daughter reported that while her father lay on his deathbed, his frontier adventures had flooded back into memory: "Especially was the California trip present in his fevered mind," she wrote, "and incidents and scenes were once more vividly before him."[36] Evidently the great sensitivity of these artists caused the spectacle of the 1850s to register upon their minds with a greater intensity than that experienced by other participants.

In the early spring of 1892, the fortieth anniversary of the season J. D. had set out for California's Southern Mines, he experienced a strange hoarseness. Over the weeks his voice continued growing more husky, as if he were suffering from laryngitis, yet strangely enough there was no pain in his throat. When he finally sought medical advice, his doctor regretfully informed him that he was suffering from cancer of the larynx, probably brought on by an overfondness for the pipe. As the cancer spread, it became increasingly difficult for J. D. to swallow; by winter he was scarcely able to eat. On hearing of her brother's illness, Janet Nicholson sent her daughter Lucy to London to care for him. Sensing death was at hand, J. D. bequeathed his few possessions to those he was about to leave behind. Lucy Nicholson, a spinster in her late twenties, provided loving care for her sixty-eight-year-old uncle, remaining at his bedside up to the final moment. He died four days before Christmas.[37]

As evidence of the small amount of fame his painting had brought him, the obituary in the *London Times* lists his single claim to distinction as having been the son of a distinguished father. Among those listed as having died on December 21, 1892, was "John David Borthwick, younger son of the late George Augustus Borthwick MD FRCP Edinburgh."[38]

Of the immediate family of Dr. George and Janet Borthwick, only three members now remained. Besides Janet Nicholson, there was Fearne, who survived until 1903 and George, who died in 1906 with a daughter at his bedside.[39]

Though John David Borthwick is represented by one oil painting in the museum kept by the Society of California Pioneers, his works do not hang in London museums. But if he failed to achieve his dreams of immortality as a painter, he at least died with the satisfaction of knowing he had waged a heroic fight. Recalling the optimism his father had shown during his own final illness, J. D. may have lain on his deathbed with a lingering hope that the worth of his London paintings would still be recognized some day.

If the life of this artist is perceived in the same manner in which he perceived the events of the 1850s—that is in perspective of the entire history of civilization—it becomes obvious that he made his unique contribution to the world while still a very young man. His vision of the Gold Rush as "a soul-expanding" experience, a steady progression toward universal equality, provides inspiration for a troubled world. John David Borthwick has captured images that enable Americans to better visualize their heritage, precious images of a brief moment in time when men of all nations, such as the Flying Dutchman and his multilingual company, demonstrated that humanity is capable of uniting in pursuit of a common dream.

NOTES

INTRODUCTION

1. John David Borthwick, *Three Years in California* (Edinburgh: Blackwood and Sons, 1857), 91.

2. Erwin G. Gudde, *California Gold Camps* (Berkeley: University of California Press, 1975), 386.

PART I: BOYHOOD AND YOUTH IN SCOTLAND

1. Scott mentions Borthwick Castle in his *History of Scotland, The Monastery, Provincial Antiquities,* and *Tales.*

2. John Dickson, *The Ruined Castles of Mid-Lothian* (Edinburgh: Robert R. Sutherland, 1894), 50–54.

3. Joseph Irving, *The Book of Scotsmen* (Paisley: Alexander Gordon, 1881).

4. Halsey M. Borthwick, *The Borthwick Family* (Cornwallville, N.Y.: Greene Company, 1936), 5–6; "Clan Borthwick Association Brochure."

5. Borthwick, *The Borthwick Family*, 48.

6. Emma Siggins White, *The Kinnears and their Kin* (Kansas City, Mo.: Tiernan-Dart Printing Company, 1916), 1, 4.

7. *Post Office Annual Directory for 1876*–77 (Edinburgh: Ballantyne, 1876).

8. Deeds and Probates, Edinburgh, Scotland; Old Parochial Registers, Edinburgh, Scotland; *Edinburgh Academy Register (Edinburgh: Constable, 1914),* 59.

9. *Post Office Annual Directory for 1829–30* (Edinburgh: Ballantyne, 1829).

10. A. J. Youngson, *The Making of Classical Edinburgh, 1750–1840* (Edinburgh: Edinburgh University Press, 1966), 222.

11. Ibid., 218–21.

12. Ian G. Lindsay, *Georgian Edinburgh* (Edinburgh: Scottish Academic Press, 1973), 42; Youngson, 156–58.

13. *Edinburgh Academy Register*, 74; R. Stevenson, *Annals of Edinburgh and Leith* (Edinburgh: J. Hutchinson, 1839), 172.

14. Plantagenet and Fiona Somerset Fry, *The History of Scotland* (London: Routledge and Kegan Paul, 1982), 217.

15. Ibid., 216–17; Edinburgh *Post Office Annual Directory and Calendar*; Death Records, Edinburgh, Scotland.

16. Moray McLaren, *Understanding the Scots* (London: Frederick Mullen, 1956), 117.

17. Neil McCallum, *It's an Old Scottish Custom* (London: Dennis Dobson, 1951), 136.

18. Census of Scotland for 1841.

19. Dickson, 37–38.

20. Ibid., 38–43; *Oliver and Boyd's Guide to Edinburgh* (Edinburgh: Oliver and Boyd, 1860), 64; Borthwick, *The Borthwick Family*, 25–28.

21. Borthwick, *The Borthwick Family*, 28; *Oliver and Boyd's Guide to Edinburgh*, 64; Dickson, 32.

22. Borthwick, *The Borthwick Family,* 29.

23. Edinburgh *Post Office Directory for 1829–30.*

24. Stevenson, 181.

25. Wills, Edinburgh, Scotland.

26. *The Edinburgh Academy Register,* 59.

27. Stevenson, 179–80.

28. William Downie, *Hunting for Gold: Reminiscences of Personal Experiences* (San Francisco: California Publishing Company, 1893), 8.

29. *The Edinburgh Academy Register*, 59.

30. Census of Scotland for 1841.
31. Wills, Edinburgh, Scotland.
32. Ibid.
33. Marriage and Death Records, Edinburgh, Scotland; Census of Scotland for 1851; Edinburgh *Post Office Annual Directory and Calendar*.
34. Edinburgh *Post Office Directory for 1840.*
35. *Illustrated London News,* 24 January 1852, 73.
36. Deeds and Probates, Edinburgh, Scotland.

PART II: ADVENTURES IN THE NEW WORLD

1. Borthwick, *Three Years in California*, 145.
2. Robert Burns, "Is There For Honest Poverty," 1795.
3. Borthwick, *Three Years in California,* 1, 3.
4. Ibid., 3–5.
5. Ibid., 4–5.
6. Ibid., 5.
7. Ibid., 6–7.
8. Ibid., 6; Bayard Taylor, *Eldorado; or Adventures in the Path of Empire* (New York: Alfred A. Knopf, 1949), 24–25.
9. Borthwick, *Three Years in California,* 7.
10. Ibid., 8.
11. Ibid., 7.
12. Ibid., 9.
13. Bayard Taylor, 13.
14. Ibid., 21.
15. Borthwick, *Three Years in California,* 15.
16. Ibid., 13.
17. Ibid., 15.
18. Ibid., 16.
19. Ibid., 18.
20. Bayard Taylor, 11.
21. Borthwick, *Three Years in California,* 20.
22. Ibid., 22–23.
23. Ibid., 24.
24. Ibid., 26.

25. Ibid., 27–28.
26. Ibid., 29.
27. Ibid., 32.
28. Ibid., 30, 33–34.
29. Ibid., 34.
30. R. R. Taylor, "A Letter from Panama," in John and LaRee Caughey, *California Heritage: An Anthology of History and Literature* (Los Angeles: Ward Ritchie Press, 1962), 45–47.
31. Borthwick, *Three Years in California*, 37–38, 40.
32. Ibid., 42.
33. Ibid., 44, 50; John David Borthwick, *The Gold Hunters* (Cleveland: International Fiction Library, 1917), 73.
34. Borthwick, *Three Years in California*, 51–52.
35. Ibid., 53.
36. Ibid., 49–50.
37. Stephen J. Field, "Personal Reminiscences of Early Days in California," MS, Cecil H. Green Library, Stanford University, 6–7.
38. Borthwick, *Three Years in California*, 90.
39. *London Times,* 16 September 1848.
40. James H. Carson, "Recollections of the California Mines," *San Joaquin Republican* (Stockton), Special Edition, 1852.
41. C. W. Haskins, *The Argonauts of California* (New York: Fords, Howard, and Hulbert, 1890), 48.
42. Bayard Taylor, 226.
43. William Shaw, *Golden Dreams and Waking Realities* (New York: Arno Press, 1973), 31–32.
44. Borthwick, *Three Years in California*, 74–76.
45. Ibid., 49.
46. Ibid., 66, 69.
47. Ibid., 67.
48. Michael Scott, *Writings* in Thomas A. Bailey and David M. Kennedy, *The American Pageant* (Lexington, Mass.: D. C. Heath, 1979), 194.
49. *Congressional Globe,* Thirty-seventh Congress, 2:58–59.
50. Borthwick, *Three Years in California,* 67.

51. Ibid., 65.
52. Ibid., 82.
53. Ibid., 69–71.
54. Ibid., 83–85.
55. Ibid., 77–78.
56. Ibid., 49, 74.
57. Ibid., 48.
58. Ibid., 55.
59. Ibid., 75.
60. Ibid., 78.
61. Ibid., 92.
62. Ibid., 51.
63. Ibid., 57.
64. Ibid., 62.
65. Ibid., 61–62.
66. Ibid., 57, 63–64.
67. William Perkins, *Three Years in California: William Perkins' Journal of Life at Sonora, 1849–1852*, edited by Dale L. Morgan and James R. Scobie (Berkeley: University of California Press, 1964), 87.
68. Borthwick, *Three Years in California*, 96.
69. John W. Audubon, *Audubon's Western Journal: 1849–1850* (Glorieta, N. Mex.: Rio Grande Press, 1906), 196.
70. Borthwick, *Three Years in California,* 54.
71. Ibid., 94.
72. Audubon, 196.
73. Frank Marryat, *Mountains and Molehills* (Philadelphia: J. B. Lippincott, 1962), 117.
74. Borthwick, *Three Years in California,* 102.
75. William Swain, Letters, in J. S. Holliday, *The World Rushed In: The California Gold Rush Experience* (New York: Simon and Schuster, 1981), 322.
76. Audubon, 233.
77. Ibid.
78. *Placer Times* (Sacramento), 28 April 1849.
79. Hubert Howe Bancroft, *History of California* (Santa Barbara: Wallace Hebberd, 1888), 6:450–59.
80. Marryat, 116.

81. Alonzo Delano, *Life on the Plains and Among the Diggings* (Ann Arbor, Mich.: University Microfilms, 1966), 291.

82. Borthwick, *Three Years in California,* 103–5.

83. Ibid., 107–8.

84. Ibid., 109.

85. Ibid., 110.

86. Ibid., 111.

87. Ibid., 112.

88. Ibid., 113–14.

89. Ibid., 114–15, 117.

90. Ibid., 115.

91. Ibid., 123–24.

92. Ibid., 124.

93. Gudde, *California Gold Camps*, 269–70.

94. Edward Gould Buffum, *Six Months in the Gold Mines* (Philadelphia: Lea and Blanchard, 1850), 83–85.

95. Borthwick, *Three Years in California,* 119.

96. Ibid., 125–27.

97. Ibid., 124.

98. Ibid., 126–27.

99. Ibid., 128, 132.

100. Ibid., 134.

101. Ibid.

102. Ibid., 128, 135–36.

103. Ibid., 136–37.

104. Ibid., 137.

105. Ibid., 137, 139.

106. Ibid., 141–42.

107. Ibid., 144.

108. *Nevada Journal* (Nevada City, Calif.), 5 May 1854.

109. Borthwick, *Three Years in California*, 146, 150.

110. Ibid., 154.

111. Ibid., 154–55.

112. Ibid., 156.

113. James Mason Hutchings, "Introduction to Three Years in California," *Hutchings California Magazine* 2 (1857) 2:72.

114. Fred S. Cook, ed., *Historic Legends of El Dorado County* (Volcano, Calif.: California Traveler, 1974), 32.

115. Sarah Royce, *A Frontier Lady: Recollections of the Gold Rush and Early California* (New Haven: Yale University Press, 1932) in Robert V. Hine and Edwin R. Bingham, eds., *The Frontier Experience* (Belmont, Calif.: Wadsworth Publishing Company, 1963), 223.

116. Borthwick, *Three Years in California*, 158.

117. Ibid., 158–59.

118. Ibid., 128.

119. Ibid., 118.

120. Ibid., 147.

121. Ibid., 159.

122. Ibid., 162.

123. Ibid., 164.

124. Ibid., 166.

125. John A. Stone, ed., "Hunting after Gold," *Put's Original California Songster* (San Francisco: D. E. Appleton, 1868), 23.

126. Erwin G. Gudde, *Sutter's Own Story,* Reminiscences dictated to H. H. Bancroft (New York: G. P. Putnam's Sons, 1936), 66–67, 97.

127. Erwin G. Gudde, ed., *Bigler's Chronicle of the West; As Reflected in Henry William Bigler's Diaries* (Berkeley: University of California Press, 1962), 89.

128. Ibid., 110.

129. Holliday, 31.

130. "Marshall's Own Account of the Gold Discovery," Statement to Charles B. Gillespie, *Century Magazine* 41 (1891) 2:537–38.

131. *New York Herald*, 11 January 1849.

132. Shaw, 98.

133. John A. Stone, ed., "The Unhappy Miner," *Put's Golden Songster* (San Francisco: D. E. Appleton, 1858), 36– 37.

134. Borthwick, *Three Years in California*, 167.

135. Delano, 351–52.

136. Borthwick, *Three Years in California*, 168.

137. John David Borthwick, "Gold in California," *Illustrated London News,* 24 January 1852, 73–74.

138. Borthwick, *Three Years in California*, 168–69.

139. Ibid., 170.

140. Ibid., 172.

141. Ibid., 173–74.

142. Ibid., 181.

143. Ibid., 186.

144. Ibid., 186–87.

145. Ibid., 201.

146. Ibid., 202–3.

147. Ibid., 204.

148. Ibid., 205.

149. Ibid., 206–8.

150. Ibid., 209.

151. Ibid.

152. *Gleason's Pictorial Drawing Room Companion* (Boston), 27 March 1852, 197.

153. Borthwick, *Three Years in California*, 210.

154. Ibid., 214–16.

155. W. H. Hutchinson, ed., *History of Plumas, Lassen and Sierra Counties*, reproduction of *Farris and Smith's History, 1882* (Berkeley: Howell-North, 1971), 456; Gudde, *California Gold Camps,* 100.

156. Borthwick, *Three Years in California*, 221.

157. *Alta California* (San Francisco), 14 July 1851.

158. "Hanging a Woman," *Sacramento Times & Transcript* in *Alta California*, 14 July 1851.

159. Borthwick, *Three Years in California,* 216.

160. Ibid., 217.

161. Ibid.

162. Ibid., 218; James J. Sinnott, *Downieville: Gold Town on the Yuba* (Volcano, Calif.: California Traveler, 1972), 124.

163. Hutchinson, 445; Downie, 147–53.

164. Sinnott, 48.

165. David Pierce Barstow, *Recollections of 1849–1851 in California* (Inverness, Calif.: Press of Inverness, 1979), 21.

166. Hutchinson, 446.

167. Sinnott, 48.
168. Ibid.
169. Hutchinson, 446; Downie, 150; Sinnott, 48.
170. Hutchinson, 446.
171. Sinnott, 49.
172. Ibid.
173. Barstow, 22.
174. Sinnott, 49.
175. Hutchinson, 446.
176. Barstow, 23.
177. Sinnott, 49.
178. Barstow, 23.
179. "Hanging a Woman," *Sacramento Times & Transcript* in *Alta California*, 14 July 1851.
180. Barstow, 23–24.
181. "Hanging a Woman," *Sacramento Times & Transcript* in *Alta California*, 14 July 1851.
182. *Mountain Messenger* (Downieville, Calif.), 1 April 1876.
183. Borthwick, *Three Years in California*, 224.
184. Barstow, 23.
185. Borthwick, *Three Years in California*, 237.
186. Ibid., 240–42.
187. Ibid., 243.
188. Ibid.
189. Ibid., 246.
190. Ibid.
191. Ibid., 179.
192. Ibid., 248.
193. Ibid.
194. Audubon, 233.
195. Ibid., 232, 227.
196. Borthwick, *Three Years in California*, 183–84.
197. Ibid.
198. Ibid., 249.
199. Ibid., 253.
200. Ibid.
201. Ibid., 254.

202. Ibid., 254–55.
203. Ibid., 259–60.
204. Ibid., 268.
205. Ibid.
206. Ibid., 269.
207. Ibid., 270.
208. Ibid., 273.
209. Ibid., 276.
210. Ibid., 278.
211. Ibid., 279.
212. Ibid., 280.
213. Ibid., 281.
214. Borthwick, "Gold in California," 73–74.
215. *Gleason's Pictorial,* 197. Borthwick evidently relied on the date of this article in setting the end of March as the time of his second departure from San Francisco; however, it would have taken nearly two months for the periodical to have reached him.
216. Audubon, 206, 217.
217. Borthwick, *Three Years in California,* 288.
218. A. P. Nasatir, "Guillaume Patrice Dillon," *California Historical Society Quarterly* 35 (1956) 4:309–24; Fred S. Cook, ed., *Legends of Calaveras County* (Volcano, Calif.: California Traveler, n.d.), 13.
219. Borthwick, *Three Years in California,* 291.
220. Ibid., 293–94.
221. Ibid., 297.
222. Ibid., 298.
223. Ibid.
224. Ibid., 292.
225. Ibid., 302.
226. Ibid., 302, 289.
227. Ibid., 311.
228. Ibid., 308.
229. Ibid., 310–11.
230. Ibid., 312.
231. Ibid., 313–14.
232. Ibid.

233. Ibid., 315.
234. Ibid., 316–17.
235. Ibid., 319.
236. Ibid., 320–21.
237. Ibid., 321.
238. Ibid.
239. Ibid., 324–26.
240. Ibid., 323.
241. Ibid., 323–24.
242. Thomas Robertson Stoddart, *Annals of Tuolumne County* (Tuolumne County Historical Society, 1963), 55.
243. *History of Tuolumne County, California* (Tuolumne County Historical Society, 1973), 263.
244. Ibid., 264.
245. Ibid., 18.
246. Perkins, 101.
247. Ibid., 101–2.
248. Ibid., 102–3.
249. Ibid., 104–7.
250. *History of Tuolumne County*, 21.
251. Perkins, 404.
252. Borthwick, *Three Years in California*, 331.
253. Ibid.
254. Ibid., 328.
255. Marryat, 137–39.
256. Borthwick, *Three Years in California,* 332–33.
257. Marryat, 142.
258. Borthwick, *Three Years in California,* 335–39.
259. Ibid., 344–45.
260. Ibid., 345–46.
261. Ibid., 346–47.
262. Ibid., 348.
263. Ibid., 350.
264. Ibid., 351–2.
265. *History of Tuolumne County*, 25–26.
266. Gudde, *California Gold Camps,* 78–79.
267. *History of Tuolumne County*, 25–26.
268. Borthwick, *Three Years in California,* 353–55.

269. Ibid., 355–57.
270. Ibid., 342–43.
271. Ibid., 375–77.
272. Bancroft, 6:465–66.
273. Taylor, 60.
274. Marryat, 199.
275. Audubon, 187–88.
276. Perkins, 92.
277. Borthwick, *Three Years in California*, 377–78.
278. Ibid., 379–80.
279. Marryat, 179–80.
280. Roger R. Olmstead, ed., *Scenes of Wonder and Curiosity from Hutchings California Magazine 1856–61* (Berkeley: Howell-North, 1962), vi.
281. John Paul Dart, "A Mississipian in the Gold Fields," *California Historical Society Quarterly* 35 (1956) 3:209.

PART III: OTHER TRAVEL IN THE NEW WORLDS

1. Charles Ferguson, *The Experiences of a Forty-Niner in Australia and New Zealand* (Melbourne, Australia: G. Renard, 1979), 2.
2. Ibid., 4–5.
3. Ibid., 4.
4. Ibid., 4–7.
5. Ibid., 13–14.
6. Ibid., 16–17.
7. Amos S. Pittman, "The California and Australia Gold Rushes," *California Historical Society Quarterly* 30 (1951) 1: 29–30.
8. *Empire* (Sydney), 22 October 1851.
9. *Morning Herald* (Sydney), 9 January 1849.
10. *Melbourne Argus,* 11 March 1852.
11. *Alta California,* 14 December 1849.
12. Ferguson, 51.
13. Ibid.
14. Jay Monaghan, *Australians and the Gold Rush* (Berkeley: University of California Press, 1966), 232.
15. Borthwick, *Three Years in California*, 371–72.

16. Ferguson, 52–53.
17. Ibid., 53.
18. Ibid., 54.
19. Ibid., 60.
20. Ibid., 62.
21. Ibid., 69.
22. John David Borthwick, "Nicaragua and the Filibusters," *Blackwood's Edinburgh Magazine* 79 (1856) 3:315.
23. Borthwick, *Three Years in California*, 382.
24. Borthwick, "Nicaragua and the Filibusters," 316–17.
25. Ibid., 317.
26. Ibid.
27. Ibid., 318.
28. Ibid.
29. Ibid.
30. Ibid., 316.
31. Ibid., 319–20.
32. Ibid., 315.
33. Ibid., 314.
34. Ibid., 326.
35. Ibid., 314.
36. Ibid., 322–23.
37. Ibid., 324.
38. Ibid.
39. Bancroft, 6:593.
40. Borthwick, "Nicaragua and the Filibusters," 327.
41. Ibid.
42. Ibid., 323.
43. Ferguson, 2.
44. *Gleason's Pictorial*, 197.

PART IV: RETURN TO THE OLD WORLD

1. "The Land of Gold," *Blackwood's Edinburgh Magazine* 81 (1857) 4:487; Borthwick, *Three Years in California*, 79.
2. McLaren, 132.
3. John David Borthwick, "Mining Life in California," *Harper's Weekly*, 3 October 1857, 634.
4. Ibid., 632.

5. Ibid., 633.

6. Ibid., 634.

7. John David Borthwick, "Three Years in California," *Hutchings California Magazine* 2 (1857) 2:72–79, 3:121–27, 4:169–74, 5:216–21, 6:271–74; 2 (1858) 8:359–62, 9:411–16.

8. "The Land of Gold," 480–81.

9. Ibid., 480.

10. Ibid., 487.

11. Ibid., 488; Borthwick, *Three Years in California,* 374.

12. Borthwick, *Three Years in California*, 149–50.

13. Ibid., 106.

14. Ibid., 60.

15. Ibid., 68.

16. Borthwick, "Nicaragua and the Filibusters," 324.

17. Borthwick, *Three Years in California*, 101.

18. Ibid., 384.

19. Ibid.

20. *Gleason's Pictorial*, 197.

21. Borthwick, *Three Years in California*, 107–8.

22. Audubon, 185.

23. Marriage Records, Edinburgh, Scotland.

24. Census of England for 1861; *London Directory* for 1858, 1859, 1861.

25. Jane Johnson, *Works Exhibited at the Royal Society of British Artists 1824–1893* (Suffolk: Baron, 1975), 49; Borthwick, *Three Years in California,* 368.

26. Algernon Graves, *The Royal Academy of Arts: A Complete Dictionary of Contributors and Their Works from Its Foundation* (London: Henry Graves, 1905), 2:244.

27. Marriage Records, Edinburgh, Scotland.

28. Borthwick, *Three Years in California*, 368.

29. Graves, *The Royal Academy of Arts,* 2:244.

30. Algernon Graves, *The British Institution: A Complete Dictionary of Contributors and Their Works from the Foundation of the Institution* (Bath: Kingsmead Reprints, 1857), 405.

31. Algernon Graves, *A Dictionary of Artists Who Have Exhibited Works in the Principal London Exhibitions from 1760 to 1893* (Avon: Kingsmead Press, 1901).

32. Census of England for 1871.
33. Census of England for 1881.
34. Death Records and Wills, Edinburgh, Scotland.
35. Borthwick, *Three Years in California*, 370.
36. Audubon, 38.
37. Death Certificate of John David Borthwick.
38. *Obituaries from London Times, January to June 1892,* 151.
39. Death Records, Edinburgh, Scotland; Death Certificate of George Borthwick.

BIBLIOGRAPHY

BOOKS

Audubon, John W. *Audubon's Western Journal: 1849–1850.* Glorieta, N. Mex.: Rio Grande Press, 1906.

Bancroft, Hubert Howe. *History of California.* 23 vols. Santa Barbara: Wallace Hebberd, 1888.

Barstow, David Pierce. *Recollections of 1849–1851 in California.* Inverness, Calif.: Press of Inverness, 1979.

Bone, James. *Edinburgh Revisited.* London: Sidgwick and Jackson, 1911.

Borthwick, Halsey M. *The Borthwick Family.* Cornwallville, N.Y.: Greene Company, 1936.

Borthwick, John David. *The Gold Hunters.* Cleveland: International Fiction Library, 1917.

________. *Three Years in California.* Edinburgh: Blackwood and Sons, 1857.

Buffum, Edward Gould. *Six Months in the Gold Mines.* Philadelphia: Lea and Blanchard, 1850.

Caughey, John and LaRee. *California Heritage: An Anthology of History and Literature.* Los Angeles: Ward Ritchie Press, 1962.

Clark, C. M. H. *History of Australia.* 6 vols. Melbourne: Melbourne University Press, 1978.

Cook, Fred S., ed. *Historic Legends of El Dorado County.* Volcano, Calif.: California Traveler, 1974.

________. *Legends of Calaveras County.* Volcano, Calif.: California Traveler, n.d.

Craigh, W. S. *History of Royal College of Physicians.* Edinburgh: Blackweel Scientific, 1976.

Delano, Alonzo. *Life on the Plains and Among the Diggings.* Ann Arbor, Mich.: University Microfilms, 1966.

Dickson, John. *The Ruined Castles of Mid-Lothian.* Edinburgh: Robert R. Sutherland, 1894.

Downie, William. *Hunting for Gold: Reminiscences of Personal Experiences.* San Francisco: California Publishing Company, 1893.

Edinburgh Academy Register. Edinburgh: Constable, 1914.

Ferguson, Charles. *The Experiences of a Forty-Niner in Australia and New Zealand.* Melbourne, Australia: G. Renard, 1979.

Fry, Plantagenet and Fiona Somerset. *The History of Scotland.* London: Routledge and Kegan Paul, 1982.

Gudde, Erwin G. *California Gold Camps.* Berkeley: University of California Press, 1975.

________. *Sutter's Own Story.* Reminiscences dictated to H. H. Bancroft. New York: G. P. Putnam's Sons, 1936.

Gudde, Erwin G., ed. *Bigler's Chronicle of the West: As Reflected in Henry William Bigler's Diaries.* Berkeley: University of California Press, 1962.

Graves, Algernon. *A Dictionary of Artists Who Have Exhibited Works in the Principal London Exhibitions from 1760 to 1893.* Avon: Kingsmead Press, 1901.

________. *The British Institution: A Complete Dictionary of Contributors and their Works from the Foundation of the Institution.* Bath: Kingsmead Reprints, 1875.

________. *The Royal Academy of Arts: A Complete Dictionary of Contributors and their Works from its Foundation.* 2 vols. London: Henry Graves, 1905.

Haskins, C. W. *The Argonauts of California.* New York: Fords, Howard, and Hulbert, 1890.

History of Tuolumne County, California. Tuolumne County Historical Society, 1973.

Hogarth, Paul. *Artists on Horseback: The Old West in Illustrated Journalism, 1857–1900.* New York: Watson–Guptill, 1972.

Holliday, J. S. *The World Rushed In: The California Gold Rush Experience.* New York: Simon and Schuster, 1981.

Hutchinson, W. H., ed. *History of Plumas, Lassen, and Sierra Counties.* Reproduction of *Farris and Smith's History, 1882.* Berkeley: Howell-North, 1971.

Irving, Joseph. *The Book of Scotsmen.* Paisley: Alexander Gordon, 1881.

Johnson, Jane. *Works Exhibited at the Royal Society of British Artists 1824–1893.* Suffolk: Baron, 1975.

Lindsay, Ian G. *Georgian Edinburgh.* Edinburgh: Scottish Academic Press, 1973.

London Directory for 1858, 1859, 1861, 1862, 1868, 1871, 1875, 1878, 1888.

McCallum, Neil. *It's an Old Scottish Custom.* London: Dennis Dobson, 1951.

McLaren, Moray. *Understanding the Scots.* London: Frederick Mullen, 1956.

Marryat, Frank. *Mountains and Molehills.* Philadelphia: J. B. Lippincott, 1962.

Monaghan, Jay. *Australians and the Gold Rush.* Berkeley: University of California Press, 1966.

Oliver and Boyd's Guide to Edinburgh. Edinburgh: Oliver and Boyd, 1860.

Olmstead, Roger R., ed. *Scenes of Wonder and Curiosity from Hutchings California Magazine 1856–61.* Berkeley: Howell-North, 1962.

Perkins, William. *Three Years in California: William Perkins' Journal of Life at Sonora, 1849–1852.* Edited by Dale L. Morgan and James R. Scobie. Berkeley: University of California Press, 1964.

Post Office Annual Directory and Calendar. Edinburgh: Ballantyne and Hughes, 1840.

Post Office Annual Directory for 1829–30. Edinburgh: Ballantyne, 1829.

Post Office Annual Directory for 1876–77. Edinburgh: Ballantyne, 1876.

Post Office Edinburgh and Leith Directory for 1864–65. Edinburgh: Ballantyne, 1864.

Prestor, Richard, ed. *Contemporary Australia: Studies in History.* Durham, N.C.: Duke University Press, 1967.

Royce, Sarah. *A Frontier Lady: Recollections of the Gold Rush and Early California.* New Haven: Yale University Press, 1932. In Robert V. Hine and Edwin R. Bingham, eds. *The Frontier Experience.* Belmont, Calif.: Wadsworth Publishing Company, 1963.

Scott, Michael. *Writings.* In Thomas A. Bailey and David M. Kennedy. *The American Pageant.* Lexington, Mass.: D. C. Heath, 1979.

Shaw, William. *Golden Dreams and Waking Realities.* New York: Arno Press, 1973.

Sinnott, James J. *Downieville: Gold Town on the Yuba.* Volcano, Calif.: California Traveler, 1972.

Steel, Tom. *Scotland's Story: A New Perspective.* London: Collins, 1984.

Stevenson, R. *Annals of Edinburgh and Leith.* Edinburgh: J. Hutchinson, 1839.

Stoddart, Thomas Robertson. *Annals of Tuolumne County.* Tuolumne County Historical Society, 1963.

Stone, John A., ed. *Put's Golden Songster.* San Francisco: D. E. Appleton, 1858.

________. *Put's Original California Songster.* San Francisco: D. E. Appleton, 1868.

Swain, William. Letters. In J. S. Holliday. *The World Rushed In: The California Gold Rush Experience.* New York: Simon and Schuster, 1981.

Taylor, Bayard. *Eldorado;* or *Adventures in the Path of Empire.* New York: Alfred A. Knopf, 1949.

Taylor, R. R. "A Letter from Panama." In John and LaRee Caughey. *California Heritage: An Anthology of History and Literature.* Los Angeles: Ward Ritchie Press, 1962.

White, Emma Siggins. *The Kinnears and their Kin.* Kansas City Mo.: Tiernan-Dart Printing Company, 1916.

Younger, R. M. *Australia and the Australians: A New Concise History.* Adelaide: Rigby, 1970.

Youngson, A. J. *The Making of Classical Edinburgh 1750–1840.* Edinburgh: Edinburgh University Press, 1966.

ARTICLES AND NEWSPAPERS

Alta California (San Francisco). 14 December 1849, 14 July 1851.

Borthwick, John David. "Gold in California." *Illustrated London News*, 24 January 1852, 73–74.

———. "Mining Life in California." *Harper's Weekly,* 3 October 1857, 632–34.

———. "Nicaragua and the Filibusters." *Blackwood's Edinburgh Magazine* 79 (1856) 3:314–27.

———. "Three Years in California." *Hutchings California Magazine* 2 (1857) 2:72–79, 3:121–27, 4:169–74, 5:216–21, 6:271–74; 2 (1858) 8:359–62, 9:411–16.

Carson, James H. "Recollections of the California Mines." *San Joaquin Republican* (Stockton). Special Edition. 1852.

Dart, John Paul. "A Mississippian in the Gold Fields." *California Historical Society Quarterly* 35 (1956) 3:205–16.

Empire (Sydney, Australia). 22 October 1851.

Gleason's Pictorial Drawing Room Companion (Boston), 27 March 1852, 197.

"Hanging a Woman." *Sacramento Times & Transcript.* In *Alta California*, 14 July 1851.

Hutchings, James Mason. "Introduction to Three Years in California." *Hutchings California Magazine* 2 (1857) 2:72.

Illustrated London News, 24 January 1852.

London Times. 16 September 1848.

Obituaries from London Times, January to June 1892. Microfilm at The Church of Jesus Christ of Latter-day Saints Genealogical Library, Salt Lake City.

''Marshall's Own Account of the Gold Discovery.'' Statement to Charles B. Gillespie. *Century Magazine* 41 (1891) 2:537–38.

Melbourne Argus. 11 March 1852.

Morning Herald (Sydney). 9 January 1849.

Mountain Messenger (Downieville, Calif.). 1876.

Nasatir, A. P. ''Guillaume Patrice Dillon.'' *California Historical Society Quarterly* 35 (1956) 4:309–24.

Nevada Journal (Nevada City, Calif.). 5 May 1854.

New York Herald. 11 January 1849.

Pittman, Amos S. ''The California and Australia Gold Rushes.'' *California Historical Society Quarterly* 30 (1951) 1:15–37.

Placer Times (Sacramento). 28 April 1849.

Sonora Herald. 1851.

''The Land of Gold.'' *Blackwood's Edinburgh Magazine* 81 (1857) 4:480–89.

UNPUBLISHED MATERIAL

Barstow, Alfred. ''Statement of Alfred Barstow, A Pioneer of 1849.'' MS, H. H. Bancroft Collection, Bancroft Library, University of California, Berkeley.

Borthwick, Charles Stuart. Letter to R. E. Mather and F. E. Boswell, 13 April 1988.

Borthwick, Joseph T. Letter to R. E. Mather and F. E. Boswell, 5 April 1988.

''Clan Borthwick Association Brochure.''

Field, Stephen J. ''Personal Reminiscences of Early Days in California.'' MS, Cecil H. Green Library, Stanford University.

PUBLIC DOCUMENTS

England. Census of 1861, 1871, 1881.

England. Death Records.

Scotland. Census of 1841, 1851, 1861.

Scotland. Edinburgh. Death Records.

Scotland. Edinburgh. Deeds and Probates.
Scotland. Edinburgh. Marriage Records.
Scotland. Edinburgh. Old Parochial Register.
Scotland. Edinburgh. Wills.
Washington, D.C. *Congressional Globe.* Thirty-seventh Congress.

INDEX

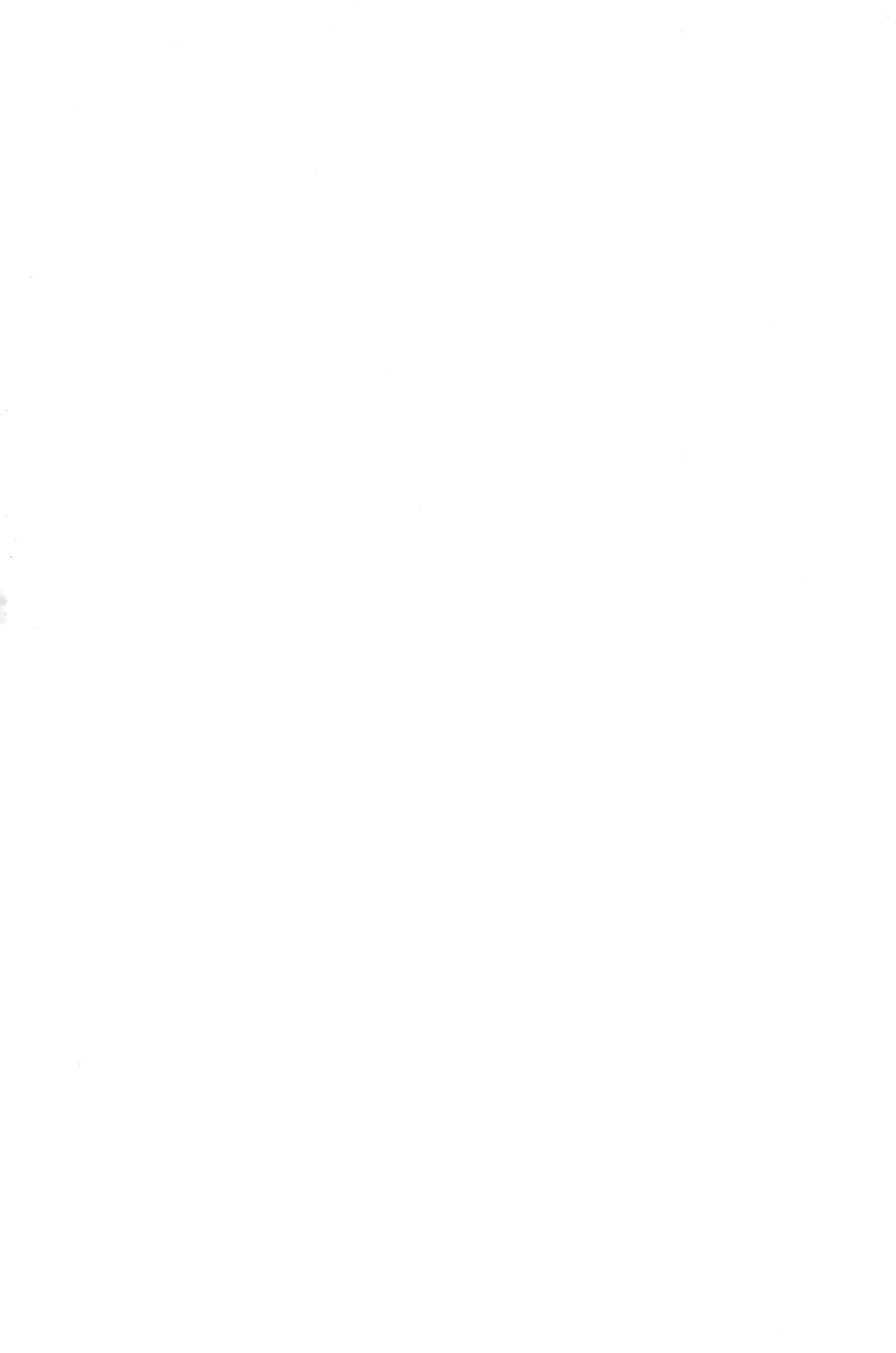